THE VISION OF SELF IN EARLY VEDĀNTA

THE VISION OF SELF IN EARLY VEDĀNTA

WILLIAM BEIDLER, B.S., M.A., Ph.D.
Department of Philosophy, Guilford College
Greensboro, North Carolina 27410 U.S.A.

MOTILAL BANARSIDASS
Delhi :: Patna :: Varanasi

Indological Publishers & Booksellers
Head Office : BUNGALOW ROAD, JAWAHARNAGAR, DELHI-7
Branches : 1. CHOWK, VARANASI-1 (U. P.)
2. ASHOK RAJPATH, PATNA-4 (BIHAR)

ISBN 0 8426 0990 3

First Edition : *Delhi*, 1975
Price : Rs. 46.00

Printed in India
BY SHANTILAL JAIN, AT SHRI JAINENDRA PRESS, A-45, PHASE-1, INDUSTRIAL AREA, NARAINA, NEW DELHI - 28 AND PUBLISHED BY SUNDARLAL JAIN, FOR MOTILAL BANARSIDASS, BUNGALOW ROAD, JAWAHAR NAGAR, DELHI-7

To
Tad Ekam
Who made it all possible

PREFACE

The present work is an attempt to apply the methods and tools of philosophy to the investigation of religious texts. To the degree that revelation can be cast into language and the categories of thought, a work such as this can be successful. Within the limitations of the scope of a Doctoral thesis such an investigation has been carried out on texts that purport to be the foundation for the Hindu religion as well as Indian philosophy.

The author is greatly indebted to the authorities of Osmania University for the fellowship and opportunities so graciously given to carry out the present research.

He is also deeply indebted to Dr. K. Sachchidananda Murty, Head of the Department of Philosophy, Andhra University, for the guidance and criticism so kindly rendered during the period of residence by the author at Andhra University.

He is also very grateful to Mr. Shiv Mohan Lal, Reader in the Department of Philosophy, Osmania University under whose guidance this research has been carried out. Also the kind suggestions and guidance of Dr. S. Vahiduddin, Reader in the Department of Philosophy, Osmania University, have been of inestimable value. The counsel of Dr. Mir Valiuddin, Head of the Philosophy Department, has also been a source of constant encouragement.

The work as now published is substantially an edited edition of the original dissertation. Looking back over fifteen years there is much that could be changed; especially in the Upaniṣads and in the conclusion. There is much here that warrants, for instance, a more thorough study of nothingness than is embodied in the present conclusion. As it stands the study hopefully will offer an "einleitung" into the fascinating period of early classical Hindu thought. If it shows the richness of philosophical thought to be found in the Upaniṣads and the Bhagavad Gītā, then its task will have been fulfilled.

CONTENTS

INTRODUCTION

PART I

THE CONCEPT OF SELF IN THE UPANIṢADS

INTRODUCTION

I. *Statement of the Problem* :

It is a common observation that objects in our environment are readily amenable to tests of most any sort. We can measure them, describe them, and catalogue them in any manner we please. Equally common an observation, however, is that the subject for whom the above objects are items of interest is not to be so easily catalogued, described or measured. Rather in trying to view the subject of self, an entirely new logic must be employed; and even so it seems that try as we might to grasp the subject it merely becomes an object in our endeavour.

The difficulty of knowledge of the subject has stimulated thinkers from earliest times to explore the realm of self. These explorations have become the basis for much philosophical and religious literature which has diversified from such beginnings much like the analogous broadening of self in the maturation of the individual.

Probably one of the most outstanding examples of such exploration is to be found in Early Vedānta in the three treatises: *The Upaniṣads* (first ten), *The Brahma-Sūtras*, and the *Bhagavad Gītā*. From these three sources has developed much of later Indian thought. It would be of some value, then, to explore the concept of self to be found in Early Vedānta; for thereby not only could we trace the origins of later systematic development through this concept but also some external evaluation of its insight could be had by asking common questions of a metaphysical, moral, and religious nature which any concept of self should give answers to. Through the exploration of self in early Vedānta then, we find a twofold benefit, indirectly the illumination of the beginnings of the later systems; and we also obtain some insight into the Prasthānatric view of self and therefore into much of its metaphysics. Moreover, we should be able to evaluate the later systems of Indian Philosophy in terms of how they have preserved and developed the major elements of the Early Vedānta concept of self.

In our analysis we shall take the first ten *Upaniṣads*, which according to philologists are most probably pre-Buddhist and so presystematic and also the *Bhagavad Gītā* which largely represents a later, yet Upaniṣadic synthesis. The *Brahma Sūtras* will not form part of this study because it is cursory in nature and without the commentaries is not too rewarding a study.

Our study then shall have a duty of developing the Early Vedānta concept of self in such a fashion that our analysis of it can be critically evaluated and compared to the concepts which the later systems found in these works and claimed to be their teachings.

II. *Historical Introduction* :

In this study we have had many illustrious predecessors who, although not often directly concerned with the concept of self, did throw light on the concepts through their study of the two texts of the present work. One of the earliest and most influential to later thought was Śaṅkara, who in the ninth century of our era wrote commentaries on most of the major works of Indian thought and rescued Vedānta from its temporary submersion by Buddhism. It is not an exaggeration to say that Śaṅkara's influence is still felt more strongly than perhaps any other of the ancient teachers; and an important part of our work shall be to see just how Śaṅkara treats our two texts. Not only does Śaṅkara try to interpret the *Upaniṣads* and the *Gītā* for his age, thereby supplying a direct link back to the Vedas, but he also links these early texts with his predecessors such as Gauḍapāda who equally were interpreters for their age of that forest which constitutes Upaniṣadic thought. In our study of the *Māṇḍūkya Upaniṣad* we shall consider Gauḍapāda's *Kārikā* also which should give us valuable insights into the sources of Advaita thought. Śaṅkara's attempts were not without opposition by later sages. Indeed, Rāmānuja and Madhva loom large as opponents to Śaṅkara's interpretations of our texts and his monistic thought in general. Entering fully into the differences between the beliefs of these three Ācāryas would make this work unnecessarily cumbersome, but we can achieve a more direct way of considering their difficulties. Through our independent development of the concept of self in our two texts we can see just how far they go toward justifying each of the Ācārya's claims to teach what the Upaniṣads and the *Gītā* teach. In the case of Rāmānuja and Madhva we are not so fortunate as to have commentaries on all the Upaniṣads. Only on the *Īśa Upaniṣad* will we consider Madhva and Veṅkaṭanātha, the latter a student of Rāmānuja. In the case of the Gītā, however, the Bhāṣyas of all three Ācāryas will illumine both our problem and their difficulties.

Modern studies of the Upaniṣads and the Gītā have largely been of a different character. On the one hand we have the work of Western scholars on both our texts, among whom we shall have occasion to consider the work of Deussen, Garbe, Otto and Keith. On the other hand there are the modern Indian scholars such as Dasgupta, Radhakrishnan, and Ranade. In both of these groups the approach has departed from that of the ancient studies. The modern studies seem to be more critical in their analysis of the texts both because of their greater distance in time from the texts, and, in the case of the European scholars, a chasm also in cultural outlook. The combination of the ancient and the modern studies on our texts shall be an invaluable aid in examining the concept of self. As in the case of the ancient studies, we cannot enter fully into the manifold arguments which rage among the modern scholars. Full criticism will be made more directly by comparing the concept of self developed by our analysis with that of the various scholars. This method will have the advantage of revealing the problems raised by the early works in their most basic and general form at the same time that it eliminates the need for detailed criticism of the later commentaries.

From a survey of the literature one is immediately struck by the lack of systematic works on the concept of self. This is especially true of the *Upaniṣads* and the *Gītā*. With the exception of Narahari's thesis of *Ātman in Pre-Upaniṣadic Vedic Literature* no other work of comparable nature has been done. This is particularly puzzling in view of the great controversies which have developed from the two texts we have selected. Many of the works of the above-mentioned scholars consider the various terms for self in these two texts and even admit that the *Upaniṣads* have as their main aim the teaching of self (Adhyātma Vidyā).[1]

1. Cf. Radhakrishnan, *Indian Philosophy*. 1, Chap. IV, Sect, II.

None of these, however, have focused their major attention on the concept of self. It is expected that much new light can be thrown on the basis for the later systematic development, especially Sāṅkhya, Yoga, and Vedānta, through a study of the concept of self.

The problem of developing a concept of self has vast dimensions, and it is to the credit of the Upaniṣadic sages to have seen the issue and made it a central element in their teachings. It is for this reason that our present study can meet the important need of offering critical judgment in comparing the later systems to the Early Vedānta; for later thought carried the concept of self also as a fundamental element in its various systems.

Even beyond our present aim, a study of history shows that in nearly all our acts when we choose some object or action we at the same time, whether we are aware of it or not, "choose ourselves." Thus we might say the exploits of Paraśurāma when compared to those of Kṛṣṇa or Rāma show a Self of a much less developed order, just as the actions of a child show much less awareness and control of self than the adult. To put the matter simply, each objective action has its subjective counterpart which reveals a certain degree of awareness of self. Because, as was stated on page one, the self cannot be easily grasped and studied, the study of self is often neglected in favour of the easier consideration of objective phenomena. Our present study then makes a broad appeal, both to the past and the present in its attempt to lay bare the teachings on self by the *Upaniṣads* and the *Bhagavad-Gītā* which loom large in the world's religious and philosophical literature.

III. *Linguistic difficulties and a tentative solution* :

We might have equally well stated the problem before us as one of elucidation of the term 'puruṣa', 'Ātman', 'Jīva' and such words as 'Ahaṅkāra' and 'Antaḥkaraṇa' which are the major terms used in our two texts for what we have titled in our above discussions as the "concept of self". Since Sanskrit is no longer a common medium of communication and a manifold common usage has not developed around these terms, the problem before us is largely just that,an elucidation of the above terms. In our discussion above the reader may have at times asked himself : Why is the delineation of a concept of self such a major problem ? Everybody knows what 'self' means, that is given, what we start with. We would not say the same regarding the above Sanskrit terms however; and it is finding and critically developing their referents that shall occupy us in the following pages. The difference between the 'self' and the Sanskrit terms is due in part at least to the above observation that we do not use 'Ātman' etc., in common parlance; but also this difference may, in addition, be due to the fact that the cultural associations which underlie such words as 'self', 'soul', and 'God' do not come to our aid, and we are thrown back on our powers of comprehension and analysis in seeking to understand the Sanskrit terms in context instead of relying on the intuitions associated with the word 'self'. Indeed, the words 'self', 'soul' and 'God' have developed within a Judaco-Christian tradition which has conditioned these concepts to the somewhat extreme theism characteristic of the Hebrews and late Christians. To make a simple translation of our texts, then, may well lead us into the dangers above, of instinctively associating 'Ātman', for instance with 'self' or 'soul' which are referents conditioned by the Western Judaco-Christian tradition. Indeed in our later discussion of the work of some of the Western scholars we shall have just this criticism to make. To avoid this difficulty we shall treat the above Sanskrit terms and any technical terms which may be ambiguous due to their multiple associations as proper nouns and seek a contextual definition such that the Vedāntic association of the terms may be brought out rather than their normal English counterpart. Such a procedure can be easily defended and shown to be required both linguistically and psychologically. Linguistically for instance, the proper name 'Mohan' has no descriptive content apart from a given context. Thus, if we are to understand the referent to 'Mohan', we have either to ask for a descriptive phrase or ask that the referent, Mohan, be pointed out to us. Nouns such as 'self', 'soul', and 'God', however, to anyone using the English language have descriptive phrases associated with them. That such descriptions are not univocal in the case of two different users, the history of philosophy stands in moot testimony. Such words as 'puruṣa', 'Ātman', 'Jīva', on the other hand seem to be used rather consistently in the texts before us. When we consider the fact that these terms are largely confined to such contexts as ours, then our definition of the problem as one of elucidation of the above Sanskrit terms becomes even more meaningful, since we will not have the manifold associations of popular usage to consider were we to translate these terms directly into 'soul', 'self' etc.

In addition to the linguistic reasons for our procedure there are analogous and equally important psychological reasons. We shall find in our texts the injunction to self inquiry (Ātma-vicāra), a seeking which is the cornerstone of philosophy. The various Mārgas outlined for this search will occupy much of our attention. We can see that this self inquiry provides an analogue to what we have forced the reader to do in treating the Sanskrit terms as if they were proper nouns for which one must seek the referent instead of calling to mind the ready-made categorial structure associated with 'self','soul' and 'God'.

Another problem with the above and other technical terms in Sanskrit is the distance between literary usage and modern uses in many cases, as well as the frequent occurrence of apparently symbolic meanings. This latter problem will become clearer to us in the next section when we discuss stylistic problems associated with our analysis. The chronological disparity is treated in the English-Sanskrit problem just discussed.

IV. *Methodology* :

Our present study is to be compared and contrasted with both the ancient and modern studies mentioned under II above. If we take Śaṅkara as an example, we can ascertain that the Upaniṣads were for him Śruti and were to be reconciled with each other no matter how divergent individual passages may be; thus we might say that Śaṅkara relates to our texts more as an apologist than as a critical investigator. The reader of the numerous Bhāṣyas of Śaṅkara is, however, struck by apparent attempts to fit the teachings of the text to some doctrines either current in his day or supposed to be found as the dominant thread by the Mīmāṁsā process to which he adhered.[1]

The modern scholars are largely critical in their orientation and interested in interpreting these texts to a modern audience. All too often we will find that they overlook the vast difference in cultural outlook which separates them from the Upaniṣadic Ṛṣis. German scholars such as Garbe and Otto might be cited as examples of those who expect to find the *Gītā* presented in the rationally complete fashion of Kant or a continental rationalist. Such failure to appreciate the difference between ancient Indian and modern German styles cannot help but result in a failure to appreciate the full meaning of the text.

Our attempts to avoid these pitfalls shall be twofold, a different posture to the texts than Śaṅkara and the ancient commentators, and the adoption of an analytical system to fit the level of language of the texts, applying external criticism only by way of conclusion after the meaning of the texts has been developed. In sum, our posture shall be sympathetically critical.

Nor shall we apply a system of logic in our analysis, since western logic as the child of rational and empirical philosophy may not extract from our texts their whole meaning. Can one imagine, for example, the inclusion of Russell's logical atomism in Biblical exegesis in order to extract the full meaning from the Bible ?

This last analogy is actually quite close, for the *Upaniṣads* and the *Gītā* represent to Indian thought what the *Bible* represents, directly and indirectly, to European philosophers and theologians. In both texts, the language is largely authoritarian and of a "revealed" character rather than discursive and argumentative, and by extension the style is more descriptive of something which is usually held not to be of an intellectual nature but rather requires a "perception", a spiritual perception or better insight or intuition (Vijñāna). We have only to stop and search ourselves to see the reason for this vast difference

1. Radhakrishnan, loc. cit. II, 467. Also Deussen, *System of Vedānta*, p. 95; see *Mīmāṁsā Sūtras* I. 2.46.

in approach. In the Statement of the Problem, above, we noted that self cannot be easily catalogued, described or measured as an object. Thus we can at best merely give different views of the self grasped from different standpoints, since we cannot remove it and stand off from it to treat it discursively. Not surprisingly we also find the frequent use of allegories and occasionally symbolic expressions in our texts.[1]

In the light of these observations we can see that simply making a conceptual analysis may not do justice to the text. Thus, if we find a certain concept in the reading of our texts and proceed to analyse it into its component parts, which is the typical procedure of modern linguistic analysis,[2] we would be assuming that the concept under examination could be divided into parts and yet analysed as a whole. Symbolically it would be much like the following :

$$f(x)=f(a).\ f(b).\ f(c).\ f(d)\ldots.f(n)$$

The first thing to realize about our texts, is their inherent wholeness : they may not be analyzable into parts when dealing with the concept of self except at the risk of losing their meaning. Another problem develops from this posture. If our concepts of self are for the large part organic wholes, then we cannot expect to find a discursive style which will conclude with an inferred concept of self, integrating the many parts discussed in the body of the text. Rather we may expect a "revelation", or better, an intuitive description of the self followed by further such descriptions from other standpoints. What we cannot expect is an integration of these different descriptions into the whole intuition of self. Each description is made in the hope of evoking in us that intuition or perception of self which the writer purports to have and which each description or allegory tries to engender. In the words of W. T. Stace[3], religious and much abstract language can only hope to be a "language of evocation" not a "language of meaning". In the latter case

1. See especially the creation stories in *Bṛhadāraṇyaka Upaniṣad* and the symbolism of OM in *Māṇḍūkya Upaniṣad*.

2. See for example, Russell : *Mysticism & Logic*, especially *Logical Atomism*; Moore : *Ethics* for such models.

3. See *Time and Eternity*, Chap. VI.

we would have a common sensory experiences, in the former only the hope of bringing up a common intuition from unconscious areas of our being. It is possibly the failure to appreciate this difference which has led so many to find nothing but nonsense in religious writings. If we are to avoid such difficulties, we must try to develop a method of analysis which will bring out the full import of the texts, taking each description and relating it to other descriptions in such a way that some organised picture may develop and lead us to that intuition ourselves.

Our first observation is that in discursive texts we try to state the problem first in a concise manner, then consider each part into which the problem has been broken critically and finally find if each part is valid in itself from the grounds of the text and whether the parts among themselves are not self-contradictory at the same time that they implicate the conclusion.

This technique is not strictly applicable to our texts without a slight adaptation. Instead of finding the premises valid and implicative of the conclusion, we will use the criterion of "coherence" since we shall not be concerned internally with ordinary implications. Thus, if each description of self purports to be the same object of discussion viewed from a different standpoint, there should be coherence of these various descriptions; they should not be psychologically contradictory, and moreover, they should be recognized to be contained in each other if we have the correct intuition of the whole. One other concept which will serve as our judge of the texts is that of "completeness". Thus, in discursive texts the parts of the subject analysed either relate to the whole as species to genus or part to whole; that is if we were studying animals, we could analyse the genus, animal, into species homo sapiens, old world monkies, gastropods etc. Since in our texts the subject cannot be so broken down into specie genus relation of part to whole, the concept of completeness is its substitute, i.e., one concept may be more complete than another when it can include the other in its own with a satisfactory degree of coherence. In other words coherence and completeness taken together, will enable us to evaluate our texts internally and to classify the various concepts of self.

There are certain difficulties with the above scheme of

analysis which must be proleptically raised and set to rest. First the critic may say that "completeness" is no concept for the most complete concept possible is a. which implies everything. This is true in material implication as everything in the universe must be either a or not a. Yet clearly, it does not tell us anything. Moreover our criterion of coherence mitigates against it; since it functions as a safeguard against such contradictions . The second difficulty is that one may say that our concepts are no concepts because they will not weed out the unrelated and superfluous material from the delimited scope of our analysis. This argument would be quite damaging if applicable. First of all, the cursory often almost aphoristic style, does not admit of loose accretions of the material and moreover, our interest in the two texts is concerned with the concept of self, itself a one-pointed interest. Indeed there will be some material with which we will not be concerned, except peripherally. Further, the criterion of coherence will eliminate unrelated material at the same time that will not determine relatedness on rational grounds alone. An example of the dangers of applying the latter criteria to our texts, appears in the concept of a dominant thread in Mīmāṁsā.[1] The Bhāṣyas of Śaṅkara, biased as they are, towards Jñāna Mārga as the dominant thread, illustrate just that sort of error of applying inapplicable criteria of analysis; for Bhakti Karma and are only to be explained away when that side of the vision or intuition comes up for discussion. Since these two are placed in a decidedly subordinate position, the whole intuition is missed; the sole aspect (Jñāna) which gives a rationally appealing system, becomes the thread of continuity.

In short, our procedure shall be to consider the material of our two texts related to the concept of self, the various terms of III; and from this material, keeping in mind the needs of coherence and completeness, we will classify the various descriptions of self under those headings which our criteria of analysis seem to dictate. More detailed consideration of the categories into which our problem is divided for analysis will be given in the introduction for each section.

1. See *Mīmāṁsā Sūtra* 1.2. 46.

Part I

THE CONCEPT OF SELF IN THE UPANIṢADS

Chapter I

INTRODUCTION TO THE STUDY OF THE UPANIṢADS

A. *Historical Introduction*

The Vedas are the oldest body of religious thought in India and seem to bear many affinities to other Indo-European religions. The origin of these Vedas is shrouded in the mists of time; some date them at 1500 B.C.,[1] others at 4500 B.C.[2] the former date seeming more probable. It was not until considerably later that they were written down and grouped together. It is not unexpected, therefore, that they bear the stamp of the thought of many ages. The periods of these thoughts may be roughly divided into the Saṁhitā or Hymn period, the Brāhmaṇa or ritual, and Āraṇyaka or forest book period. These periods are roughly the chronological order of their inception, varying considerably from one Veda to another; for instance, the *Ṛgveda*, the earliest Veda, seems to be largely ritualistic and devotional; although as would be expected with different authors and different times one finds spiritualistic, monotheistic and philosophical and even sceptical hymns. The *Sāma* and *Yajurveda*, composed somewhat later, are largely liturgical and contain many hymns found in the *ṚV*. Some scholars such as Whitney have remarked on the changes in ritual and acts of devotion from the Ṛk and Sāman gradually crystallizing into a formula; and such can be seen in the *Yajurveda*. The *Atharvaveda*, composed much later and for a long time not recognized as a Veda, seems to have largely lost the ritualistic spirit and preoccupies itself with magic and sorcery. The different views as to the origin of this magical tendency need not occupy us, though the reader may refer to Radhakrishnan[3] or Dasgupta[4] for some insight into the problem. All we need to recognize

1. Radhakrishnan, *Indian Philosophy*, I. 67.
2. Tilak, B.G., *Orion*, Poona (1893).
3. Radhakrishnan, loc. cit. I. 117ff.
4. Dasgupta, *Hist. of Indian Philosophy*, I. 12 f.

here is the chronological nature of the teaching of the four Vedas both within themselves and between each other.

The Brāhmaṇa portions of the Veda are a later development than the above Saṁhitās and show to an even greater extent the crystallization of the rituals and devotional hymns of the ṚV. By this time religion had grown complex, the ritual was largely conducted by specially trained priests. The Brāhmaṇas as a result are largely formal, divided into schools and preoccupied with sacrifice and ritual of many sorts suitable to a more complex society.

One development during this period was the institution of Āśramas, the division of duties in a person's life into periods, the Brahmacārī or student, the Gṛhastha or householder, the Vānaprastha or forest dweller and lastly the Sannyāsin or mendicant. There is reason to believe that these Āśramas were not hard and fast categories at this early period.[1] We might say however that, as time went on, the differences between the various sections of the Vedas became more clearly foci for study at different periods of one's life. The Āraṇyakas or "Forest Books" first bring out this development and tradition places them in the Vānaprastha stage when the couple had turned the household fires over to their children. It is interesting to note that while the early hymns in the ṚV were developed by people living close to nature, a philosophy of nature, it seems, could only be developed in the Āraṇyakas at a later age after religious formalism had taken over. The Āraṇyakas, then, go a long way towards showing that Hinduism of that age was perhaps not wholly formalism of ritual and sacrifices, etc. The Āraṇyakas served largely as objects of meditation on the spiritual and symbolic aspects of the sacrifices of the Brāhmaṇas.

It is at the end of the Āraṇyakas that the *Upaniṣads* are to be found. These sections are largely intended for the Sannyāsin, the one who has renounced all, or so orthodoxy would claim. Indeed we find many Upaniṣads extolling renunciation and the life of the Sannyāsin. The universal acceptance

1. See Radhakrishnan, loc. cit. I 222-3, also Keith, *Religion and Philosophy of the Veda and Up.*, p. 587 f.

of this practice and the Āśramas in general, however, may be doubted on the basis of the Upaniṣads themselves.[1] Yet the Upaniṣads are "Vedānta" or end of the Vedas, both chronologically and logically, is quite clear.

By contrast, the position of the Upaniṣads in relation to the Saṁhitās and Brāhmaṇas and Āraṇyakas is much less clear.[2] The traditional view, cited above, avers that the Upaniṣads represent the culmination of the Vedic Ritualism and philosophy, as "Vedānta". Indeed, Narahari[3] has made great efforts which, if not wholly satisfactory, at least suffice to show that Upaniṣadic speculation has deep roots in the Saṁhitās and Brāhmaṇas. Deussen[4], among many scholars and even some of the Upaniṣads themselves[5] look upon their position as a reaction against Vedic ritualism, roundly condemning all institutionalism. Whether the Upaniṣads are to be looked upon as a reaction against traditional modes of religious expression and the "dawning" of the philosophical spirit or as culmination of the Saṁhitic and Brāhmaṇic thought is a question that we need not attempt to settle here; it would be a thesis in itself. Suffice it to note here that in the Upaniṣads themselves there is not a uniform view on this matter. Consequently, we should not be surprised to find more than one school of thought taught in the Upaniṣads.

In spite of the divergency of opinion on the philosophical status of the Upaniṣads within the Vedas, the content of Upaniṣadic teaching is clear. On either interpretation the dominant interest is Adhyātmavidyā or self knowledge.[6] There are exceptions such as the erotic ritualism of the *Bṛhadāraṇyaka Upaniṣad*, but largely the reader is struck by the preoccupation with self inquiry even when imbedded in rituals, cosmology, theology, psychology, philosophy, or mysticism. These categories are found abundantly in the Upaniṣads and perhaps represent chronologically and logically different levels

1. Cf. *C.U.* 8.15, 223, 1. 5. 10; *B.U.* 4.2.22, 3.8.10.
2. See especially Keith, loc. cit. 499-500.
3. Narahari, *Ātman in Pre-Upaniṣadic Vedic Philos.*, Intro.
4. Deussen, *Philos. of the Up.*, p. 2ff, 10 ff.
5. See B.U. and especially *Muṇḍaka Up.*
6. Radhakrishnan, loc. cit. I chap 4, sect 2, p. 145f, 162.

of thought into which has been imbedded the teachings on self. We may be led to expect, then, concepts of self characterized by variant degrees of sophistication.

One short word about the word 'Upaniṣad' might be in order before going on to consider the chronological and Vedic ordering of the Upaniṣads. The most general interpretation and that given in the Brāhmaṇas[1] and Upaniṣads[2] themselves, is that it means "secret teachings", the rahasya of the Veda. Other interpretations give it as Upaniṣad, "sitting close by with devotion"[3] or even Śaṅkara's interpretation[4] "that which removes obstacles". The first is perhaps the better interpretation as indeed it was only the śiṣya initiated by the Guru who could undertake the study of such teachings.

Upaniṣads have been written for an indeterminable time in the case of the older Upaniṣads usually set before 600 B.C.[5] and continued to be written even up to modern times. It is clear, then, that we shall have to select only those which will suit our present purpose, since our job is to develop and compare the early Vedantic concept of self with later views. The first criterion of selection which appears is that they should be presystematic either in date or content. Also to afford us some idea of how much Buddhism may have influenced later systematic thought, it would be desirable to have these Upaniṣads free from Buddhist influence, preferably prior in time, as near as that can be determined. A third criteria for simplicity's sake would be to select those which do not duplicate one another excessively. Some stories will be unavoidably common but only those which show sizable lack of originality will be eliminated.

Every philologist and philosopher of the Upaniṣads has tried to date and arrange chronologically the Upaniṣads; mostly all admit that any arrangement is quite vague[6] and indeed

1. Keith 2.1.2; see also *Taittirīya Brāhmaṇa* ending "iti Upaniṣad".
2. See S.B. on *B.U.* intro, *Kaṭha Up.*, p. 73, *T.U.*, p. 9; *Muṇḍaka*, p. 261.
3. See Radhakrishnan, loc. cit. I 137.
4. Ibid, also S.B. on *T.U.* intro.
5. See next page for discussion of chronology.
6. See Keith, loc. cit. p. 501f; Deussen, loc cit., p. 22f; Radhakrishnan, *Indian Philosophy*, p. 141.

Muller[1] claims it quite hopeless a task, even attacking the validity of relative dating. For one thing many Upaniṣads, especially the larger older ones, have had more than one author and are of clearly different times.[2] Since our purpose is quite definite, then our task is made easier by the almost unanimous agreement among modern scholars[3] and ancient ones,[4] that, of the various reckonings of the number of Upaniṣads as 253,[5] 170[6] and 108[7] (the most common reckoning), only twelve of them are to be considered "Principal" Upaniṣads and of ancient date; these are the ones (with the exception of one) which Śaṅkara has commented on, another factor in our selection. Of these twelve, following is a table of what little is known as to the chronological ordering given by Keith,[8] Deussen[9], Muller[10] and Ranade.[11]

Keith	Date	Deussen	Date	Muller	Ranade	
Aitareya		Bṛhad.		Up. that are	Bṛhad.	I
Bṛhad.	I	Chānd.	I	in Saṁhitās	Chānd.	
Chānd.	600 B.C	Taitt.	600 B.C.	Brāhmaṇas &	Īśa	II
Kauṣī.	ancient	Aitareya	ancient	Āraṇyakas of	Kena	
Taitt.	prose	Kauśī	prose	Vedas prior	Aitareya	
Kena		Kena		to 600 B.C.	Taitt.	III
Kaṭha		Kaṭha	II Met.	probably.	Kauṣī.	
Īśa	II	Īṣa	contem-	Nothing		
Śveta	400 B.C	Śveta	porary	beyond this	Kaṭha	
Mund.	Metrical	Muṇḍ	Buddhism	can be	Muṇḍ.	IV
				given.	Śveta	
Praśna	III ?	Praśna	III ?		Maitrī	
Māṇḍ.	later prose	Māṇḍ	later prose		Māṇḍ.	V

1. Muller, F.M. *Upaniṣads*, S.B.E. Vol. I, LXX.
2. See Keith, loc. cit. p., 497f
3. See Radhakrishnan, loc.cit, Vol.I, p.141; Dasgupta, loc.cit, Vol.I, p. 26. Ranade, *Constructive Survey of U. Philos.*, pp. 11, 16. Deussen, loc. cit., p. 5 ff.
4. Cf. especially Śaṅkara's bhāṣya on only 10 of these
5. Weber, *Hist. of Sanskrit Literature*, p. 155.
6. See Adyar library edition of unpublished Upaniṣads making the total 170.
7. The generally accepted figure, See Radhakrishnan, loc.cit. Vol. I. p. 141, cf. also Mahadevan, *Upanishads,* G. Natesan, introduction, p. xxii.
8. Keith, loc.cit, p. 498-500.
9. Deussen, loc.cit. p.23-6.
10. Muller, F.M. *Upanishads,* S.B.E. Vol. I, LXXVI.
11. Ranade, loc.cit., p. 16.

Of these twelve Upaniṣads we shall fully consider only ten of them, the other two shall be referred to only. The first not studied is the *Kauṣītaki Upaniṣad* which while being an early Upaniṣad and most probably presystematic is largely ritualistic, copies much from the *Bṛhadāraṇyaka Upaniṣad*,[1] and with the exception of the doctrine of transmigration, offers little to our subject of inquiry. Clearly these reasons in the light of the criteria for selection mitigate against it. In addition we do not have a Bhāṣya by Śaṅkara on it, which the other ten have. Another Upaniṣad which shall not be taken up fully, but will be used as reference in our study is the *Śvetāśvatara Upaniṣad*. The conclusion of this Upaniṣad is a theistic system comprising what were later Sāṅkhya, Yoga, and Vedānta and is quite close to the *Gītā*; but we shall not consider it fully both because the technical use of the terms differs markedly from the other ten Upaniṣads which seems to strongly indicate systematic influence; and also because use of the word 'Māyā' stands out from the use in the other ten and the *Gītā* where it usually means "the power of creation," strongly suggesting later sectarian formations. Now these objections are themselves not beyond questioning; and so to avoid begging the question of our thesis we should keep in mind the contents of the two Upaniṣads and refer to them where needed in our discussion. One point in regard to our selection of the *Kaṭha Upaniṣad* should be mentioned. Many writers have remarked on the appearance of both Sāṅkhya and Yoga elements in this Upaniṣad.[2] A close inspection of the passages,[3] however, shows to the contrary only such general references as might be found in other Upaniṣads more definitely free of any systematic influence. Rather it appears that here as in the *Gītā*, although the germs of these two systems are there, a presystematic use is more probable. We shall have more to say about this when discussing the *Kaṭha Upaniṣad* and the *Gītā*.

As to the Vedic order of the twelve Upaniṣads, there is not such doubt as with the Chronological order. Just how integrated they are with other portions of the Veda is quite

1. See Deussen, loc. cit., p.24.
2. Radhakrishnan, loc.cit. I 142.
3. II 18-19, II 6, 10-11.

variable and full consideration is not necessary,[1] except to note that Upaniṣads such as *Bṛhadāraṇyaka*, which is part of the *Śatapatha Brāhmaṇa*, show strong Brāhmaṇic influence as noted above, while the *Praśna* and *Māṇḍūkya*, much later Upaniṣads, seem associated little more than in name only. One might conclude that these, like the minor Upaniṣads, coming as they did much later, associated with various Vedas for their own purposes.[2] Below is the Vedic order of the twelve Upaniṣads:

TABLE OF VEDIC ORDER OF UPANIṢADS

Ṛv.	Sāma	Yajur: Black	Yajur: White	Atharva
Aitareya	Chāndogya	Taittirīya	Bṛhadāraṇyaka	Praśna
Kauṣītaki	Kena	Kaṭha	Īśa	Muṇḍaka
		Śvetāśvatara		Māṇḍūkya

Since the doctrines of the Upaniṣads are largely independent of the other sections of the Vedas in which they are found, especially in regard to our topic, then the above table will not greatly influence our analysis, except to note that the Atharva Veda Upaniṣads are considered to be the latest of the twelve and indeed as Keith rightly observes, presupposes the material of the others. As we shall see in our conclusions, these Upaniṣads consciously or unconsciously sum up the concepts of self found in the others.

It was observed in the General Introduction that there had been surprisingly little work done with major interest on the concept of self. Narahari's thesis[3] was mentioned, but his interest is largely pre-Upaniṣadic and complimentary to ours. There have been many ancient and modern studies of the Upaniṣads and their treatments of the concept of self will be considered in our present work, especially in the conclusions.

1. Deussen, loc.cit., p. 25 also Keith, loc. cit., pp. 498-500
2. Loc. cit., p. 500
3. See p. iii Intro.

Of the ancient writers on the Upaniṣads, Śaṅkara is undoubtedly the most influential. The concept of Ātman-Brahman, as is commonly known, is a key concept in Advaita Vedānta, the popularization of which Śaṅkara is largely responsible. He clearly claims authority of our two texts, especially the Upaniṣads for his views. To what degree his claims are valid, we shall have occasion to consider. Śaṅkara, however, whatever the source, clearly owes much to Gauḍapāda, whose teachings Śaṅkara learned through his Guru, Govinda, a student of Gauḍapāda. Gauḍapāda's *Āgama Śastras* are one of the earliest works on Advaita Vedānta and the *Kārikā*, which is its first chapter is related to the *Māṇḍūkya Upaniṣad* usually considered a commentary on it.[1] We shall have occasion to discuss this work when taking up the *Māṇḍūkya Upaniṣad.* In addition, when considering the *Īśa Upaniṣad* the Bhāṣyas of Madhva and Veṅkaṭanātha will be referred to as an aid in unravelling its rather difficult passages.

Deussen is one modern supporter of Śaṅkara's views, and believes him to be correctly interpreting the Upani adic teachings on Ātman-Brahman. In the conclusions when more general matter will be discussed, Dasgupta, Radhakrishnan, and Ranade along with Deussen will provide some assistance in classifying the Teaching of the Upaniṣads on self. Such scholar's works as Keith's and Deussen's are indispensable for anyone attempting to unravel the vast lines of thought found in the Upaniṣads; the divergency of opinion among them, and these latter two are good examples, illustrate a difficulty with the text itself, and perhaps the approach used in the Upaniṣads. Indeed some basis for this difficulty has been already discussed in the General Introduction. We shall now consider this matter in more detail as it relates to the Upaniṣads.

B. *Linguistic Problem*

Much has already been said regarding language problems in the General Introduction and we need here only to empha-

1. See Bhaṭṭācārya's introduction to his translation of Gauḍapāda's *Āgama Śāstra.* He tries to show that the Kārikā is on the *Brahma Sūtras* and is before the *Māṇḍūkya.* Consensus of opinion is that the bhāṣya is on the *Māṇḍūkya Up.*

size that aspect related to the Upaniṣads. The profuse use of myth, allegory, and symbolism was observed earlier, and it applies especially to the Upaniṣads. We must observe at first with Radhakrishnan[1] that "The Upaniṣads are essentially the outpourings or poetic deliverances of philosophically tempered minds in the face of the facts of life." Moreover since according to the Historical Introduction, above, there have been many authors and different eras, sometimes even for one Upaniṣad, we cannot expect anything like systematic use of language; indeed as we would not so expect of poetry. Passages are often cursory, almost aphoristic and usually cast in dialogue form, being the teachings attributed to various sages. Our task, then, will be much like developing the concept of self that might be found in a body of poetry, hence our categories of analysis outlined in the General Introduction.

Most important of our considerations of linguistic problems which arise from the above discussion is the difference in Upaniṣadic and later systematic terminology. For example 'prāṇa': where in the later systems it seems usually to refer to "vital force", in the Upaniṣads it is so occasionally used, but seems more often to be used in its general connotation as "life" or "life breath." Another more obvious case is the use of 'manas' which in systematic use[2] generally refers to the internal sense organ, i.e., the unifying factor of the indriyas. Many uses were made of it in the Upaniṣads,[3] sometimes even to refer to what we might use 'Buddhi' or 'Vijñāna' for, in later philosophy. It is apparent, then, that the procedure of the general introduction to retain Sanskrit terms where possible is of special value in this case; for we might conclude from the two examples above—which only represents a host of others—that the Upaniṣadic use is less fixed, often showing effects of different individual usage in the absence of a technical vocabulary. In addition to this varied use of some of our terms, there is also their symbolic nature to consider. 'Anna' for instance is possibly the most outstanding. While often translated by scholars as 'food', as indeed is its common meaning,

1. loc.cit. I 138.
2. See *Sāṅkhya Kārikā* XXVII.
3. See Bloomfield, *Vedic Concordance*.

one feels the symbolic use of it almost continually in the sense of "stuff" or the basic matter, the material out of which all phenomenal things are shaped. It is truly, then, "food" for the created world, much like Aristotle's "Hyle". Another example is 'Vāyu' which is usually translated "wind" and seems to be the cosmic equivalent of 'prāṇa' which is usually used in reference to man. One might say that it is the same vital force in the cosmos or "macrocosm" which man finds in his "microcosm".

If this is sufficient warning about the language to be found in the Upaniṣads, the methodology to be used in the face of such language should be briefly considered.

C. *Methodology*

The remarks in the General Introduction as to the intuitive and supra-rational nature of the teachings to be considered, apply especially to the Upaniṣads. One could hardly expect a systematic treatment of the concept of self as an individual philosopher would develop a cosmological or linguistic system. Because in the language of the Upaniṣads, then, they may hardly be said to present us a systematic treatment of our topic. The criteria of our analysis, coherence and completeness, already given, were constructed with this in mind.

Before considering our technique in detail, some general remarks on procedure should be given. First, since we shall not consider the Upaniṣads to be śruti, as Śaṅkara for example does, our task is not one of resolving the manifold "revelations" to some rational system, but a critical one of developing in a coherent manner the concepts of self to be found in the vast outpourings of the ten Upaniṣads chosen. Secondly since the ten Upaniṣads were written, as was observed in section A, over different periods of time and by different authors, we can hardly take them as one unit as would be done were they considered śruti or had they a single author. Indeed Śaṅkara's treatment can be seen immediately to be quite inadequate in view of the style, different authorship, etc., which render a "dominant passage" all but impossible.

In our texts, as in any works written by various authors

and over a period of time, one finds different philosophical levels of presentation. Thus in our ten works ritual, theology, cosmology, psychology, and mysticism all occur. The casual reader in philosophy soon becomes aware of the order of the above. The beginnings of philosophical thought seem often to be found in a search for the first principle, the essence of the cosmos and its source, which has been termed theology here. This early interest, then, is focused entirely on environment; and the same personality underlying the observer is projected so to speak in the form of a God or first principle. Prajāpati or Hiraṇyagarbha might be examples of this. Interest is then focused on cosmology, how this first principle has created or projected the world and what is its structure. The many descriptions of creation we shall consider will well illustrate this level. It seems that after the world is created and understood, only then does man's interest focus on man, on psychology. At this point consideration in vision of self really begins. Perhaps at first, as we shall see, relating organs and powers of the body to those in nature is a preoccupation. Finally the thinker is led to consider problems of purpose and the ultimate destiny of the self, after he has some knowledge of the self as he immediately finds it. For the lack of a better word this endeavour will be termed eschatology, the study of last things. All these levels are to be found in the Upaniṣads and shall be studied by our consideration of the concept of self. Our work, then, is the discovery of the orderly steps which lead to understanding of the nature of self. To forestall objections which may be immediately made against such an analysis, we might emphasize that the above structure is a logical arrangement, not necessarily a chronological one. Rather referring to our general introduction, the above structure is arranged according to the criterion of completeness in its formulation of a concept of self. In other words the theological view, insofar as it is self-projected into nature or beyond, is the most incomplete level of a concept of self; precisely because it is considered objective and is a projection. The steps that lead through cosmology gradually to psychology and eschatology are more "complete" because the problem is treated more directly whereby much that could not be objectified in the wloer levels can then be taken up.

This logical order of completeness will be more clear in our analysis of the concept of self, especially as we reach the more complete concepts of self such as Ātman and Brahman. Our consideration of the material will be centred around the three main terms representing "self" in the Upaniṣads—'Puruṣa', 'Ātman', and 'Brahman'. Although these three terms are used quite differently in different Upaniṣads and different contexts, we can assign a meaning to them which will have both etymological and textual support, thereby giving us criteria for analysis. Like the above logical order of completeness, these three terms will be seen to represent three different levels of considering self, each more complete in its coverage till with 'Brahman' we have a term for the ultimate reality. Thus, for example, 'Puruṣa' although it is used in contexts ranging from those describing the egocentric immediate self, the individual, to those contexts discussing Brahman and creation, the majority of passages discussing self in its individual and immediate sense use only 'Puruṣa'. Therefore we shall merely limit its denotation to this level in our analysis. Likewise 'Ātman' and 'Brahman' each denote higher and more complete senses of self which include both the macrocosmic universe and in the case of Brahman also the ultimate reality. By carefully studying the uses of these three terms in our ten Upaniṣads, not only will we be afforded an adequate cross-section of the concept of self in the Upaniṣads, but also by the nature of the three concepts connoting each a broader sense of self, we can, in the light of the order discussed above, find the logical development of the concept and any chronological development that presents itself. Our first task in each chapter will be to consider the various uses of the term and attempt to find its primary and most direct meaning. When this task has been accomplished we can then proceed to consider the term, keeping in mind the above progression from theology to eschatology insofar as it is applicable to the term under consideration. In the conclusions some attempt will be made to classify the various senses of self found in the connotation of the terms of our analysis. If this classification is successful we may then go on to apply external criticism, such as finding in what sense we can say the Upaniṣads teach one doctrine, the claim of orthodoxy. Also this classification would be expected to throw much light on the Gītā's treatment of the concept of self as well as the source of the Dārśanic views. Let us proceed, then, to consider 'Puruṣa', 'Ātman', and 'Brahman' each in its turn.

CHAPTER II

THE SELF AS PURUṢA

A. Introduction :

The use of 'Puruṣa' reaches all the way back to the Ṛgveda.[1] There it seems Puruṣa is viewed in one context as the first principle. Elsewhere[2] Puruṣa becomes literally "man". Although such a broad extension would seem to vitiate its effectiveness as a term for our analysis, we can see nevertheless a common intention in all the uses of 'Puruṣa'. Thus even in the creation myths of the Ṛgveda, mentioned above, Puruṣa is viewed as a cosmic man, i.e., a personality. This concept of personality, in other words the individual, what we normally refer to as a 'person', seems to be the root meaning found in all uses of 'Puruṣa', as might be verified by reference to Bloomfield's *Vedic Concordance*.

The use of 'Puruṣa' in the Upaniṣads, it should be noted, differs greatly from the *Gītā* and later Darśanas. There 'Puruṣa' takes the place largely of all three terms of our investigation here, 'Puruṣa', 'Ātman', and 'Brahman'. Qualifying adjectives such as 'kṣara', 'avyakta' etc. are used with 'Puruṣa' to adequately distinguish the different senses of the term. This use has many important philosophical implications which will be considered in the conclusion to the chapter. We might recognize at the outset, however, that the *Gītā* and later uses of the term carries the sense of personality into areas transcendent normally of such distinctions. The Upaniṣads seem more to limit 'Puruṣa' to the personal, individual sense of self. At least we might say that when the individual is referred to, 'Puruṣa' is almost invariably the term used, even though in other contexts it may be used where 'Ātman' might seem to be called for.

In our analysis, then, we shall merely delimit its intention to its root application, to the personality, the person, the indivi-

1. Ṛgveda X. 90.

2. See Jacobs, C., *Concordance to the Principal Upaniṣads and Bhagavad Gītā*, Motilal Banarsidass, Delhi, 1961.

dual. This shall be the preoccupation of this chapter. We might realize at the beginning that it may be impossible to realize a clear separation of what would apply to 'Puruṣa' and that which would apply to 'Ātman'; rather we must recognize that Puruṣa in its higher reaches may blend into what will be discussed under Ātman. This point will not in any way vitiate our analysis and its full significance may be realized, perhaps after taking up 'Ātman' in the next chapter.

B. Analysis of Puruṣa :

First let us see just how our ten Upaniṣads view self on the most basic level of physiology and psychology. Perhaps the oldest analysis in point of time, having roots in the Brahmanical portions of the Vedas, are the analyses of man in terms of his senses. Thus we find in the *Kaṭha Upaniṣad*[1] the description of the body as the town of 11 gates, presumably referring to the seven openings in the head, the navel, the two lower openings and the one in the middle of the head, the ending of the suṣumnā. Parallel with this eleven-fold analysis one finds a five-fold[2] and a three-fold analysis[3] both related and somewhat symbolic. The five-fold analysis, in addition to its symbolic relation to the individual, is also part of the creation stories we shall take up in the third chapter. The parts of Puruṣa and their symbolic relations are as follows[4]—

1)	Mind (Manas)	.. Husband
2)	Speech	.. Wife
3)	Life (Prāṇa)	.. Work (Karma)—offspring
4)	Eye	.. Wealth
5)	Ear	.. Knowledge

This analysis of man is largely sensory and egocentrically oriented, i.e., both the eleven-fold and the five-fold analysis presupposes man on the body and sensory level. A third analysis even more common to earlier parts of the Veda is derived from the above five-fold analysis, i.e., mind, life, and speech, the three-fold offspring of Prajāpati[5]. This three-fold analysis seems to

1. *Kaṭha Upaniṣad*, 5.1.
2. See *B.U.* 1.4.17.
3. *Ibid.*, 1.4.3.
4. *B.U.* 1.5.
5. *Ibid.*, 1.3.

be directly linked in the *Chāndogya Upaniṣad*[1] to the culmination of all physical and physiological analyses.

Faculty	*Constituent*	*Symbol*
Mind	Anna (food)	black
Life	Apas (water)	white
Speech	Tejas (heat)	red

Unlike the previous two analyses which have *largely only* cosmological significances linking the various faculties represented to corresponding deities, this analysis reaches out into what was to be the Guṇa-theory of the *Gītā* and later Darśanas. Its relation can be seen when it is realized that all existence is composed of these triune elements. Thus the *Chāndogya* says, "The redness of the sun is due to heat, its whiteness to water, and its darkness to earth. Hence the sun ceases to be the sun, it is nothing but a word; it is an effect and is nominal. Its three forms alone are true."[2] Thus all creation is a mixture of these three elements. Man, for instance, bodily is analysed as follows under this scheme :

Gross element	*Gross particles*	*Middle particles*	*Fine particles*
Food	.. Solid waste	Flesh	Mind
Water	.. Liquid waste	Blood	Breath (Prāṇa)
Heat	.. Bones	Marrow	Speech

Thus we see that the gross element is itself triune, giving rise to three different particles. The *Chāndogya* does not seem to clearly differentiate between the three subtle qualities and their gross representations in the above table as does Sāṅkhyan metaphysics later. The analysis clearly does, however, lay the foundation for the guṇa theory and the analogy is quite clear when viewed in terms of red-white-and black.

Symbol	*Element*	*Guṇa equivalent*
Red	Tejas	Rajas
White	Apas	Sattva
Black	Anna	Tamas

Others, such as Deussen, have also recognized this analysis as the foundation for the later guṇa theory.[3] Although Śaṅkara

1. See also *Śvetāśvatara Upaniṣad.*
2. *C.U.* 6.4.2.
3. Deussen, *Philosophy of the Upaniṣads*, p. 250 ff.

criticizes this view and sees no connection, only an affirmation of the one being of which all are modifications (vikṛti), in the *Śvetāśvatara* he finds only reference to the enlightened and unenlightened (C.U. 6.4. Bhāṣya and *Śvetāśvatara* Bhāṣya).

Thus the early symbolic analyses of Puruṣa, largely sensorily oriented, culminate in the physical analysis of man and material creation. This has manifold consequences not only to our present analysis of man but we will see also later in the chapter when trying to show man's relation to the Universe and in later chapters when treating self in its more universal senses.

Parallel to these analyses is another which leads to a more comprehensive analysis of man. In this analysis, which likewise reaches back to the Brāhmaṇas,[1] man is viewed as sixteen-fold. Only vague references at first reach us in the *Bṛhadāraṇyaka*[2] and the *Chāndogya*[3] which are not elaborated. Śaṅkara somewhat gratuitously identifies those analyses with their elaboration in *Praśna Upaniṣad.*[4] Even here, however, the significance of "sixteen" is not made clear and the enumeration is not unequivocally sixteen-fold. The many references to the sixteen-fold man as mentioned above stem from the *Śata-Br.*, where it is given as the sixteen symbols of the words loman, tvac, asṛj, medas, māṁsam, snāyu, asthi, majjā (hair, skin, blood, sap, flesh, sinew, bones, marrow).

It seems most probable that in view of the Upaniṣadic vagueness about the sixteen parts that it served primarily to give Vedic authority to their analyses of man; and sixteen-fold divisions were obtained by truncating certain elements into a single unit. Therefore, let us expand each of these analyses to be found in the Upaniṣads to find certain basic trends, if any in them.

1. See *Śata. Brāhmaṇa,* X 4.1.17.
2. *B.U.* 1.5.17.
3. *C.U.* 6.7.
4. *Praśna*, 2. 2. 6; 6.5-8.

Praśna 6.4	*Praśna* 4.8		*Deussen*, p. 268
Prāṇa (Life)	Earth (Pṛthivī)	5 gross elements	Earth (Pṛthivī)
Śraddhā (Faith)	Apas (Water)		Apas (Water)
Kham (Ether)	Tejas (Light)		Tejas (Light)
Vāyu (Air)	Vāyu (Air)		Vāyu (Air)
Jyoti (Light)	Ākāśa (Ether)		Ākāśa (Ether)
Āpaḥ (Water)	Subtle earth	5 subtle elements	Eye
Earth (Pṛthivī)	,, water		Ear
Indriyam (Sense Faculty)	,, light		Smell
Manas (sense Mind)	,, air		Taste
Anna (Food)	,, ether		Skin
Strength (Vīryam)	Eye object	Jñānendriyas	Speech
Tapas	Ear object		Hands
Mantras	Smell object		Organs of generation
Karmaḥ	Taste object		Organs of excretion
Lokaḥ (The worlds, effect of work)	Skin (Tvak) object		Feet
Nāman	Speech object (speakable)	Karmendriyas	Manas
	Hands object (graspable)		
	Organs of generation object (enjoyable)		
	Organs of exertion object		
	Feet object (What is movable)		
	Manas object		
	Buddhi object		
	Ahaṁkāra (ego) object		
	Citta object		
	Tejas object		
	Prāṇa all to be supported		

The first list, that associated directly with the term sixteen-fold, can be seen to contain in the last five elements much of the earlier Brāhmaṇic material in its use of name, mantras, action and the *Worlds* of action. Moreover, it seems highly gratuitous that the Indriyas are considered as one instead of ten, which had been known much earlier.[1] If considered as ten there would be twenty-five elements; indeed not the Sāṅkhyan twenty-five elements, however. The second, however, does give an analysis remarkably close to the later Sāṅkhyan, enumerating twenty-six. The similarity between these two is borne out by the third, which is a sixteen-fold enumeration based upon a more elaborate material and sensory analysis than given in the five-fold or three-fold analysis above.

Perhaps these sensory analyses, with the exception of the three-fold analysis, would give us little help in understanding Self as Puruṣa were it not for a chapter in the *Chāndogya*,[2] "The teachings of Sanatkumāra to Nārada", in which a sixteen-fold analysis of Puruṣa ('Ātman') is used, giving order to the analysis. Here, of course, there are some elements of the above analysis not to be found and others in their place.

1) Name
2) Speech
3) Manas (Feeling or sense mind)
4) Saṅkalpa (determining reason, will)
5) Citta (thought, intellect)
6) Meditation, reflection (dhyāna)
7) Vijñāna (insight)
8) Power, strength (Balam)
9) Anna (food)
10) Apas (Water)
11) Tejas (heat)
12) Ākāśa (ether)
13) Memory (connectivity)
14) Āśā (hope)
15) Prāṇa (Life)
16) Puruṣa (Ātman)

The importance of this analysis lies in its assertion of order to the enumeration, which is not to be found in the previous attempts. Thus elements one to seven, of name to Vijñāna, represent epistemologically an increasing order of completeness in consciousness of Puruṣa. Elements eight to twelve represent the physical and vital basis for the expression of this consciousness of Puruṣa in the world. The last two, memory or connectiveness and hope, represent, it seems, what we might call the world ground, that which lays the purpose for existence and unfoldment of all the elements from Prāṇa. This last point, the nature of memory and hope, is admittedly a speculation, but is based

1. *B.U.* 2.4.11; 4.5.12.
2. See Chap. VII.

upon the clearer analyses of the other elements which we have already considered. Śaṅkara at this point gives us little help because at the beginning of the chapter we have been informed that it is about "lower things". Further on 'truth' (Satyam) and insight (Vijñānam), zeal, faith (Śraddhā), Niṣṭhā (reverent service), balanced and controlled mind (Kṛti), happiness (Sukham), and finally bhūmā or the infinite is given as the means and ground of Prāṇa's unfoldment. The two terms hope and connectivity, then, are given in an expanded sense and are linked to the first seven elements of name to insight. The crown of the analysis lies in Bhūmā—immensity or the infinite and this as we shall see later in discussing the triune—Brahman-Sat-chit-ānanda or satyam-jñānam-anantam—sheds more light on memory and hope as world and personal grounds for the unfoldment of the entire order from Prāṇa in Sanatkumāra's analysis, i.e., memory, hope and Bhūmā are perhaps precursors of anantam and ānanda given in *Taittirīya* as the basis for Brahman's creation.

Now the reader undoubtedly has seen a trend in the above analyses of Puruṣa. The early symbolic analyses led in two directions, one to the triune physical analysis anticipating the later guṇa theory of Sāṅkhya; the other to the more complete analysis of the physical, vital and mental levels, seeming to anticipate the Sāṅkhyan twenty-five-fold analysis and culminating in Sanatkumāra's teaching which has given order and arrangement to the other attempts. This order can clearly be seen to be ontological in nature; that is elements 1 to 7 clearly are the mental levels and are shown to rest upon the vital level-element 8 and physical level-elements 9-12 and finally all three are given teleological grounds of memory and hope leading ultimately to rest in the concept of immensity or infinite (bhūmā). We might infer a relation between Sanatkumāra's analysis and that in the *Taittirīya*[1] and in the *Kaṭha*,[2] both of which show more clearly in ontological character than our previous analyses. This is the concept of the Pañcamayakoṣas, which was to be the dominent theory in the later Dārśanic analyses. The nature

1. *T.U.* 2. 15.
2. *Kaṭha Upaniṣad*. 2. 6; 7. 8.

of these five kośas, or Sheaths of Puruṣa, and their relation to our above analyses is shown below :

Taitt. Kośa analyses	*Sanatkumāra and Praśna*	
1) Annakośa (Food sheath)	(1) Anna, Apas, Tejas, Ākāśa of Sanatkumāra	(2) 5 gross and subtle elements of Praśna analyses
2) Prāṇakośa	(1) Balam—power—of Sanatkumāra	(2) Vīryam—strength—of Praśna
	Sanatkumāra	*Praśna*
	Name—speech as Indriyas	
3) Manaḥkośa	Manas Saṅkalpa Citta Dhyāna	Manas Buddhi ahaṁkāra Citta
4) Vijñānakośa	Vijñāna	
5) Ānandakośa	Memory—hope and immensity	(none)

From this table interesting conclusions can be obtained in support of the above discussion of Sanatkumāra's analysis. First we see that the Praśna's sixteen-fold analyses fail to give order or purpose to Puruṣa, i.e., their analyses fail insofaras they are incomplete on the higher levels of mind (Vijñāna and dhyāna of Sanatkumāra) and lack any reference to the Ānanda or immensity level of Sanatkumāra's. These two additions by the Sanatkumāra and *Taittirīya* analysis give clear ontological order to the entire 25 elements. These additions were not in any way new additions, but go back to the earliest considerations of Ātman and Brahman in the Vedas to which they are the link of Puruṣa. The *Praśna* analysis merely stops short of providing this link of Puruṣa to Ātman and confines itself to a more phenomenal analysis. Secondly, we can see that the Koṣa analysis brings out the full import of an ontological analysis of Puruṣa as well as illuminating the meaning of Brahman being food, Prāṇa etc. which we shall find in the chapter on Brahman. In addition, much of the symbolism of earlier analyses will show up clearly in the light of the Kośa analysis of Puruṣa of the *Taittirīya Up.* Thus the chariot allegory of the *Kaṭha* is given import by this analysis. The body as the chariot, buddhi (reason) as the charioteer, and manas (mind) the reins, and the senses the horses, all point to the same conclusion, the need to direct the senses by the mind, the body by the Prāṇa etc., otherwise it is like the chariot with uncontrolled (wicked) horses which never attains its goal. This is merely saying all five Kośas are part of a team, the Puruṣa, like the chariot, horses etc. There is an order to their function, therefore, and so there is the need to control the lower anna and Prāṇa Kośas, for instance, by the Manas and Buddhi levels; or as it is said in the *Taittirīya* in presenting the Kośa, analysis, each higher level is the inner soul (Śarīra-Ātmā) of the next lower ones. From this, then, we may reach the important conclusion that the five Kośas, standing for the twenty-five elements and other analyses set out in the other Upaniṣads, is not an analysis of Puruṣa in extenso but represents an intensive analysis, an ontological analysis in which each level of being is summed up (as the embodied soul of the lower) in the higher till a complete expression of the Puruṣa is attained in passing from the fifth Kośa—ānanda. Even greater importance of this conclusion will be seen as we proceed. One observation which might be made regarding the Kośa analysis is the general agreement by all the ācāryas on its being an analysis of the different levels of reality. The only difference arises over whether they are to be taken as layers of ignorance over the one Brahman—Śaṅkara's adhyāsa—or as grades of bliss, grades of proximity to Brahman which is more the Taittirīya's own view.

The above Kośa analysis claims that as one ascends from the anna to the ānanda Kośa there is a 'more complete' expression and consciousness of Puruṣa. At first glance this may seem contrary to the many passages in the Upaniṣads seeking the primary psychophysical principle. Thus the organs quarrel in the *Chāndogya*[1] as to which is 'chief'. Of them, Manas, Prāṇa, speech, eye, and ear—Prāṇa is given the victory. In other Upaniṣads[2] the same conclusion is reached. This is not to say that Prāṇa is a more complete expression of Puruṣa than Manas, but more 'basic' to bodily existence. 'Manas' here does not stand as in the Kośa analysis for all mental principles from Manas to Vijñāna but merely as the basic meaning of inner sense organ. This conclusion, then, is merely saying that Prāṇa, life force, is the ground of bodily existence, without which manas and the rest could not function through the senses. In other words as the tree depends upon its roots, the Puruṣa depends upon its roots in Prāṇa. Elsewhere,[3] anna is joined to Prāṇa as fundamental principles of our existence in bodily form. For instance, the 15 days Śvetaketu[4] drank water (prāṇa) but did not take anna or food he lived but Prāṇa could not manifest through hearing, sight or thinking, action or acquiring knowledge. All this seems to bear out the idea that each higher Kośa is the 'embodied soul' of the lower one, for Prāṇa is the necessary inner activation of the sense, as organs of the anna or food sheath. Therefore those passages are not contrary to the conclusions of the Kośa analysis but supplement the concept and merely illustrate that the Puruṣa's expression is grounded in the two lowest Kośas, in the food and vital sheath, without which Puruṣa would not have bodily existence.

This point sheds light not only on the eschatology of Puruṣa, which we shall take up later, but also upon another factor of the Upaniṣadic analysis, the study of the three states of man, waking, dream, and deep sleep. In the waking state Puruṣa expresses itself through the senses and the food sheath. It conceives, desires, does actions and reaps fruit of those actions. The dream state, on the other hand, seems to be considered a transition state between 'this world' as *Bṛhadāraṇyaka*[5] terms the waking state, and the other world; the world of death, the next world where one retires in deep sleep. In the dream state Prāṇa retires from the senses and the Puruṣa then constructs

1. *C.U.* 5. 1.6-16.
2. *B.U.* 6.1.7-13; *A.U.* 2.1; *P.U.* 2.2-4.
3. *C.U.* 7.9; *T.U.* 3.2; 2.1.
4. *C.U.* 6.7.
5. *B.U.* 4.3.9.

a 'dream body'[1] and all things of this world; and so experiences pleasures and pains. It seems that impressions from this world are acted out as well as visions of the next world in this dream state. Since the Puruṣa is agent of this dream world there are no impressions remaining as in the waking state. This view of the dream state is highly significant in terms of modern thought; for it seems that the Upaniṣadic Ṛṣis have seen the transitory and subjective nature of the dream state. As is said in the *Praśna,*[2] the mind (Manas) is the enjoyer of dreams; it is as if all the senses were collected in manas where this transition world is constructed and experiences acted out purely subjectively within the prāṇa kośa. This view of the dream state seems like that of modern psychology at many points.

From a study of the deep sleep state, on the other hand, there are novel ideas to contribute to our consideration of Puruṣa. Unlike modern consideration of deep sleep state as a negative or blank state, the Upaniṣads show us its positive character. Various terms are used to describe it; the Puruṣa "dwells within itself",[3] "it takes on the nature of bliss,"[4] it becomes self illumined, effulgent in light of self.[5] Here the Puruṣa dwells, it seems, in its own nature in bliss, effulgence, and at rest, the subject object state of the waking and dream state having been dropped.

We might observe at this point the significance of these three states to the previous Kośa analysis, and also to eschatological considerations found in the pseudo-physiological analysis of the heart and 'nāḍī' structure which occurs in many passages. In these passages it is said that the self ('Puruṣa', 'Ātman' or 'Brahman' is used depending on context) dwells within the "ether of the heart"[6] (antahṛdya-ākāśa); and that the various aspects of personality revolve around this as the spokes and rim of a wheel to its nave.[7] It is said that from the heart spread 101 nāḍīs connecting all aspects of personality and even extending

1. See *B.U.* 4.3.13.
2. *P.U.* 4.5.
3. *B.U.* 43.19, 23; *P.U.* 4.6.
4. *B.U.* 4.3.17.
5. *B.U.* 4.3.6; *P.U.* 4.6.
6. *T.U.* 1.6.1.
7. *Praśna* : 2.6.3, 3.4, 3.5.7.

beyond into macrocosmic realms. The 'nāḍīs' are often mistranslated as 'veins',[1] or as 'nerves'[2]; but it seems that any attempt to take such views literally and think that the heart as a physiological organ is referred to physiological nerves or veins reduces the passages to nonsense and lies counter to the physiological knowledge of the most rudimentary sort which the culture of the time possessed. Rather it seems that the nāḍīs as carriers of Prāṇa to the manifold aspects of personality are more nearly what later Yoga-darśana has considered them to be simply carriers of Prāṇa and are psychic and not physiological; the heart more nearly approximates the later Hṛdpadmam. If this be the case, then, we can see that it is saying that the self retires to the manas and eventually to nāḍīs surrounding the heart in the dream state[3]. We may translate these obtruse passages in terms of the kośa analysis whereby the Puruṣa withdraws from the food sheath and expresses itself on the vital level which is the transition between "this world" (body considered as anna and prāṇa kośas) and the "next world" (the subtle body 'Sūkṣmaśarīra' considered as Prāṇa and manas kośas). In this stage we might observe that, as discussed above, manas as the enjoyer of the dream seems to construct all objects through the agency of Prāṇa. What is most important is that in deep sleep it is said that Puruṣa retires into the ether of the heart and 'leaving Prāṇa to keep watch in the sleeping city,'[4] Puruṣa becomes the nature of bliss, self-effulgent. The kośa analysis interprets this literally as a retiring from the manas—vijñāna level into the ānanda or bliss kośa, its 'own nature', and truly so being the highest ontological level and so most complete in its expression of Puruṣa.

Although the interpretation of the nāḍīs and heart as we have done is admittedly a speculation based upon later, less symbolic terminology of the Darśanas, nevertheless the passages lend themselves to this interpretation, and indeed interpret the sleep-waking-dream analysis in terms of the Kośas most coherently. Śaṅkara often speaks of the gross and subtle bodies but

1. Keith, *Religion and Philosophy of the Veda and Upanishads*, p. 566. Deussen, loc. cit. p. 286-90.
2. Radhakrishnan, Tans., 1. *Praśna Up.* 3.6.
3. *Māṇḍūkya Up.* 4; *Kaṭha Up.* 6.16; *B.U.* 2.1.19; 4.3.10-14.
4. *P.U.* 4.3.

he seldom makes the correlation[1] with the kośa analysis, although he does speak as the texts do of "the Self retiring into its own nature of bliss" etc., in deep sleep. Our interpretation is merely one of linking various passages which mutually support one another and not an interpretation of our own. Aurobindo seems to have made the same correlation,[2] as well as Rāmānuja,[3] although the latter not in Upaniṣadic context.

The consideration of the three states when so linked to the Kośa analysis might also afford us some insight into the essential nature of Puruṣa. Thus, just as the dream state is a freeing of Puruṣa from the anna level, with its requirements of action binding the Puruṣa, into a level of Prāṇa where it is self-creative of its objects, so the deep sleep state is a dropping the activity of Prāṇa and Manas to a level to retire into its own nature of bliss and self effulgence. We can see, then, that the three state analysis and the psycho-physiological analysis culminating in the kośas both agree that the essential nature of the Puruṣa is bliss (ānanda), self-effulgence, and a consciousness free from the subject-object structure of the waking and dream states where it does not abide in its own nature.

This then is the analysis of Puruṣa, the foundation for the concepts of self in the Upaniṣads. We must not fall into the misconception, as some do,[4] that this analysis of Puruṣa represents "the teachings of the Upaniṣads". This analysis is only the metaphysical culmination of all the analyses given here and indeed what most passages speaking of the Ātman and Brahman seem to presuppose when referred to Puruṣa or the individual. Actually there are many conclusions in the Upaniṣads as to the nature of Puruṣa; practically all the above sensory, psycho-physical and metaphysical analyses represent such. We could infer, however, that the tripartite analysis anticipating the Guṇas, and the sixteen-fold analysis are the culmination of the analysis of self, for those who claim the self to be ego-centric individual bound to Vedic works etc. If we understand this, let us go on to consider now these concepts of Puruṣa are related to the conception of the universe as a whole.

1. *B.U.*, *Śāṅkara Bhāṣya* 4.3.36; *P.U.*, Ś.B. 5.
2. See *T.U.*. 2, *Life Divine*, p. 238.
3. See Rāmānuja Bhāṣya on *Kaṭha Up.* 6.16.
4. Especially the Three Ācaryas.

C. Puruṣa and the Universe :

From the above consideration of Puruṣa in the three states, one might ask the question, "Why, if in deep sleep, Puruṣa retires into its "own nature", does it return to the trials and tribulations of the waking state?" It is, in answer to this question that the real difference between the dream and waking state is shown most poignantly, and at the same time points up the different Upaniṣadic outlooks on Puruṣa and the Universe. In the dream state Puruṣa is the agent of the entire experience and no impressions (Saṁskāras)[1] are left when leaving the state. To the contrary, in the waking state impressions are left, implying Puruṣa is not the agent of all the experience. These impressions bring the Puruṣa back to the waking state to take them up further.[2] Thus we have in this the basis for the Upaniṣad's treatment of the Puruṣa "Vaiśvānara", active in this world. Before going on to consider this posture to works and actions by the Puruṣa, let us consider briefly just how physically and physiologically Puruṣa may be related to the universe by continuing the psycho-physical analysis to find any linking factors to the macrocosm.

In the various analyses above we find, for instance, a common physical basis for both the microcosm and the macrocosm in the three physical elements which made up both. This parallel extends to the Prāṇa also. In earlier literature the life force when considered in relation to the microcosm was termed 'Prāṇa' and in relation to the microcosm 'Vāyu'. The two were linked later[3] in talking of the Prāṇa as the outside and inside breath. Perhaps the earliest attempts to link the micro and macrocosmic features, however, are the many attempts to identify the eye with Āditya (the Sun), the mouth with Agni, nose with Vāyu and ears with Diś[4] and the like. Moreover we shall see in the chapter on Brahman that the Kośa analysis can be taken as levels of reality as well as levels of self. Thus along the entire gamut of the analysis of Puruṣa, from the early

1. *B.U.* 4. 3.16.
2. See *B.U.* Yājñavalkya portion.
3. *P.U.* 3.8.
4. *Aitraya Up.* 1. 1-2.

symbolic analyses to the later Kośa view, there is an attempt to link the microcosmic and macrocosmic orders in claiming a common substratum for both. From this it seems necessary to conclude that on the level of Puruṣa there must have been general agreement in the Upaniṣads that the microcosm was not different in its basic structure from the macrocosm both having common characteristics and hence these two terms 'macro' and 'microcosm' are truly applicable to the Upaniṣadic analysis.

It is understandable, then, to find in many of our ten Upaniṣads, especially in the earlier, more Brāhmaṇical and Āraṇyaka Upaniṣads, the extolling and explanation of ritual and sacrifices. We cannot dismiss this posture to works and action as merely 'earlier material', not part of the Upaniṣads, but included for weak minds,[1] since for example we find the Naciketas fire sacrifices an integral part of the *Kaṭha*[2] or at the end of the *Muṇḍaka* extolling a fire sacrifice. Rather it seems that sacrifice and ritual fit in with the earlier sensory and ego-centric analyses of Puruṣa; and this is the position Śaṅkara gives it; but he rejects this view as a conclusion of the Upaniṣads saying it is for those not fit for Jñāna. From our analysis it would seem necessary to make it a conclusion on a par with others, but by different schools of thought. According to this view the Puruṣa is a unit, an individual, and his posture to Brahman or the Gods, is one of worship and propitiation through ritual and sacrifice, such as the Satyakāma portion of the *Bṛhad. Up.* lays out. Now this view is not by any means metaphysically the most complete view given in the Upaniṣads as we have seen in our analysis of Puruṣa, but we must be careful to recognize that not all the ten Upaniṣads take a negative view of this level of self. The development of Theism in the *Śvetāśvatara* or the continuation of ritualistic interest from the *Bṛhadāraṇyaka* right through to the *Muṇḍaka* places this ego-centric view of self as one stage of the Upaniṣad's concept of self.

There is another positive posture to works and action taken in the Upaniṣads. Here, as it is said in the *Muṇḍaka*, the self is to be obtained by "constant practice of truth devo-

1. *Muṇḍaka Up.*, Śāṅkara Bhāṣya, 1.4.
2. *Kaṭha Up.* 1.3 6.18.

tion; of perfect knowledge and duty".[1] Some of the Upaniṣads teach practices of duty and works in the form of the Āśramas. Thus the *Taittirīya* presents the Guru's closing remarks to his pupil about to take up the Gṛhastha stage. Their duty to fore-fathers, sacrifice, and begetting of offspring is enjoined. After this stage is completed then the posture to works and actions seems in many passages to change to renunciation in the third and fourth āśrama of Vānaprastha and Sannyāsa. The āśramas as stages on life's way involve a definite metaphysical commitment to the value of work and actions, although the Upaniṣadic authors occasionally seem not to recognise its presuppositions. Works and actions prepare the Puruṣa for the stage when one devotes all his attention to knowledge and meditation. Those passages extolling such a view would seem to imply the two—works and knowledge—are mutually exclusive. The one interfering with the other, and so must be arranged in form of periods of one's life. There are passages in many of the Upaniṣads in addition to the above Āśrama description, however, which seem to take another view. Thus the *Iśa* enjoins one to works (Karma) and to live a hundred years so doing. Thus we are to follow both the path of vidyā (knowledge) and avidyā (action).[2] The same is put forth in the *Bṛhadāraṇyaka*.[3] This view in contrast to the above āśrama concept seems to enjoin action and knowledge and lies closer to what we shall find in the *Gītā* as Niṣkāma Karma. What is important to us in our present discussion is the implication on the concept of self as Puruṣa of these two postures to works and action.

To fully appreciate the difference between the two, we first must consider the negative stands on work and action, i.e., the ideas of desire and bondage. In our consideration of the three states of Puruṣa we found that Puruṣa makes the rounds of the three states because there are impressions left in the actions of the waking state which draw it back from deep sleep. This is otherwise characterized[4] as desire, and represents the bondage of the Puruṣa to these three states instead of abiding in its own nature in deep sleep or a fourth state which infuses

1. *Muṇḍaka Up.*, 3.1.5.
2. *Iśa Up.* 2.
3. *B.U.* 4.4.10.
4. *B.U.* 2.4.5., 14.

the other three[1]. The basis for this desire is well stated by the *Kaṭha* in its remark that "the doors of the body face outwards (The senses turn to external objects); therefore man sees the external objects not the internal self."[2] Here it is said, as above, that the senses should be controlled by the Manas and Manas under the inspiration of Vijñāna. Thus the Puruṣa like the chariot with well-controlled horses reaches its goal. On the other hand for those whose senses roam free they are said to "childishly follow desires, turning to external objects."[3] Thus we might characterize desire as the turning to external objects without the inner guidance and control proper to the ontological character of the Puruṣa. There is general agreement of most of the Upaniṣads and even in the Gītā on this as the nature of desire, the uncontrolled action of the senses. In considering the path out of this bondage we do not find unanimity of opinion however; and indeed here the above two views can be inferred. One view, the more monistic view, characteristic of the Yājñavalkya portions of the *Bṛhadāraṇyaka* and parts of the *Kaṭha*, says that Puruṣa is bound to the three states by desire. Thus its expression in the world is largely ignorance. We see, then, this view as the origin of the āśrama stands to actions and works above. Works merely work the desires out of Puruṣa so that it can eventually turn, free of desire, to the contemplation of self. The other view, although not as explicit as the first, seems to make a more positive claim to Puruṣa's expression in the world, and although in agreement with the first that ignorance is the cause of bondage, it differs in its interpretation of ignorance. Perhaps the difference in views is shown up by the reference to the "two sciences" in the *Muṇḍaka*[4] and analogous passages through the other ten Upaniṣads. Vedic work, ritual, sacrifices and the Vedāṅgas—constitute the lower science and the "life of a mendicant (Bhaikṣacaryā)—subduing the senses by knowledge, faith and tapas (austerities)—constitute the other, the "higher science". The two sciences set forth here appear on the surface exhaustive of the postures to work and action and would require the Āśramas as a consequent rule of life. If this were the case

1. See *Māṇḍūkya Up.*, 7, 12.
2. *Kaṭha Up.*, 2.4.1.
3. *Ibid.*, 2.4.2.
4. *Muṇḍaka Up.*, 1.1.5,8; 2.1.10; 1.21-6.

the passages of the *Īśa* and *Kaṭha* mentioned above enjoining both work and knowledge would be in open contradiction to the passages extolling knowledge solely. We are even more puzzled when in the same Upaniṣads setting up the two sciences we are later told that the self is to be obtained by "constant practice of truth, duty, tapas (devotion), and perfect knowledge."[1] The idea of constant practice would seem to call for action in addition to meditation and knowledge. The two positive postures to work and action, the one making it the lesser science to be supplanted later by the higher science, and the other enjoining both work and knowledge, can now perhaps be seen to be not openly contradictory but talking about different things. Thus the higher science is opposed to action in the form of the earlier more egocentric posture to sacrifice and ritual as "Vedic work". The 'karma" of the *Īśa Upaniṣad* perhaps is not this "Vedic work" as Śaṅkara[2] so interprets it. Rather it may be the constant practice of truth knowledge, etc. Both views according to this interpretation would be against work interpreted as desire or egocentric action[3] and so there is no open contradiction, just a difference of interpretation of 'work'.

We are now in a position to more fully grasp the different Upaniṣadic views regarding the nature of Puruṣa. These positions can be seen more fully in the light of the eschatology of Puruṣa; and here the postures to work just discussed point up this difference clearly. First we have seen that one view, the earliest, extols ritual and sacrifice—Vedic work—which calls for an egocentric view of the Puruṣa as a unit or individual. Directly opposed to this view is the second claiming action through the senses to be due to desire; and therefore ignorance is to be overcome if Puruṣa is to escape bondage to the three states. Here Puruṣa becomes "An Ātman" that which is not real self, i.e., ignorance or illusion. This is the monism familiar to all in later Dārśanic literature. In the light of our analysis of Puruṣa we have found another view, however, one that occupies much of the attention of the Upaniṣadic Ṛṣis. This view, for which the ontological analysis of the Puruṣa is the basis, accepts the first or egocentric view as the first stage of an unfoldment to

1. *Muṇḍaka Up.*, 3. 1.5,
2. See Ś.B. on *Īśa*.
3. See *Īśa* 1, for confirmation on this point.

higher and more complete expressions of Puruṣa, whose true nature is Bliss and self effulgence. Under this view the Puruṣa becomes at first more an individual, but something more complete in essence through unfoldment which requires both knowledge and action to realize.

If we keep these three positions in mind let us proceed to consider the eschatology of Puruṣa before treating these three more fully.

D. The eschatology of Puruṣa :

Just as in the consideration of works and actions, so in the eschatological views, a range of interpretations can be recognised; the earlier more Brahmanical material resulting in one view, another arising by the rejection of this, and a third growing out of the earlier.

Let us first consider the physiological descriptions of death before considering the states after death. In consonance with the earlier sensory analyses of man, the process of death in such contexts is described as the dissolving of the senses, the fifteen parts, into their elements, and the organs to their presiding deities.[1] One description gives them in the order of their withdrawal as[2] :

i) speech to fire
ii) prāṇa to Vāyu (wind)
iii) eye to sun
iv) ear to quarters
v) mind to moon
vi) body to earth.

There are also descriptions of a symbolic nature based upon the nāḍī and heart concepts mentioned above. Basically it is said that the self dwells within the ether of the heart; and at death the Puruṣa goes out of the body taking Prāṇa with it, and as the *Praśna* terms it "becomes united with light which is the ascending air (Udāna)." Various other passages speak of becoming dissolved in light[3]. The more developed physiological analyses in conjunction with the Kośa analysis explains some of this otherwise impenetrable allegory. We found out in the physio-

1. *Muṇḍaka Up.* 3.2.7; cf. also *C.U.* 6.8.6.
2. *C.U.* loc. cit.
3. *C.U.* 6.8.6; 6.15, 2.

logical analysis that the Puruṣa in the 'ether of the heart' was connected to all parts of the personality and the macrocosmic world through the nāḍī, which were carriers of Prāṇa. This physiology will be considered later in relation to Ātman, and Brahman and creation, where we will find that Ātman-Brahman has entered the body, through the suṣumnā-nāḍī from the top of the skull and has entered the ether of the heart. In death the organs (Prāṇas) retire to the nāḍī; and when Puruṣa leaves the ether in the heart taking Prāṇa with it, it leaves by one of the 101 nāḍī, only one of which leads to immorality according to the passages.[1] The others lead to eventual rebirth. We might see in this the basis for the Kośa explanation. The one nāḍī leading to immortality seems interpretable as the process of Puruṣa retiring from the Annakośa where it dwelt in the heart to the Ānandakośa where it dwells in its 'own nature', as mentioned above when considering sleep. The other nāḍī leading to other worlds and rebirth are the various possibilities of the other three Kośas becoming the seat of Puruṣa in the process of death. No clearer picture of the physiological aspects of death can be made both because the few passages discussing it are quite occult; and also perhaps because they could only be interpreted fully by further appreciation of the pseudo-physiology than so far presented. For our purposes, however, the physiological aspects have shown us the necessary points; that is, there are various 'paths' which the soul follows after death according to the texts and these paths are directly connected with the life which the Puruṣa has led while in the body. Thus in terms of our discussion, of works and action of Puruṣa, which path Puruṣa follows depends upon how free he is of bondage to the 'ignorance' which keeps him on the round of the three states. This freedom requires, as some passages state, a 'knowledge' (vijñāna) of the Puruṣa in the ether of the heart; and this is what the more developed physiological analysis seems to describe, in the Puruṣa retiring through one of the five gates in the heart, only the top one leading to immorality as a *Chāndogya* passage puts it,[2] the others to symbolic deities and return to birth.

Let us proceed on this basis and consider the various paths followed after death and their development. In the Vedas

1. *Kaṭha Up.* 2.6.16; *P. U.* 3.7; *T. U.* 1.6; *A. U.* 1.3.12; *C.U.* 8.6.6.
2. *C.U.* 2.1.3.

themselves two paths were early considered, the Pitṛyāna (path of the forefathers) and the Devayāna or path of the Gods. Initially implying the paths through which one's sacrifice was borne to the Gods,[1] only later has it become used in the eschatological views of the Puruṣa with the addition of another, the path of men.

The Pitṛyāna, apparently, we are to take literally to be the result of sacrifice, gifts, austerities; in other words, the traditional duties which bring the deceased to the world where his forefathers dwell. This path seems much like what the Western spiritualists speak of as the 'Astral world'. One finds there not only relatives but all the things he found here on earth. This path, however, is claimed even in the earliest Upaniṣads[2] to lead to eventual rebirth by a long symbolic process after the fruits of his action in this world have been exhausted. Thus we seem to have a round of rebirths much like the round of the three states.

In the Devayāna, however, we have a path which leads to 'no return to birth'.[3] Man is first carried on to the world of the Gods, where he apparently enjoys a godlike position in the company of the gods receiving the oblations of his offspring and like a god granting them boons. He eventually travels to Āditya, thence to Vidyut and finally to the Brahmaloka where he 'dwells never to return'.[4] This path, it is said, is taken by one who meditates on the truth and has the knowledge of Brahman.[5] We may say, then, that the first and foremost requirement to follow the Devayāna is knowing the Puruṣa.

The path of men seems to be viewed as damnation to immediate rebirth 'becoming small creatures of repeated birth. They are born and they die'.[6] Thus we have in this early view three paths, one the path of man brings immediate rebirth in low forms in consequence of a low and reprehensible life while in the body; the Pitṛyāna brings eventual rebirth in form according to merit after enjoying the fruits of their actions among the

1. See Deussen, p. 334 f. for support of this view.
2. *B.U.* 4.4.4-6; cf. also *C.U.* 5.10.7.
3. Śāṅkara Bhāṣya on *C.U.* 5.10.1.
4. *C.U.* 5.10.1, 4.15.
5. B.U. 6.2.15.
6. *C.U.* 5.10.8.

forefathers; the Devayāna brings the Puruṣa eventually through the world of Gods and a path of light (Arci) to the Brahmaloka wherefrom it seems one does not return.

We may conclude from this that the basic egocentric view of Puruṣa had largely the view of "conquering the various worlds"[1] and dwelling with God, certainly in consonance with its concept of self. We find, however, the germs of the more developed views within this three-fold path. The more monistic sections truncate this three-fold path to a two-fold one. Bondage to rebirth (the Pitṛyāna is not elaborated in this context), or liberation and complete identity with Brahman.[2] Liberation here is not only identity with Brahman to be discussed later, but essentially what was described in the psycho-physiological analysis as the return of Puruṣa to his true nature as bliss and self effulgence in deep sleep. This is then a return, permanently in the form of a liberation. This two-fold path is quite in harmony with the stand to works and actions whereby Puruṣa is anātman or ignorance. Thus, one remains bound to the three states in life and the round of births so long as self is confused with anātman. Knowledge alone brings liberation, a return to self's true nature, as in deep sleep and death, although the later state of Puruṣa there is return because the illusion of anātman has not been conquered by knowledge (Vijñāna).

The less monistic view takes a positive stand to knowledge and action in the bodily state. It is the view whereby the Kośas are levels of expression of Puruṣa, an ontological and teleological order; this view also grows out of the three-fold path of the early more symbolic material. The paths here are bondage and liberation as above, but not so contrasted because of the more positive view to works and action. Rather than a process of rejecting the illusion of anātman, the process is one of unfoldment to eventual self-realization. In other words, this growth through the Kośas perhaps explains the passages hinting at gradual liberation[3] and which seems to more fully develop the earlier Pitṛyāna-Devayāna view rather than simply rejecting it. We may infer this as a conclusion not only from our discussion of this view's stand on works and action, but also upon

1. cf. *C.U.* 2.24 passim, *B.U.* 1.5.16.
2. See *B.U.* Yājñavalkya portion.
3. See *Taittirīya Up.* 2.6; cf. also *C.U.*, Chap. 7-8.

such passages as in *Taittirīya* setting forth a calculus of Blisses. "This joy of man, taken a hundred fold—is one joy of men who have attained the state of Gandharvas......" etc. through many levels to Brahman[1]. Also the passages emphasizing graded teachings of self, such as Prajāpati's teachings to Indra[2] where self is taught gradually from body to its true nature, represents a view that the bliss and self effulgence will be obtained only by this unfoldment through the Kośas. This view and the others on eschatological matters will be even clearer after considering Ātman and Brahman which such a discussion presupposes; it will suffice at the moment to see the physiological and psychological basis for self both in action and in eschatological matters. With this understanding let us sum up our conclusions on the self as Puruṣa.

E. Conclusions—the concept of self as Puruṣa :

We have so far discovered three different views to the psycho-physiological treatment of self we have termed Puruṣa. The difference between them lay primarily in their view on works and action and their outlook on eschatological matters.

The first view of Puruṣa is as egocentric immediate self of our normal experience. We found in our analysis that the earlier more Brahmanical material reflected this view in extolling the virtues of sacrifice and ritual, and in pre-occupation with relating microcosmic factors to macrocosmic 'deities'. In the psycho-physical analysis there were various analyses of eleven, five, and three elements and they culminated on the one hand in the triune analysis of tejas, apas and annam which was anticipatory of the Sāṅkhya guṇa theory; and on the other hand it culminated in a sensory analysis of the five Prāṇas or the ten indriyas, or sense organs and manas. With such an analysis the outlook on works and action was not surprising; a view extolling offspring, maintenance of household fires, gifts to Brāhmaṇas etc., put forth as the duty of the individual. The very positive attitude coupled with the integral interweaving of such claims into many of the Upaniṣads prevents us from dismissing this as earlier, non-Upaniṣadic material; and so we are

1. *Taittirīya Up.* 2.8.
2. *C.U.* 8.

forced to recognize this posture to works and actions to follow from the more restricted psycho-physical analysis of man, which represents one of the Upaniṣadic views about self. Eschatologically we found the process of death spoken of as a dissolving of the senses into their deities and the Puruṣa being set free to follow one of three paths, the path of man, the Pitṛyāna, or the Devayāna, whichever his works here in bodily existence, merited him.

It is quite clear that this view of self is basically that of simple theism quite familiar in the early mantras of the Vedas. It represents the ground floor of the idea of self. Important to us is that, contrary to Śaṅkara[1] and the Ācāryas, this represents a view which the Upaniṣad does put forth positively as self, whatever the motive—perhaps as representing one level of expression of self found in our ordinary experience.

From out of this basic material we found a more developed view of the psycho-physical analysis arising. There did not appear to be any disagreement; and the various symbolic analyses purporting to be sixteen-fold resulted in the ontological analysis of the five Kośas under which we found all twenty-six, twenty-one and sixteen elements could be ordered, and indeed for which the Kośas were merely labels. Their correspondence was as follows :

5 gross elements 5 subtle elements	))	represented by Annakośa
Balam, Vīryam Prāṇa	))	represented by Prāṇakośa
Indriyas, Manas, Saṅkalpa, Citta Dhyāna	)	represented by Manaḥkośa
Vijñāna (insight)	..	represented by Vijñānakośa
Memory, hope, immensity and various expressions of bliss in other passages	)))	represented by Ānandakośa

1. See *Muṇḍaka Up. Ś.B.* 1.4.

When applying this analysis of Puruṣa to works and actions and eschatological matters we found two separate views over this psycho-physiological analysis and earlier more Vedic material. The first view was a more monistic interpretation, perhaps best represented in the teachings of Yājñavalkya in the *Bṛhadāraṇyaka*[1] or in the *Muṇḍaka*[2] in its theory of two sciences and consequent praise of ritual and sacrifice only to later call it a "fool's" pastime.[3] Here the entire psycho-physiological analysis of Puruṣa is viewed as veils of ignorance over the true nature of the self which is bliss and self effulgence found in deep sleep. In other words Puruṣa as we have analysed it is anātman, merely ignorance. Therefore in considering action, this view puts forth the Āśramas as the way to overcome the ignorance; and from this it can be implied that meditation and knowledge (Vijñāna, insight) is the ultimate means, action being only a preparation, a satisfying or sublation of the desires prior to the Sannyāsa efforts. We shall examine this point of Vijñāna and its opposition to action in our criticisms of the views put forth. In eschatological considerations, this view, we found, carried out its concept of action and bondage consistently and made a contrast between bondage, which was a round of three states and births so long as self was considered Puruṣa or anātman; and liberation, which was a return to a state analogous to deep sleep, a loss of particularity. When this ignorance was dispelled, then the self was realized in its true nature as bliss and self effulgence etc.

The third view of self as Puruṣa, while also seeming to arise out of the earlier egocentric material, interpreted actions and work in a diametrically opposed manner. Ignorance it is agreed was the cause of bondage, but ignorance there was a sense of unfoldment through the Kośas expressing the true nature of Puruṣa in an ever more complete manner; and hence the ignorance was more a veil over that which is yet to be realized. This view emphasized that knowledge (Vidyā) or action alone led to further bondage[4] and that the two combined were necessary for the realization of the higher levels of Puruṣa.

1. *B.U.* 2.4.
2. *Muṇḍaka Up.* 1.2, 3.2.
3. *Ibid..* 1.2.7.
4. See *Iśa Up.* 1-3.

The various eschatological passages putting forth a gradual liberation, and other less monistic passages discussing both the Puruṣa and Brahman seem to carry out this posture to works and action consistently into eschatological considerations of Puruṣas.

If these are the three views to come out of our analysis of Puruṣa, in the way of critical reflections we can see that the key point of difference between the two more developed views is over 'Knowledge' and 'Ignorance'. They both admit that in understanding of the true nature of Puruṣa cannot be had on the lower levels of manas; and it is only 'Vijñāna'—direct insight—which affords this understanding. From this agreement it would seem that disagreement is only minor, over the nature of 'ignorance', but within this disagreement is an entire difference in metaphysics such as to take diametrically opposed stands to the physiological analysis. We can see perhaps, then that disagreement is really over what the term 'Vijñāna' means. Is 'Vijñāna' purely "knowledge" in the same sense and acquired by the same way that Jñāna is so acquired ? or does the "insight" require a total effort of the organism including both an effort of the mind in knowledge seeking and an effort of the body in action ? If the body and mind were merely an ātman then only by sublating these obstructions could vijñāna be obtained. If the body and mind are really Kośas or levels of expressions of Puruṣa, then a positive attempt to unfold them would result in a permanent return to the bliss and the self effulgence of its real nature. Some light could be shed on this matter by recalling that in the later Yoga Darśana there appear different types of Samādhi one of which may be nirbīja (without seed). One is permanent (in kaivalya), the other is not.[1] The former can only be obtained by *practice*; and this accords with the remarks above that practice and effort were recognized even by some of the more monistic Upaniṣads. We shall have opportunity to consider these three concepts of self further as they will be met in both analysis of Ātman and Brahman.

Another point worthy of note is the Sāṅkhyan character of the psycho-physiological analysis. The actual origin of the Sāṅkhyan system cannot be placed with any certainty; so it is

1. See *Yoga Sūtras* 1.51, see also Dasgupta, *Yoga Philosophy*, p. 52n.

an empty question to ask whether the Upaniṣads, considered here, borrowed from Sāṅkhyan doctrines or *vice-versa*. At best all we can do is to point out the close relationship between the elements found in our analysis and those of Sāṅkhya. Below is a table of the analysis of the *Praśna* along with the later Sāṅkhya and Vedānta analysis[1].

Sāṅkhya	*Vedānta*	*Praśna* (4.8)
Puruṣa	Parabrahman	Prāṇa
Prakṛti)		Tejas
Mahaḍ)	Brahman with	Citta
Ahaṁ-kāra)	limiting adjuncts	Ahaṁkāra
		Buddhi
Manas		Manas
5—Organs of knowledge		5—Jñāna Indriyas
5—Organs of action		5—Karma Indriyas
5—Tanmātrās		5—Subtle elements
5—Gross elements		5—Gross elements

We may conclude from this that in the Upaniṣads, insofar as a phenomenal analysis of self (on a level of Puruṣa) is made, then the Sāṅkhyan analysis is metaphysically the conclusion of these attempts. Moreover, the triune analysis tejas, apas, and anna or red, white, and black unquestionably anticipates the guṇa theory with its important consequences both physically, which the Upaniṣads (*Chāndogya* and *Śvetāśvatara*) did seem to realize, but also its important moral conclusions we will find only later in the *Gītā*.

One concluding observation which might be made concerns the change in use and root meaning of 'Puruṣa'. Even in the Vedas where 'Puruṣa' is used in a non-phenomenal context it still bears the reflection of man, a personality in our ordinary sense; this was observed in the introduction.[2] Our analysis has shown considerable preoccupation with psycho-physiological matters in which context 'Puruṣa' or 'embodied ātman' is used. It seems that only in the *Gītā* does 'Puruṣa'

1. See Tilak, *Gītā Rahasya* for a discussion of this and a similar table.
2. See p. 36-38.

qualified by Akṣara or Avyakta etc., come to be used in place of the more frequent and broader term 'Ātman' or even 'Brahman'. This point of usage is of interest not only because it might afford a calculated guess as to the period of the precipitation of the Sāṅkhya system from the context of the Prasthāna-traya but also because it shall provide us an important clue as to the nature and cause of the splitting up of Early Vedānta into Vedānta and Sāṅkhya-Yoga, which will be discussed in the final conclusion to the present work.

CHAPTER III

THE SELF AS ĀTMAN

A. Introduction:

'Ātman' like 'Puruṣa' is a very ancient term in Indian thought. In its root sense Ātman means in the *Veda*[1] breath or vital force. In later literature it seems to be translated by 'soul' or 'self' both so vague in the English as to be of little help. From an inspection of the *Vedic Concordance* (Bloomfield) we can see that Deussen's classification of the various connotations of 'Ātman' is correct.[2]

1. *The corporeal self*, the body (usually called Śarīra Ātman).
2. *The Individual Soul* free from the body, which as knowing subject is contrasted with and is distinct from the object.
3. *The supreme soul* in which subject and object are no longer distinguished from one another.

In the last chapter we spoke of the various uses of 'Puruṣa' and that both 'Ātman' and 'Brahman' in some contexts overlapped each other. There we limited 'Puruṣa' more to its root meaning as 'man' or 'personality' in its more phenomenal sense. Our preoccupation was with the psychological and physiological level, roughly what Deussen above considers the first level of the usage of 'Ātman'. At many places we have used 'True nature of Puruṣa' or just 'self' in the last chapter. It was at those places that the concept of Puruṣa overlapped our present discussion of 'Ātman'. For of the many uses of 'Ātman', some talking in the sense of what Deussen has termed supreme or universal soul, of these uses 'Ātman' will overlap 'Puruṣa' at one end and 'Brahman' at the other end. While we might do away with it entirely and just consider self under the headings of Brahman and Puruṣa, the absence of 'Ātman' would leave a gap in the Upaniṣad's concept of self. Puruṣa

1. Ṛgveda, X.16.3;
2. Deussen, *Philosophy of the Up.* p. 94.

seems to be the embodied self multiple and phenomenal, which in its true nature is, what we might term, the active side of Ātman, active in phenomenal existence. On the other hand 'Brahman' as we shall see almost always implies a cosmic and supreme sense of being, which leaves the many contexts putting forth a universal principle, often in a personal sense unanswered. Therefore, Ātman, although a via media between Puruṣa and Brahman, shall have a definite usage in our analysis. It shall stand for the manifest principle of being, both active in phenomenal existence and as a universal sense of self. 'Ātman' then shall be considered under two headings 'Ātman and the Individual' and 'Ātman and the Universe'. Let us proceed, then to consider the first.

B. Ātman and the Individual :

If 'Ātman' has a sense in which it stands for something multiple and active, which might be called self, then let us investigate more completely not only its relation to what we have considered as Puruṣa but also any individuality apart from what we find connected with body and the three states.

We found Puruṣa to be a sense of self which was associated with a body and bound to three states, none of which seemed to carry any conviction of being Puruṣa in his true nature, the ultimate sense in which we say 'I'. The teachings of Prajāpati to Indra in the *Chāndogya*[1] well illustrate this feeling. One aspect of our earlier discussion which would help elucidate the way in which Ātman may be connected to Puruṣa is the various discussions of the embodiment of self, some of which we have presented in considering the 'ether in the heart' and also the process of death and the Nāḍīs and the heart. Many passages are to be found giving special emphasis to the heart lotus as the centre of our being and all being, as the dwelling place of Brahman[2] or of Ātman in addition we find special mention in the *Aitareya*[3] and in the *Taittirīya*[4] of the entrance of Ātman

1. *C.U.* 8.
2. *Muṇḍaka Up.* 2.1.10, 21; *Kaṭha Up.* 2.20.
3. *A.U.* 1.1; 1.3.12.
4. *T.U.* 1.6.

into the body by way of the top of the head and through the suṣumnā to the heart lotus, from where it rules the microcosm as the inner guide. In the last chapter we found we were hard pressed to interpret this as anything but symbolic unless by the Kośa analysis the "ether in the heart" was the center of all levels of the Puruṣa, the various bodies gross, subtle and causal, around which they revolved as the spokes and rim around the nave of the wheel.[1] This interpretation was further strengthened by the remark that Puruṣa retired into his true nature through the nāḍī to the ether of the heart in both sleep and death and this nature has been characterised as bliss (ānanda) and self-effulgence (jyotirmaya) which is what the Ānandakośa purports to be.

We may conclude from this that the Upaniṣads at this point are claiming some sense of self previously unembodied because when embodied it lodges in the heart lotus or ether in the heart, from where it rules as inner guide. Perhaps now some distinction between Ātman and Puruṣa can be made. Ātman is this core of the sense of self from which Puruṣa proceeds bound to the rounds of the three states or in another expression in the three Kośas—anna and prāṇa as the waking state, prāṇa, vijñāna, and manas as the dream state and vijñāna and ānanda as deep sleep state. Ātman then remains in this last kośa and is only united with Puruṣa in death and deep sleep; otherwise its influence is felt from the heart indirectly by way of these nāḍīs to the Puruṣa in the waking of dream state. What this is saying, then, is that Ātman is the essence, the ultimate and true nature of Puruṣa expressed on the highest, the ānanda level of its ontology. This is the meaning that Ātman is the eye of the eye etc., which eludes us otherwise in passages of the *Kena*[2] culminating in predication of contradictory qualities to this Brahman or Ātman. The claim in *Praśna*[3] that all functions rest on Ātman is similarly illuminated. This is not to say that the particular author of these passages openly subscribed to the above Kośa analysis of Puruṣa and Ātman as its culmination, but only that it is implied metaphysically and what are otherwise obscure and allegorical passages are given form,

1. See *B.U.* 1.5.15; *Muṇḍaka Up.* 2.2.6, for this wheel analogy.
2. *Kena Up.* 1.2-8.
3. *P.U.* 4.9-11.

such as these flashes of intuitions about Ātman can be coherently connected into a fuller description. Ātman as the inner guide in the ether of the heart also explains the various Upaniṣadic passages voicing a dissatisfaction with identification of self in its true form with the deep sleep state,[1] and whereupon a fourth or turīya state is set up which infuses the other three; that is to say, this state has the unity felt in deep sleep and yet the consciousness of the dream and waking state, but yet is not changing from one state to another; it is rather permanent. This permanent fourth state is the Ātman residing in the heart lotus, that upon which the entire ontological structure of Puruṣa depends.

If we realize Ātman to be the fourth state of Puruṣa, as embodied yet not changing its states as does Puruṣa in the waking state, in other words if Ātman is the true nature of Puruṣa much like the deep sleep state but endowed with consciousness and permanence, then from this, questions naturally arise. First one wishes to know just in what way Ātman is active, i.e., connected with the activity of Puruṣa; and secondly the related question "Why is Ātman embodied?"

The answers to these questions lay in the nature of desires and actions which was discussed in the last chapter. If we summarize briefly the conclusions reached there, then it will suffice to see just what answers we can find in our texts as to Ātman's embodiment and activity.

In the last chapter there were three postures to work and action. The first which we might call Vedic work enjoined sacrifices, rituals and the various methods of worshipping the Gods laid out in the Brāhmaṇas. This view of action was purely an egocentric action done basically for the desire of conquering the "various worlds". From this basic view two more developed views of desires and action arose. The first is to be found in Yājñavalkya's philosophy in the *Bṛhadāraṇyaka Upaniṣad*. Actions are done from a sense of ignorance of Puruṣa's true nature in deep sleep (Ātman or Jīvātman). Desires and impressions of the waking state bring him back to take up family, sacrifices etc. Thus we may conclude that the

1. See *C.U.* 8, *Māṇḍūkya Up.* 7, also *Kārikā* 3.33f, Deussen *Philos. of Up.* p. 309.

criterion of action is desire and this desire is only for something other than self as Yājñavalkya puts it.

The path out of bondage to action for monism is to realize the Puruṣa to be really ignorance or a veil over the Ātman which in itself is analogous to deep sleep. When this true self is realized then there "is no consciousness of particulars" (Saṁjñā) and the illusory Puruṣa dissolves. Until this realisation is made, Ātman carries this veil or latent "Saṁskāras" with it from the round of the three states and also the round of births. What is really the nature of Ātman for Yājñavalkya and the monistic view will be taken up in the next section. At the moment we have only to recognize that Ātman is not of itself active, having no consciousness of otherness; and only "ignorance", conceived as desire, brings by reflection a substantive value to an egocentric state which is Puruṣa or Anātman. This quality of apparent substantiative value of egocentric Puruṣa is illustrated by the *Kaṭha* passage[1] in which the two beings in the cave (of the hṛdguhya) are likened to shadow and sunlight. Thus, we may conclude that there is no Ātman which is individual and having intercourse in any manner with the worlds of dream and waking. Once egocentricism is overcome by knowledge (Vijñāna) then consciousness of multiplicity vanishes as a mirage in liberation.

The second view, that one centred around the Kośa analysis of Puruṣa in the *Taittiriya*,[2] agrees with the first in claiming that ignorance keeps the Puruṣa bound to action; but because of the ontological analysis of Puruṣa this ignorance is not to be equated with the ignorance one might have of a solution to a mathematical problem; but better it is ignorance one may have an unexplored territory or even of his own abnormal mental states of the unconscious areas of mind. The solution of the ignorance does not come by knowledge but by experience which involves the total organism of the individual, cognitive as well as volitional aspects, not simply the cognitive alone. This same misunderstanding regarding ignorance of true nature of self is to be found in the writings of the Platonic Socrates who thought the immoral actions of his fellow citizens were from a "double ignorance" which could be removed simply by

1. *Kaṭha Up.* 1.3.1.
2. *T.U.* 2.

pointing it out to them. His condemnation by the Athenians is a pointer to the fact that the "ignorance" is a special ignorance not simply the antonym of knowledge. This is what the second view, the less monistic, seems to be claiming in regard to bondage to action. Thus, this posture to action is perhaps best stated in the *Īśa Upaniṣad* where the removal of the veil of ignorance is only achieved by both vidyā and avidyā.[1]

Perhaps, then, as mentioned in the first chapter, the Vijñāna is not to be translated by knowledge but immediate experience. It is to be noted that Śaṅkara does use 'anubhava' as a cognate of Vijñāna not simply 'vidyā'; but his contrast in several places[2] of Vijñāna and action (which we remember can only arise from desire and so a sense of otherness) would seem to indicate that he thinks the cognitive and volitional faculties are separated on a level of Vijñāna as is the case with jñāna (knowledge Vs. will). As we can see from the second view of actions and desires, the Ātman is the essence of the Puruṣa's growth as the full grown neem tree is to its seedling. In this case one can conclude that the Ātman, while not itself active as Puruṣa, underlies as adhiṣṭhāna or substratum of the Puruṣa's growth through the Kośas surrounding the Ātman which is fourth state, the Ātman in the heart.

We can now see more clearly the different views in the Upaniṣads as to Ātman's relation to action. One view, the earlier, considers action to be Vedic phenomenon and looks positively upon egocentric action, and so has no developed view of Ātman. The first of the more developed views casts all action in the model of this earlier egocentric view. Such passages condemning worship saying the worshipper becomes a "lapdog of the gods" illustrate this feeling.[3] Accordingly Ātman is wholly actionless yet supporting action of the egocentric Puruṣa or anātman through ignorance which is cast as desire; or in the words of Yājñavalkya[4] "when Brāhmaṇas know (Vid) this Ātman, then elevating themselves from the

1. *Īśa Up.* 1. 2.
2. *B.U.* Ś.B. 2.4.14, *Īśa*.9, *C.U.* 8.1.1., *T.U.* 2.9; cf. Deussen, loc. cit., p. 150 f.
3. *Māṇḍūkya Up.* 1.2.7. See Radhakrishnan, loc. cit., I. 147 f. for further discussion on this point.
4. *B.U*, 3.5.1.

desire of obtaining a son from the desire of wealth and from desire of gaining the worlds, they lead the life of wandering mendicants." Even though Puruṣa, locked in ignorance, conceives action egocentrically as desire for another, we might ourselves question desire as the sole basis of action. The full import of this will be taken up only after considering the Universal Ātman.

Ātman is itself actionless and not multiple according to the monistic view. The less monistic view, however, says the egocentric self is the lowest sense of self-centered in the manas as the sense mind and is the basis for growth through higher levels of manas and vijñāna Kośas. Ātman is the adhiṣṭhāna; itself not active, but acting as the pattern or goal and the reference to which all actions are done. Exactly why Ātman who is the perfected sense of individual self should support growth of Puruṣa through the Kośas is not considered at all in this context, although in discussing Brahman in the next chapter some attempt will be made to solve the problem in a wider context to which the present one is related.

The answer to the second question "why is the Ātman embodied ?" would come from the above discussion. In the first, the monistic view, Ātman is embodied because of ignorance, the results of which cause action and bondage to Puruṣa as a result of desire. This seems inferred from such passages as *Muṇḍaka.* 2.2.8 (also Kaṭha 1.15) where it is said "The knot of the heart strings is rent, cut away are all doubts, and a man's works are spent and perish, when is seen that which is at once the being below and the supreme." Ātman, it is inferred, has some desires associated with it. Since the Puruṣa is claimed to be united with it in the heart lotus in deep sleep then for Puruṣa to return, losing sight of its true nature in the waking state, the desires in the heart must be primal motive forces for Puruṣa's action and not just Puruṣa's ignorance alone. This is to say Ātman itself, although not active in the world, by the above, must be linked to it by desires. When one asks the origin of this ignorance or desire and why if Ātman is bliss and self-effulgence does it acquire a pallor of darkness about it, when he asks, he finds peculiarly throughout the Monistic passages of the Upaniṣads[1]—a complete lack of interest in "origins" which so occupied the earlier Brāhmaṇic material with its descriptions of creation and entrance of Brahman into the world and later dissolution. Here, however, we see such a lack of interest leaves the whole metaphysics quite incomplete and unsatisfactory; for if ignorance is the cause of bondage, then the Ātman could hardly be the Brahman as the monist claims; and the ignorance is not simply cloudy knowledge but a lack of experience as the other view claims. This is another way, then, the monistic view is to be contrasted with the earlier egocentric material, i.e., the monistic passages seem to reject origins as being knowledgeable or applicable. Śaṅkara[2] expresses this same attitude when he rejects creation stories as the "lower science" and hence takes up only the return or liberation as the higher science.

The second, less monistic, view considers the Puruṣa to have a real growth from the egocentric position through the Kośas to Ātman which is its essence. Therefore, one would seem to be able to draw the conclusion that the Ātman is embodied according to the level of its insight into itself (vijñāna), into various "bodies" consisting of the physical-vital, the mental-vital or vijñāna-ānanda kośas. Like the first view we have difficulties when we seek further into origins, i.e., just why and how and in what sense can the Ātman be viewed as having a growth. This question can only be answered by finding the basis and cause of creation which this view accepts as real. Little is ever said in the Upaniṣads except the calculus of Blisses in the *Taittirīya*[3] and *Bṛhadāraṇyaka* as possible answers; and these are fore-runners of the later *Gītā* theories.

In the final analysis we can say, that Ātman is linked to Puruṣa in one of two ways according to the school of thought:

1. Through ignorance taken as desires or clouding knowledge whereby Puruṣa becomes really anātman.

2. Ātman is viewed as the essence of Puruṣa, the existence which is undergoing a growth.

1. *B.U.*, Yājñavalkya sections, *Kaṭha Up.* 3. 12-16, *Muṇḍaka Up.* 1.2. This is noted especially in the change of interest away from creation to Psychology in the *Kaṭha*, *Muṇḍaka*, *Māṇḍūkya* and *Praśna*.

2. *Muṇḍaka Up.* S.B. 1.1.4.

3. *T.U.* 2.8; *B.U.* 4. 3. 33.

Both these views break down when pursued for ultimate origins of the embodiment or veiling of Ātman. This is expressed both in the monistic passages of the Upaniṣads, and specifically recognized by Rāmānuja[1] and Śaṅkara[2] in their refusal to answer questions as to origins. The first view, however, seems openly contradictory claiming the Ātman to be the omnipotent Brahman and then linking the ignorance back to Ātman as we have shown above. The notion of Ātman's relation to action and Puruṣa, we shall see in the next chapter and the conclusion, is a weak point in the analysis of self in the Upaniṣads which by and large is not as concerned with the individual Puruṣa as with the universal Ātman.

Before taking up the Ātman in its universal aspect let us consider briefly the eschatological aspects of the Ātman as individual.

From the last chapter we remember that when the self left the body in death it retired through the senses to the other in the heart, and then, according to its insight, went either through the suṣumnā to liberation or through one of the other five gates to other worlds and eventual return. From the above discussion of Ātman and its relation to action, we can see that in death as in deep sleep Ātman carries latent impressions (Saṁskāras) with it according to general agreement. These are seeds then which will again sprout a body. The death of the body, as we have described in the last chapter, seems to be looked upon as the departure from the physical or gross body, of the core of self, Ātman, surrounded by the accretions of its various lives and activities, basically what one may refer to as the "personality". Thus, when the Ātman comes to some sort of self illumination (vijñāna) whereby its nature is recognized to be bliss, self-effulgence, and consciousness, mentioned in the last chapter as the return of the Puruṣa to its true nature; when this occurs Ātman is liberated and these accretions are dropped. Let us at this point take up in more detail this emancipation of Ātman. There seems general agreement in most of the

1. Rāmānuja Bhāṣya on *Brahma Sūtras*, II 1-15; I.1.21; also *Gītā Bhāṣya* II 18; VII 12, 14.

2. *Gītā*, Śāṅkara *Bhāṣya*, XIII.2.

Upaniṣads as to the psychology of liberation. Three passages of the *Kaṭha*[1] well reflect this psychology:

"The Puruṣa's being the highest self is not placed in what is in the ruler visible; none beholds it by the eyes, but by the heart, by the mind, by the illumined consciousness, is it manifest. Immortal become they who know it."

> "The state which ensures, when the five organs of knowledge rest along with the mind and reason does not strive is called the highest aim.
>
> "This they call Yoga which is the firm keeping down of the senses. Then one becomes free from distraction; for Yoga is the birth of things and their ending."

In these passages we have one of the earliest references to what is comparable to the Yoga Darśana. Had this passage not been in context describing the highest self, we might be led, in view of the negative statements, to infer a viyoga as is so inferred of Patañjali's system. Here, however, the implications are quite definite. The movements of the senses occlude the full consciousness of Puruṣa; and instead of having a clear knowledge or insight (vijñāna) of Ātman, the true nature of self, one has only its reflection into the sense mind and consequent confusion with the object's reflection brought in through the organs of knowledge. The result is the sort of statement "I saw an object". The 'I' referred to here is this reflection of Ātman into Manas, which unlike vijñāna offers only a limited and distorted image. As the passage states, liberation is "Yoga" i.e., the quieting of the senses, mind and reason, but allows the heart and intuitive faculties to bring a deeper sense of self to consciousness. A further implication from the above is that when the consciousness resides in these higher faculties, the heart and illumined mind, then Ātman is liberated, has attained "the highest aim".

From this psychology of liberation two conflicting interpretations arise, the two theories which have been following us thus far. The division is over the relation of the Ātman to the reflection in sense mind or ego. Monism claims that once the senses are quieted (by meditation and constant practice) and the Ātman is known in its purity, then no longer will the

1. *Kaṭha Up*. 6.9-11.

sense reflection confuse us. Thus far it is simply agreeing with the above passages; but it says further that when this knowledge of Ātman is attained there is "liberation" that is "consciousness of particulars" is sublated[1] and self returns to its nirguṇa state. This seems to be the import of such passages as the *Kaṭha*[2] extolling knowledge of Brahman here and now as the necessary condition for liberation. Also such passages as in the *Chāndogya*, saying we have issued from truth and yet know not our origin, indicate this clouding of the truth by the sense activity. In terms of the above psychology, the reason for the loss of truth becomes apparent to the activity of the sense mind. What marks these passages as monistic is the sharp contrast between liberation and rebirth, ignorance and knowledge of the truth. This, it seems, could only be possible by viewing the activity of the sense mind as ignorance which once put down frees Ātman from its bondage. The less monistic passages always stand out by not making this sharp contrast between rebirth and liberation. Rather in many places one finds the positive concept of gradual unfoldment such as the calculus of Bliss in the *Taittirīya*. Perhaps, then, the knowing not of the truth of our origin may not be ignorance simply in the sense of the object being clouded over, but more in the special sense mentioned above which requires an evolutionary unfoldment to fully remove. Thus the second view would not consider the putting down of the confusion of self in the sense mind as "liberation"; rather it would involve consciousness expanding to the next Kośa. This is illustrated well by Prajāpati's teaching to Indra in the *Chāndogya* where the confusion by Indra of the self for the reflection in the water does not later make the reflection disappear as an illusion or confusion when being shown otherwise, but only his understanding of self is changed, so the identification of self and body is no longer made and the confusion overcome. The whole process of "graded teachings" in which the *Chāndogya* abounds are such examples of this less immediately monistic view.

While there is some difference as to what constitutes "final liberation", the teaching to the highest self, in the Upaniṣads, as pointed out above, there is general agreement that when consciousness ceases to be linked to the Manas level of mind

1. *B.U.* 2.4.14 and Ś.B.
2. *Kaṭha Up.* 6.4.

and resides in vijñāna, then, the Ātman is no longer limited to the three states and continued rebirth. Whether all multiplicity actually ceases or just ceases for the Ātman is the metaphysical question disputed in the Upaniṣads as well as in the later Ācāryas. There is no doubt, however, that when the Ātman is so freed and returns to the fourth or turīya state and resides in the cave of the heart (hṛd-guha), then consciousness is not limited to the multiplicity of the waking state nor the transitoriness of the dream state; rather Ātman takes on a cosmic aspect of consciousness. Let us then consider this other cosmic aspect of Ātman.

C. *Ātman and the Universe*:

So far in our consideration of self we have been occupied with the self as individual. In the last section of this chapter, we have tried to explore some of the foundations for the sense of individuality. We found this basis to be the Ātman, the true self, in the ether in the heart, who was not active but supported action. Ātman also was the core of personality which survived bodily death and made the round of the births. That the foundation for self is not ultimately individual, we already have had some indication in our discussion of the self in the cave or ether of the heart, and in considering liberation directly above. It is more in the creation stories in the *Bṛhadāraṇyaka*[1] and *Aitareya* such as:

> "This was before Ātman bearing the shape of a man. Looking around he beheld nothing but himself. He said first 'this am I'. This world was before Ātman, one and nothing else whatsoever active. He reflected: 'Let me create the worlds'."
>
> (*B.U.* 1.4.1).

which bring the ultimate nature of Ātman into clearer light. From the above passage, it is apparent that Ātman is looked upon as something which has not been created like animals and trees; but itself is the ultimate reality which is yet a con-

1. *B. U.* 1.4.1.; *A. U.* 1.1.1.

sciously functioning unit, what so far has been referred to as self, a personality in a broad sense. Here unlike Puruṣa, however, there is no multiplicity. Ātman is the cosmic person or universal self often referred to in the text as "Prajāpati". This is simply to say that the Upaniṣads do not contrast personal and impersonal on the traditional subjective and objective distinctions. Rather it seems that when the subjective objective distinctions, basic to self as Puruṣa, are transcended, then individual and cosmic, personal and impersonal distinctions also disappear. Thus in the above passages we have the transpersonal sort of self, before creation, unitary and yet being viewed as personal in the sense of having consciousness which is a functioning whole, not merely the sum of unrelated parts. If this concept is borne in mind, the following *Kaṭha* passage can be properly understood.[1]

> "He is the seer that sees him who came into being before tapas and was before the waters (apas). Deep in the heart of creatures he sees Him, for there He stands by the mingling of the elements."

Were we not to be aware of this transpersonal foundation of self, Ātman here would be both universal and the first born (Hiraṇyagarbha) and in the cave of the heart, which would seem to be a hopeless contradiction. Rather we might avoid this by infering the Ātman to be dipolar, having an individual pole which is the foundation for the personality, or Puruṣa, and also a universal pole which from Puruṣa's viewpoint is the impersonal objective universe, but from this transpersonal standpoint, it is the universal pole of Ātman and so no less personal or impersonal.

Perhaps this transpersonal viewpoint will also explain the ether of the heart or cave of the heart which has followed us all along. It is because this concept, occult though it may be, is given so much emphasis in the texts of the Upaniṣads that it could not be ignored; but in addition we can perhaps now see its vital significance as the link to both individual and universal senses of self. Thus the following are a sample of the numerous[2]

1. *Kaṭha Up.* 4.6;

2. *B.U.* 4.4.22; *T.U.* 2.1; *Kaṭha Up.* 1.14; 2.20, 3.1; 4.6-7; *Muṇḍaka Up.* 2.1.10; 3.1-7.

passages in the Upaniṣads making references to the cave of the heart (guham) the ether of the heart (hṛdaya-ākāśa), the heart-lotus (hṛd-padmam); "The Ātman, which is subtler than what is subtle, greater than what is great, is seated in the cavity (guhyam) of the living Being" (*Kaṭha* 2.20).

"This (Brahman) is great, divine, of a nature, not to be conceived by thinking, more subtle than what is subtle, it shines in various ways, it is more distant than what is distant, and also near in this body; for the beholders it dwells even here in the cave." (*M.U.* 3.3.1,7).

The two poles of Ātman stand out clearly here. The self is the size of a thumb[1]; the individual pole of Ātman, the microcosm. The various analyses of Puruṣa in the last chapter, are just this microcosm here. This self in the heart is also the macrocosm in that all the deities, all the manifold cosmic aspects, are to be found here. All this makes hopeless nonsense unless it can be viewed in somewhat the same way as the Kośa analysis in the discussion of Puruṣa. Were we to take the heart-lotus, etc. literally, the confusion would be even worse, in that we would be holding that all the universe is contained in the heart-cave. Rather this concept can be interpreted best when looked upon as the core of self, the Ātman, which is the soul or inner guide of all the Kośas interpreted as "bodies", i.e. gross (physical and vital), subtle (vital and mental) and casual (bliss and vijñāna). In other words the heart is the nave around which the "bodies" and aspects of personality revolve as spokes around the wheel. In the physical body it is the locus of the vital Kośa as inner guide of soul; and in the vital body it is locus of the mind as its inner guide, and so on, each of these locuses being one, the "heart", which is the Ātman as the foundation for individuality. The Kośa analysis may also interpret the macrocosmic pole. These Kośas or "levels of being" when looked at from Ātman rather than our limited standpoint as an individual are also levels of reality, the physical is simply the level of reality composed of gross and subtle elements. The vital level is not just Prāṇa as breath but, Vāyu as vital force in creation. This

1. *Kaṭha Up.* 4.12; also *Śvetāśvatara Up.* 3.13.

sort of dual aspect of the Kośas was hinted at in the last chapter, when the senses, Prāṇa etc. were linked to Āditya, Vāyu etc., by the early more symbolic material.

This matter is yet far from clear, and indeed clarity may well be unobtainable in the light of the subject matter. It can, however, be seen in way of conclusion that the heart is the thread of self upon which is strung the micro and macrocosmic aspects. The transpersonal view of Ātman, then is just this view of the Kośas from their apex, unfolding in one direction as levels of reality in the macrocosm and as levels of being (the various bodies) in the microcosm. The heart looked at from the standpoint of Puruṣa is this locus of Ātman embodied as inner guide and true nature of self. What the Upaniṣads then say is that the microcosmic order pursued to its heart is also the macrocosmic order.

D. Conclusions :

From this concept of a transpersonal, dipolar Ātman arise three aspects which each of the three theories we have so far discussed interpret as Ātman itself. Thus to one theory, that of the early symbolic material, viewing Puruṣa egocentrically and extolling worship of the gods, Ātman of our discussion is Īśvara, Prajāpati, Hiraṇyagarbha. Such theistic views arise, perhaps from identifying self with the egocentric awareness in sense activity (discussed in the eschatological section above) as the reflection of Ātman into the sense mind. Thus the higher levels of self experienced only derivatively in sense-mind appear as another self more perfect and universal, Īśvara, Prajāpati etc. We might say here that the dipolar self is split into two separate poles, self and God.

Ātman is also the witness in some passages such as the *Kaṭha*[1] "The Knowing self is not born, nor does it die, He sprang from nothing and nothing sprang from Him. He is unborn, eternal, everlasting and ancient. He is not slain when the body is slain." This passage which occurs in the *Gītā* (which we shall consider later) seems to emphasise the Ātman

1. *Kaṭha Up.* 1.2.18.

as the witness to activity but not itself active. Thus as in the case of the Ātman's relation to the Puruṣa as inner guide but not itself active, here Ātman is transpersonal and merely a spectator like the self in dreams, a spectator but to an activity which is only evanescent upon its true nature. This, of course, seems to be more monistic in its understanding of Ātman. Ātman is viewed from the Universal pole where the activity of egocentric Puruṣa seems only a little different from dream activity.

Thirdly, there is Ātman who is active; to whom "all beings are self"[1] and who is the foundation of personality and all manifold creation.[2] This view is the Kośa analysis above which includes the witness Ātman and the more immediate sense of self the egocentric Puruṣa—as two poles of a dipolar transpersonal self.

Before trying to draw conclusions on our study of the dipolar Ātman, let us see what other scholars conclude as to the nature of Ātman in the Upaniṣads. Śaṅkara, the leading commentator on the Upaniṣads, seems to take an even stronger monistic position than Yājñavalkya's and that of parts of the *Kaṭha*. For instance, the key to understanding the two poles of Ātman, the Universal and the individual, lay in the answers to our two questions "In what way is Ātman active ?" and "Why is Ātman embodied ?" In answer to this we find direct answers only in the late Upaniṣads, such questions usually taking the form of creation stories in the earlier texts. In *Praśna* (3.1), for example, it is asked "Whence comes this Prāṇa Ātman" and "How does it enter the body ?" The answer is given "from the Supreme soul this Prāṇa originates as the shadow on a man, so he projects himself on it and he enters into this body" by the mind's action (manaskṛtena). Śaṅkara interprets this to mean entrance into a body because of his works which have originated from the will, desire etc. of the Manas."[3] While the vague statement "manaskṛtena" in the original may be a direct answer to the question, Śaṅkara interprets it as a question whence came this present embodiment not what causes embodi-

1. *Īśa. Up*. 6, 7, 16.
2. *Praśna Up*. 4.10, 11.
3. See Ś.B. on *Praśna Up*. 3.3.

ment. This is the keeping with the avoidance of questions of origin by later monists as well as Upaniṣadic monism, mentioned above. Śaṅkara seems to be saying then, what we concluded above as the second view, that works, desires etc. cloud over Ātman causing embodiment, which only knowledge of Ātman can remedy. Thus we have Śaṅkara's conclusion that the individual pole of Ātman is a superimposition (adhyāsa) upon the unmanifest Brahman[1] like his well known cliche of the snake in the rope illusion.

Now the existence of many sections of the Upaniṣads with this outlook is not to be denied, but neither is it to be denied as Śaṅkara does[2] that theism and ultimate monism also play important roles in the Upaniṣads' views on self. With Śaṅkara they are only for weak or lesser minds. Actually where the less monistic passages differ from monism and Śaṅkara, the claim that when an understanding or knowledge of the universal aspect of Ātman is obtained the individual pole does not necessarily disappear like the illusion of the snake but remains and becomes the dipolar Ātman dynamic in the world yet not active in the limited egocentric sense. In other words action and desire are not necessarily merely of individual origin and hence are not to be contrasted with inactivity of the universal Ātman.

Deussen, following Śaṅkara, also seems to think action to be from desire and hence limited to the individual which is evanescent, as might be inferred from his summary of Upaniṣadic philosophy in the following three principles.[3]

Principle :	*Confusion by weak minds demands for knowledge :*
(1) The Ātman is Unknowable	Ātman becomes an object of knowledge which in truth it is not.

1. See especially Śaṅkara's intro. to his Bhāṣya on The *Brahma-Sūtras*—his discussion of adhyāsa.

2. See Ś.B. on *Muṇḍaka Up.* 1.1.4, the discussion of the Sciences.

3. Deussen, loc. cit. p. 355.

(2)	The Ātman is the sole reality	Reality of the Universe is maintained and consequent contradiction is adjusted by the often repeated assertion that the Universe is identical with the Ātman.
(3)	Intuitive knowledge of the Ātman is emancipation	Emancipation appears finally and wrongly in the phenomenal form of causality as a becoming something which previously had no existence and in phenomenal form as the removal of a temporal and spiritual separation from the Ātman which never existed and does not need to be removed.

It is clear that Deussen thinks the "Upaniṣads" teach an immediate monism, and only in some passages which "Bring down, though illegitimately this metaphysical truth to where knowledge is possible" is there any recognition of growth and reality of the phenomenal world. Deussen seems to be confused over the word "Knowledge". In the proposition (1) the 'knowledge' of the right hand column is not empirical knowledge, as the Ātman is never claimed to be knowable by empirical or discursive forms of knowledge. Rather perhaps Deussen has not realized that 'vidyā' such as in the *Kaṭha* passage[1]; "ignorance and knowledge are known to be far asunder and lead to different goals. I think thee desirous of knowledge because many objects of desire did not attract thee". Empirical knowledge is not meant; but vidyā is here a generic term standing for all knowledge and primarily intuitive knowledge of self; all knowledge is transformed in the light of that intuition. Deussen seems also bothered by the contradiction of affirming the universal nature of Ātman and the reality of the Universe of multiplicity at the same time (see proposition 2). Thus one aspect of our experience is negated for him.

1. *Kaṭha Up.* 2.4; cf. also *B.U.* 1.5.16.

Ranade seems to point out one assumption underlying Śaṅkara's and Deussen's monistic interpretation of the Upaniṣads. Thus Ranade feels it is wholly gratuitous to say as Śaṅkara does that emancipation in reality is a corruption of the truth that intuitive knowledge is emancipation. Śaṅkara's view is that intuitive knowledge (Vijñāna) is more of the nature of vidyā than of action which can only have a motivation from desire. If, as we have seen in our discussion, Vijñāna is more of the nature of experience, having a quality of action as well as knowledge, then there is a sense in which the Upaniṣads do teach a real becoming. The monism would then merely be another theory on a par with the others, not "the true teachings from which the ultimate monism is a corruption". Ranade recognizing this says that "self already realized" is a metaphysical fact, and is not to be confused with what he terms "mystical and moral aspects". He says, for instance, "When it is said that the self is to be realized, we are asked to take into account the whole ethical and mystical process by which the allurements of the not-self naturally ingrained in the human being are to be worked out gradually and the self to be made to stand in its native purity"[1]. Ranade, then, considers it a mistake to take only the epistemological facts into account, when considering Liberation. The "mystical and moral" facts, then, when taken into account, even throw the epistemological facts of intuitive knowledge into different light, whereby Vijñāna becomes as we have said above an insight or experience rather than a knowledge.

Aurobindo in the *Life Divine*[2] throws light, perhaps in a broader context, on our problem by pointing out that the successive consideration of many gods, each extolled as the one God containing the others, are merely "poises" or faces of the one, or as he puts it "In essence the gods are one existence which the Sages call by different names". This concept of "Unity in difference" is familiar to us in later Śuddhādvaita of Vallabha. This point, then, brings to question the word 'Unity' which is

1. See Ranade, *Constructive Survey of Upaniṣadic Philosophy*, p. 30.
2. p. 144f.

applied to Ātman in the universal sense such as Śaṅkara's "One without a second" (ekamevādvitīyam)[1]. Does the realization of the universal pole of Ātman exclude the multiple pole ? That a mathematical unity is not always meant in the Upaniṣads, and that there is a sense of difference in unity or a dynamic interplay of aṁśas or aspects, will be clear from the passages considering Brahman and even more clearly found in the *Gītā*.

Both the early symbolic strain in the texts, as well as monism, then, seems to either split the two poles—universal and individual Ātman—or to deny one of the two poles in order to escape the apparent contradictions which are contained in the transpersonal view and most evident in the various "heart lotus" passages. This third more complete view is based, it seems, on these two poles as poles of our experience immediate through the senses and intellect and noumenal through the intuitive faculties. Therefore, this last view, although not standing to logic, can only be denied by claiming one or the other poles are not part of our experience of self, and there it is to be noted the "monistic passages do not deny the intuitive aspect of experience but deny the intellectual and sensory experience."

Now it will be remembered that the "heart lotus" and such terms seemed to be the linking factor to the two poles of Ātman. In spite of the many passages using this concept, it seemed somewhat occult. The only interpretation we could make was to consider 'heart' in its symbolic sense as the heart of the matter, i.e., its core, its foundation. When looked upon in this way we see it to be Ātman's link through the various Kośas or levels of being. Our concentration on this concept has not been wholly gratuitius for modern sages such as Ramana Maharshi, who claimed direct experience of such a heart-center. Ramana Maharshi[2] claimed that the heart-center physically located, was in the center of the chest to the right of the heart; but this was merely a funnel to the universal sense of self. When one wholly centered his awareness there he lost limitations of individuality and in a flood of power became permanently centered in the Ātman beyond the three states. This was

1. See *S.B.* on *C.U.* 6.2.1.
2. See Ramana Maharshi's *Who am I?* and *Upadeśa Sāhasrī*.

claimed not an intellectual knowledge by him but direct experience; it is cited here only because it points out our interpretation of the heart lotus and its importance as a link of Universal and individual poles of Ātman. For purposes of our study it can at best only illustrate the continuance of such beliefs as a fundamental part of the religious experience.

Another point to be observed is that what the above *Kaṭha* passage[1] refers to as the knowing self[2] is not what we have referred to as the Universal pole of Ātman. This knowing self, though universal in the sense of not being just individual, is not manifest or created whereas Ātman, while being a witness is within creation. This latter is the sense of Hiraṇyagarbha, Prajāpati etc., the universal pole of creation viewed as self. At this point our discussion extends into Brahman. In the next chapter some of the problems here will become clearer. Ātman is the manifest Brahman whereas the above passage seems to refer to the unmanifest Brahman.

1. *Kaṭha Up.* 2.18.
2. *Ibid.*, 2.16-17.

CHAPTER IV

THE SELF AS BRAHMAN

A. *Introduction* :

'Brahman' like 'Ātman' is found in literature back to the *Ṛgveda*, such as "Brahmaṇaspatiḥ"[1] or "Jyeṣṭharājaṁ brahmaṇāṁ brahmaṇaspate".[2] These occurrences in the Mantras, however, clearly show that Brahman as a concept of ultimate reality had not yet formed. Indeed it was only later in the Brāhmaṇas[3] that Brahman began to replace Prajāpati as the term for the first principle and ultimate reality.

The etymology of 'Brahman' like 'Ātman' goes back to a pre-Aryan past according to Müller.[4] Its origin has variously been assigned to 'prayer' (Bṛh)[5], 'growth' and 'welfare', or 'force' as manifested in nature. Deussen[6] also assigns a primary meaning 'prayer'. Müller himself carries the origin back to "word" (Bṛh, Bṛhaspati),[7] but he admits the meaning of 'Brahman' to be prayer and secondarily to grow or break forth.

The link between etymology and the later concept as we find it in the Upaniṣads and Brāhmaṇas, is indeed not clear; and it is, perhaps 'Brahman' like 'Ātman' which points up the very plastic and creative use of language by the later Vedic Aryans. This indeed is one of the major difficulties in interpreting the Upaniṣads, their free use of Vedic terms often in a symbolic way.

Since the etymology will not help us much in assigning a connotation to 'Brahman'[8] let us give as broad a sample of its occurence in the Upaniṣads as is necessary to fix its meaning:

1. *Rgveda*, II. 23. 1
2. *Ibid.*
3. See Keith, *Rel. & Philos. of the Veda and Up.* p. 449 for discussion on this point, also *T.B.* II. 2.9; *S.U.B.* III. 38.I ff.
4. Müller, *Collected works*, Vol. VI, p. 54.
5. D. Haug, Müller, loc. cit. p. 52.
6. Deussen, *Philos. of Up.* p. 10.
7. *Ibid.*, p. 68 ff.
8. See Keith, loc. cit. p. 445 f.

Brahman is the sun (*Chānd. Up.* III 19.1; *Bṛh. Up.* II 1.2)
" Manas (*Chānd. Up.* III 19.1. VII. 3.2.)
" Speech (*Śata. Br.* II 7.9.2).
" Food (*Chānd. Up.* VII 7.9.2).
" Vijñāna (*Chānd. Up.* VII 7.2).
" World (*Muṇḍaka Up.* 2.1.10; *C. II.* 11.4.26).
" all (*Muṇḍaka Up.* 1.1.5, *Īśa* 4-5).
" timeless (*Kaṭha Up.* 2.14).
" Unknown (*T.U.* 2.9; *C.U.* 6.8-16; especially *B.U.* 4.2.4;4.4.22;4.5.15; 3.9.8,6).

From these passages we can see that Brahman is the source, the underlying reality, as well as indefinable and unknowable. Some of these seem to be contradictory. Actually, however, while 'Brahman' may be unknowable or indefinable, we might recognize this to mean that the connotation of Brahman is inexhaustible and unbounded. This does not limit us from considering aspects of the connotation to obtain some insight into its implication for the concept of self.

We can see then that Brahman is the ultimate reality, whether created or uncreated, personal or impersonal. While in its broadest usages it would include what we have termed Ātman and Puruṣa, 'Brahman' does seem to refer more typically to the substratum of reality; that which one would term the cosmic and supreme sense of being. Let us then agree to limit the connotation of 'Brahman' to the cosmic and supreme sense of being and proceed to study the various passages in the texts employing the term in this sense.

Before doing so, however, we should reassess the nature of the three terms and their relation to each other in the light of the criteria of analysis "Coherence" and "Completeness". Thus we limited 'Puruṣa' to a sense of individual personality, what we normally look upon as the person with a given environment and name. Individuality in a slightly broader sense was also one aspect of Ātman, we found. Thus Ātman is a more complete concept subsuming 'Puruṣa' under its connotation. It was apparent, however, that the coherence of the particular aspects of Ātman (the individual and cosmic) was such as to lead some texts, especially the earlier more symbolic material, to take a theistic stand, making the cosmic Ātman, Īśvara or Prajāpati. One can conclude then that the Ātman with its two poles lacks the coherence that the concept of Puruṣa had. In the ensuing chapter we shall see if there is any significance between the greater completeness and lesser coherence which may appear in the concept of Brahman. More will be said on this matter also in the final conclusions to our study of the Upaniṣads.

B. *Brahman And The Universe* :

1. *Introduction* : In the Upaniṣads and even earlier in the Vedas, many passages take up the origin of this Universe. Various first principles and causes are educed, (we shall consider them shortly) but perhaps most basic to the concept of Brahman are those passages regarding 'Sat' and 'Asat'. A great deal of misunderstanding has arisen over these terms. Let us try to clear these up before considering more fully the manifest or created Brahman. Following are the passages using 'Sat' or 'Asat' in relation to Brahman.

(1) This Universe was in the beginning not being; this was being, it arose ; thereupon an egg was developed (*C.U.* 3.19.1).

(2) Not being was this in the beginning; from it being arose (*T.U.* 2.7).

(3) After he had created it (all this whatsoever; after he had entered into it he was the being (Sat) and the beyond (tyat), expressible and inexpressible...consciousness and unconsciousness, reality and unreality...As reality he became everything that existed; for this men call reality (*T.U.* 2.6).

(4) In truth there are two forms of Brahman. The formed and the unformed, mortal and immortal, abiding and fleeting, the being (Sat) and the beyond (tyam). (*B.U.* 2,3.1).

(5) Being only my good Sir, this was in the beginning, one only and without a second. Some indeed say that this was not being in the beginning, one only and without a

second; from this not being, being was born. But how my good sir could this be so ? How could being be born from not being ? Being, therefore, rather, my good Sir, this was in the beginning, one only and without a second."
(*C.U.* 6.2.1).

In passages (1) to (4) it is clear that not being cannot be a nihil or nothing; and rather perhaps if we looked upon Sat as empirical being, an existent, and Asat as reality prior to existence or creation, the passages would become clear. The *Chāndogya* passage (5) would then be using Sat in the sense of ultimate being or Reality. In this regard it is interesting to note both the *Ṛgveda* and later Upaniṣads, in some contexts, viewed Brahman before creation as neither being (Sat) nor non-being (Asat).[1] In the later Upaniṣads, creation seems to be of little interest and accordingly we find "Brahman is neither being nor not-being".[2] "Higher than that which is and that which is not"[3]. Again in *Śvetāśvatara*[4] Brahman seems to take in both empirical reality, the realm of ignorance, and the eternal reality, the Kingdom of Knowledge. We shall have occasion to consider this aspect of Brahman after the manifest and unmanifest have been considered.

We may conclude, then, the above passages refer to Asat as not being in reference to the empirical and existent Sat and not as not being in any absolute sense. This point is of considerable importance in laying the foundation for our study of Brahman. Just as we found the Kośa analysis gave order and purpose to otherwise unrelated elements in the analysis of Puruṣa, uniting them into a functioning whole which was not merely the sum of parts but showed an intensive relation of the higher Kośa being the "soul" of the lower; just as in Ātman the two aspects of individual and universal were linked into a functioning whole, the dipolar Ātman, by the concept of the heart lotus; just so in the present case of Brahman, the concept of Sat carries most generi-

1. See for example *Ṛgveda* X. 129.1.
2. *Śvetāśvatara Up*. 4.18.
3. Cf. *Muṇḍaka Up*. 2.2.1.
4. *Śvetāśvatara Up*. 5.1.

cally this same idea of a "functioning whole". In fact although the concept of being may seem to be an irreducible one, we usually predicate "being" of something which functions as a unit whatever elements it may have. Thus the human being is such a functioning unit. All the cells and organs, brain and psychic qualities all cooperating towards purposive behaviour of the man. Man, then, is not just an extensive unity of all these parts, rather there is a heirarchy of unities each being subsumed as in the Kośa analysis under the next highest level. This intensive relation of elements points out one important meaning of 'being', the sense of "levels of being". Thus we would not intend quite the same when predicating being of a rock and a man. In spite of the apparent greater permanence of the rock we feel that man partakes more widely of the possibilities of being.

Thus in the above passages considering Brahman as Sat, it must be concluded that whatever diversity may be found in Brahman it must represent a functioning unity. This conclusion is of immediate importance in considering the manifest Brahman; but also the same criterion may well follow all through the various aspects of Brahman to be found in our texts.

Creation, then, arose from Brahman as an ultimate reality which is tyam (as against Etad) or beyond. Moreover from the above passages it appears that Brahman, in some way yet to be explained, entered creation and became the foundation for all existence as soul of the universe. In this role Brahman appears as Hiraṇyagarbha or Prajāpati and overlaps our discussion of Ātman on the universal pole or as cosmic self. It is now possible, however, to consider this universal Ātman in the broader context as manifest Brahman or the creator.

The categories for our study of manifest Brahman may be realized by calling to mind the passages referring to a triune Brahman or viewing the Universe triunely. These passages are correlated in the table below :

T.U. 3.1	*C.U.* 14.1		*Ma*
Creator (that out of which creatures arise)	tad)		A
Preserver (in which they live)	Jan)	Tajjalān	U
Destroyer (to which they return)	līna)		M

Although the trinities of the Upaniṣads and earlier Vedas are quite obscure, it is apparent from the above table that the notion of Manifest Brahman as creator, preserver and destroyer was already in the Upaniṣads in a formed state and it only remained for later more religious literature to give them names Brahmā, Viṣṇu and Śiva. These three divisions also reflect the three basic divisions of man's thought about the Universe—cosmology and theology or the creation, psychology and science or the preservation and soteriology and eschatology or the dissolution. This trinity represents the logical and perhaps the chronological order of man's study of self as was discussed in the general introduction. Let us proceed to consider them in order.

2. *Brahman as Creator*: In treating Brahman as creator the implications of the dipolar Ātman must be born in mind. This is to say, creation may conveniently be divided into two orders, the microcosmic order and the macrocosmic order. This is of course an artificial distinction and may give difficulty if its position as a tool of analysis is not held in mind.

In the preceding chapters we have traced the microcosmic order in some detail. We found that in Ātman it is blended with the macrocosmic order. Let us therefore, here take up the latter order in more detail so as to understand the creation in its broader aspects.

First, there are three basic types of creation to be found in the Upaniṣads, viewed as emanations from Brahman out of his "own nature": (1) evolution, (2) involution and (3) creation of a substratum. The process of involution, somewhat analogous to Vivarta of later philosophical literature, seems to be a process of precipitation from Brahman as an unmanifest Unity. The first step in the involution is usually described as division; such as in the *Bṛhadāraṇyaka* "He (Prajāpati) was desirous of a second—He divided this two-fold. Hence were husband and wife produced"[1]. From this division or bifurcation all created things are produced by their union, in one story gradually descending from cows to the creation of ants. There are, then, two significant points in these symbolic creation stories. First, there is the con-

1. *B.U.* 1.4.3-4; 2.1.1-13; 1.5.18-21; 1.2.4.

cept that the one cannot itself unfold the multiplicity of creation; an initial division of itself producing two different forces (Male and female of the story above) is the primal cause for the created multiplicity. This doctrine of course seems highly suggestive of the Puruṣa and Prakṛti doctrine of Sāṅkhya and also precisely the meaning of the following passage of the Gītā[1]. "Whatsoever creature is born, immobile, or mobile, know thou...that it is from union between field (kṣetra) and knower of field (kṣetrajña)"; and this union is interpreted as Prakṛti being the womb and Puruṣa the seed. We shall consider this point fully in the next part when discussing the Gītā; suffice it here to recognize this first stage of involution as anticipatory of the Sāṅkhyan metaphysics. The second significant point is that in the involution we have a sense of "Unfolding" much as in the Kośas. Each previous level being the inner guide or soul of succeeding one. This solves the problem which we shall see the other two theories, evolution and creation of substratum, encounter, i.e., just in what way is the Brahman-Ātman the inner guide, and how did this universal principle enter the creations. This point will be taken up at length in discussing Brahman as the preserver, here we can recognize that involution unfolds a multiplicity, from the pre-existent Brahman and hence is really emanation rather than "creation". Simply we can see that the donkey, man, etc., all the patterns for the created multiplicity, are "patterns" inherent in the pre-existing Unity.

Another theory of creation is the creation of a substratum. The basic ideas of this mode of creation have been met with in discussing the analysis of the microcosm, Puruṣa[2]. The same elements as substratum, the primal elements of creation, have been hypothesised—Anna[3], Prāṇa[4], Tapas[5], Apas[6], and also name, form and matter[7] as well as Prāṇa and Rayi[8]. These various substrata, fall into roughly the same pattern as in the

1. 13.26; cf. also 7.6.
2. *RV*. X. 90.
3. *B.U.* 1.4.6, 1.5.2; *T.U.* 2.1-5.
4. *B.U.* 1.3; *Muṇḍaka Up.* 2.1.3; 4.8.
5. *Muṇḍaka Up.* 1.1.8; 2.1.1.
6. *C.U.* 7.10.1, 6.2; *B.U.* 1.5.13; *Kaṭha Up.* 4.6.
7. *Muṇḍaka Up.* 1.1.9; 2.1.4-9.
8. *P.U.* 1.4-10; 3.3.

Puruṣa analysis. First the most simple substratum is the attempt almost analogous to pre-Socratic searching for the primal element. Prāṇa, Anna, apas, tapas is put forth as the primal element out of which all this multiplicity arises. More sophisticated attempts anticipate largely the Sāṅkhyan evolution. We encounter for instance in *Praśna*[1] that Prajāpati (the manifest Brahman-Ātman) desired offspring and produced a couple, Prāṇa and Rayi intending that, "they should in manifold ways produce offspring for me". This, of course, strongly resembles the primal division of the involutional creation, but with this one interesting difference. Unlike the Vivarta of the involution, there is "produced" as a substratum Prāṇa and Rayi containing potentially in their natures all manifold creation, and the creation in this case proceeds more by pariṇāma, by evolution. Thus while both division and production of the two substrata resemble Puruṣa and Prakṛti of Sāṅkhya, they must be realized as quite distinct, both implying a different metaphysics. Both views, perhaps, carry over into later philosophical thought; the former as the Vivarta Vāda of Vedānta, and the latter, Pariṇāma of Sāṅkhya. It can also be seen that in both cases it is easy to negate one aspect of the creation: in the case of division, the later manifold creation; and in production of Prāṇa and rayi the "production" of them by Prajāpati, thereby giving rise to Vedāntic and Sāṅkhyan metaphysics, respectively.

Related to this two-fold substratum is the threefold substratum already discussed in the second Chapter as the anticipation of the Guṇa theory:

Red	Tejas	Speech
White	Apas	Life
Black	Anna	Mind

This three-fold division is the product of Rayi's unfoldment as Sāṅkhya has later inferred it. Not only does it create man but all created nature is said to be composed of these three elements. "The redness of the sun is due to heat, its whiteness to water and its darkness to earth. Hence the sun ceases to be the sun, it is nothing but a word; it is effect and is normal. Its three forms

1. *P.U.* 1.4.

alone are true".[1] This too, like the twofold product of division, is an unfoldment but from the substratum of creation not from Prajāpati directly i.e. evolution not involution. Thus we have in the *Chāndogya*, Sat unfolding successively the three basic principles tejas, apas, and annam. It is inferable, however, that this unfoldment produces a substratum from which multiplicity evolves rather than involution whereby Prajāpati divides himself into man and woman and they successively involve from cows to ants:

There are other attempts to find the substratum, we remember, in the many sensory analyses of Puruṣa. There we found a symbolic link between the senses and macrocosmic equivalents[2]

Mind	Husband	Water as clouds
Speech	Wife	Agni
Life (Prāṇa)	Work (Karma)	offspring Vāyu (wind)
Ear	Knowledge	moon
Eye	Wealth	Āditya (sun)

As in the microcosmic order, so here in the macrocosmic order, the Kośa analysis can be inferred to make order, out of the various strands of substrata. Thus one is hard pressed to fit ānanda or bliss into the scheme of the above evolutionary or substrata analysis; yet the *Taittirīya Up.* claims the worlds to be upheld by Ānanda. Also Prāṇa as the other element in creation, unlike the Sāṅkhya's Puruṣa, is the active element and irreducible to Rayi. The various deities of the above tables, āditya, Agni, etc. also present another irreducible element in existence : Seemingly macrocosmic counterparts of the mental levels of Puruṣa. It can be concluded, therefore, that although most of the creation stories conceive of the two-fold nature familiar in the *Gītā* and Sāṅkhya; nevertheless, the three-fold matter is not given the exclusive position so given in Sāṅkhya; and Prāṇa, ānanda, the deities, etc. are the irreducible components of an analysis of the macrocosm in some contexts not supporting the three-fold analysis. Often such

1. *C.U.* 6.4.2.

components as the above occur in more cosmological contexts. The creation stories so far narrated usually, however, fall short of a cosmological analysis so supplied in these other contexts. The Kośa analysis does supply the missing links macrocosmically just as it does microcosmically. In this case it rounds out the cosmological analysis and links it to creation. Radhakrishnan points that correlation in the following table showing the microcosmic and macrocosmic correlations.[1]

Subject (*Ātman*)	*Object* (*Brahman*)
1. Bodily self (Viśva)	1. Cosmos (Virāṭ or Vaiśvānara)
2. Vital self (Taijasa)	2. Soul of the world (Hiraṇyagarbha)
3. Intellectual self (Prājña)	3. Self Consciousness (Īśvara)
4. Intuitive self (Turīya)	4. Ānanda (Brahman)

Actually to put Ānanda as an objective element opposed to Turīya Ātman is gratuitous and perhaps if we compare microcosmic and macrocosmic components instead of limiting the correlation to Ātman as a subject and Brahman as an object, we would get the following analysis.

Microcosm (*Ātman*)	*Kośa equity.*	*Macrocosm*	*Brahman*
1. Viśva or bodily self	Anna Kośa	Vaiśvānara the Virāṭ	Cosmic Self (The Viśvarūpa)
2. Taijasa or Vital self	Prāṇa Kośa	Hiraṇyagarbha	The life or soul of the world as life force (Śakti)
3. Prājña or in tellectual self	Manas Kośa	Īśvara	The world as Ṛtam
4. Turīya or intuitive self	Vijñāna Kośa		The world as Self

——Ānanda——

It must not be assumed from the above table that this Kośa analysis is "the conclusion" of the Upaniṣads on creation nor even on puruṣa. This analysis merely cements together diverse analyses both of microcosm and macrocosm and represents

1. Radhakrishnan, *loc. cit.* I. 172.

perhaps the most metaphysically complete cosmology. Indeed it can be seen that the various creation theories remain distinct contributions by the different authors of the Upaniṣads; and the Kośa analysis as a cosmology would square best with the involutional creation. Although some modern philosophers such as Aurobindo try to fit it into the evolutional scheme,[1] the evolution creation could logically reach only the Guṇa theory which it does anticipate; for Prāṇa is merely the mate of Rayi here not as inner guide or "soul" as in involution and the Kośa analysis.

There are, then, two distinct views of Brahman as creator, both views characterize Brahman before creation as Sat, Asat and Death, Why this primal being itself a unity created multiplicity is variously given as from fear[2] and from desire of offspring[3] or from various desires.[4] Thereupon creation follows two paths, one an involution in which Prajāpati, or the first being, the creator aspect of Brahman, divides into two, a man and a woman, symbolic of two natures or creature forces. These two forces further involude from cows down into ants, creating the whole multiplicity in the creation story. According to this theory the primal being is active in creation, i.e., all the forms created are forms which he can potentially assume, just as the two primal forces are divisions of his nature "as a split pea is of the whole".[5] Thus the actual creation is, thereby, linked to a cosmology ontologically arranged as in the Kośa analysis. Each level of being, expresses the creator who is its soul or inner guide.

The other theory of creation also begins with two primal forces; but here they are products created by Brahman such as Prāṇa and Rayi, or other elements which are the substrata of creation. From these elements by an evolution all the multiplicity of forms were developed. However we interpret the substrata, Prāṇa and Rayi being the most complete concepts, they

1. Aurobindo, *life Divine* (American Edition), pp., 217-18, 744-45.
2. *B.U.* 1.4.2.
3. *P.U.* 1.4.
4. *A.U.* 1.1; 1.2; *B.U.* 1.4.17.
5. *B.U.* 1.4.34.

are not "divisions of the one Brahman" but primal elements as their English equivalents so connote, matter and life force. Both these theories of creation seem to be the cosmological basis for the two rival theories of vivartavāda and pariṇāmavāda of Vedānta and Sāṅkhya in later Dārśanic literature. The importance of these two theories will be even more evident after the consideration of other two aspects of the manifest Brahman—as the preserver and as the source of dissolution.

3. *Brahman as the source of Preservation*: Because of the disconnected nature of the Upaniṣadic texts, seldom are all three aspects of the manifest Brahman found together. Thus in the first chapter of *Bṛhadāraṇyaka Upaniṣad*[1] there are six creation stories alone, but little discussion of consequent relation of Brahman to the creation. Most of the discussion of Brahman as preserver occurs in later Upaniṣads or in other passages. Before taking them up let us gather from the previous section the implications of Brahman's relation to the created world or in more cosmological language how "Brahman entered creation". In the one theory of division and involution, Brahman clearly became active and all things are merely the coating around the manifest Brahman so divided. That is to say, Brahman unmanifest became the dipolar Ātman-Brahman; and then subsequent expansion to created multiplicity arose from inherent characteristics of an Ātman being the unity in the diversity of potential manifold Puruṣas. This point has already been discussed while considering Ātman. Here further light can be shed, in terms of creation, upon this dipolar Ātman. Thus the universal Ātman is prajāpati, Hiraṇyagarbha. The different levels of the Kośa analysis constitute the inherent nature as levels of being of this Ātman-Brahman. The story of involution symbolically points this out when the two primal forces "man and wife" pursue each other from cows down to ants: The different creatures being the result of this dipolar Ātman expressing itself on different levels of being, mental, vital, and down to physical. Thus in this theory of creation there is no problem of the relation of the world to Brahman—the world

1. *B.U.* 1.4. 1,5.

literally is Brahman as the active manifest Brahman or the dipolar Ātman. The other, substrata-evolution theory does encounter difficulty relating Brahman to creation. Indeed if the substrata are seeds of all the evolution (through the tripartite tejas, apas and prāṇa), then it becomes only a short step to reject the previous step, the creation of the two forces by Brahman, and ends up in the dualism later accepted by Sāṅkhya.

After the first four Upaniṣads—*Bṛhadāraṇyaka*, *Chāndogya*, *Taittirīya* and *Aitareya* — only in the *Praśna* do we find any theory of creation.[1] The shift from cosmology to psychology can be seen gradually taking place until by the *Taittirīya* the creation theory is largely supported by the Kośa analysis and a psychological speculation as to the motives for creation.[2] The one element of this early interest in cosmology which does survive and become the dominant means of linking Brahman with the created multiplicity is the " ether in the heart" concept which has followed us through the last two chapters, hardly less difficult than the creation stories to interpret but indeed showing more of a psychological orientation. The one line of thought on Brahman as preserver which was carried through in later Upaniṣads, then, was the heart-lotus as the seat of Brahman, the conjunction of the macrocosmic and microcosmic orders. In other than the *Taittirīya*[3] where it occurs in the context of the Kośa analysis, indeed it is the only link between the microcosmic and macrocosmic orders, and that upon which the Upaniṣads are most insistent; *viz.*, that "it is the seat of the eternal Brahman". Brahman as the preserver then is linked to the created world in later Upaniṣadic texts either through the Kośa analysis or directly through the self in the heart being "the size of a thumb" yet larger than and filling in the worlds[4]. The former, like the involution theory of creation, brings Brahman directly into the manifold world as its very core; in the latter case Brahman at best is interpreted as the

1. *T.U.* 1.4; 2.7; 3.3.
2. *Ibid.*, 2.7; 2.8.
3. *Ibid.*, 1.6.1; 2.1,7.
4 *Kaṭha Up.* 4.12; 6.17.

support and witness to the manifold creation through this centre in the individual. In fact in the *Aitareya*[1], it is so interpreted. After creating the first man, Brahman (male the first born), entered through the top of the head and took up his abode in the heart cavity.

We may conclude, then, that although interest in Manifest Brahman shifted from the creator aspect to preserver, the implications of the two theories of creation, involution and substrata evolution, were carried through in the Kośa analysis and the direct linking of the micro and macrocosm through the heart cavity as the seat of Brahman in activity. These two (The Kośa analysis and the direct linking) both imply analogously the same status of Brahman, one as the core or soul of existence, the other as the witness and support, as was concluded in the Ātman chapter.

4. *Brahman as the Source of Dissolution*: As was found in the introduction to our discussion of manifest Brahman, the number of passages referring to a triune Brahman—the creator, preserver and that to which all creatures return—are relatively few[2]. This, however, does not mean that it is not a fundamental concept in Upaniṣadic thought, rather it serves to co-ordinate much of which is found in disconnected parts like the Kośa analysis. It is Brahman as that to which all things return that rounds out and gives meaning to the picture of manifestation.

There are three aspects which we must discuss regarding Brahman as the source of dissolution. Firstly, we must examine the meaning and import of the individual or microcosm "returning to Brahman"; secondly the sense in which the macrocosm might be said to be dissolved by Brahman; and thirdly Brahman as the source of dissolution and its role in giving order and purpose to the triune manifest Brahman.

The liberation of Puruṣa has already been discussed to some extent. We found that the Individual was bound to changes from waking, dream, and deep sleep; and in the latter state he

1. *A.U*, 1.3.12.
2. *P.U.* 3; *T.U.* 3.6; *Muṇḍaka Up.* 2.14; *C.U.* 3.14.1.

was united with the Ātman in the ether of the heart; and only in liberation did he cut asunder the "Knots of the heart"[1] and enter the fourth state, liberated from the round of the three states and from limitation to the individual pole of ātman. Brahman as the source of dissolution, then, is either the "telos" of man, (that in which man finds his transcendence and the completion, if the less monistic theory of evolution and growth of self is taken), or Brahman is the ground and only reality to which the self awakes when the desires and *Knots* of the heart which bind him to existence as man are broken. The individual is thereupon said to "become one in the great inexhaustible all"[2] or in the same Upaniṣad referring to the same liberation. "In the golden highest sheath the knowers of Ātman know the Brahman who is without spot, without part, who is pure, who is the light of lights"[3]. When the self returns to the ānandamayakośa or the "golden highest sheath", then as said in the last chapter he becomes transpersonal.

Brahman in creation created also the macrocosm. In what way can it be said that the macrocosm has its dissolution or return to Brahman? This is an exceedingly difficult question, because, outside of Brahman as the source of dissolution of the creatures mentioned above, only one possible passage in our ten Upaniṣads gives any hint of dissolution of the Universe; and this speculation is doubtful:

> "As the spider casts out and draws in its web, as on the earth the animal and herbs are produced, as from living man the hairs of the head, and body spring forth, so is produced the Universe from the immutable (akṣarāt)".

The fact that the drawing in (of the web) was not followed through in the verse makes any macrocosmic dissolution highly doubtful. The first time the creation-preservation-destruction appears to be applied to the macrocosm is in the *Śvetāśvatara*

1. *Kaṭha Up.* 2.6.15; *Muṇḍaka Up.* 2.2.8.
2. *Muṇḍaka* 3.2.7.
3. *Ibid.*, 2.2.9

Upaniṣad[1] and of course in the *Gītā*.[2] Deussen[3] attributes the theory of dissolution of the universe and repeated cycles to the later Vedānta which was faced with the squaring of their theory of the beginninglessness of the Saṁsāras[4] with the numerous references in the Upaniṣads to the "Beginning". Thereby creation was a "re-creation" and all creatures are originally found with the Saṁsāras of their former existences. It seems that Brahman as the source of the dissolution of the Universe need not have its origin quite so gratuitously. Brahman clearly was viewed as creator and preserver of the Universe as well as the individual, and in addition that to which the individuals return. All this is lacking, the dissolution of the Universe seems almost a necessary inference. What seems not to be a part of the Upaniṣad's teachings, however, is the repeated creation-preservation-dissolution cycle. Deussen, however, does not distinguish between these two views of dissolution in his discussion. The Upaniṣads unequivocally were soteriologically oriented; but this seems not to include any development or liberation of the macrocosm. One might infer then that the macrocosm is really in the Upaniṣads the vehicle for the microcosm and has no telos itself as does the microcosm.

Two very important conclusions arise from this discussion: One pointing to the less-monistic theory as most coherently interpreting the diverse elements of self in the Upaniṣads, and the other indicating the purpose of creation. To consider the first one, it is evident from the above that the individual sense of self occupied an important even if different place in Upaniṣadic thought than the universal self. Should this be, if monism was more than an element in the Upaniṣadic conclusions? That is to say if there were no evolution to self, only a breaking of the knots of the heart which binds the otherwise omniscient self to the three states, then should there be any value to the individual self. The answer may be found in Yājñavalkya's philosophy, the first and most complete expression of monism

1. *Śvetāśvatara Up.*, 3.2.
2. *Bhagavadgītā IX.* esp, IV. 7,
3. Deussen, *Philos. of Up.* pp., 219-226.
4. Gauḍapāda's view as discussed by Deussen, p. 220.

in the Upaniṣads. What sets off the Yājñavalkya section of the Upaniṣad from the earlier chapters is the almost total lack of concern with creation. As mentioned in the last chapter attention was more psychologically directed i.e. the individual was recognized to be bound to states in which he did not find his true nature; and the path to this fulfilment was laid out. This theory, therefore, had no need of creation. It might be inferred, then, that such problems as we have brought up would be rejected as applicable to the monistic teachings; and indeed perhaps Śaṅkara has consistently carried these ideas out in rejection of creation as a "real creation".[1] This point shall lead us to a discussion in the next section of the unmanifest Brahman. Here, however, the question asked is both meaningful and important to the Upaniṣadic teachings. That the majority of our texts are concerned with the multiple world as a part of Brahman, there can be no doubt from the above discussion of manifest Brahman. This is also the conclusion of Deussen.[2] Yet Deussen like Śaṅkara considers it a lower position than the idealism in monistic passages. From this it can be concluded that so far as the Upaniṣads view creation as a real creation, then some development of the individual is indicated. This is precisely what the Kośa analysis of the individual imports, ontologically arranged levels of reality through which the individual expands to the transpersonal Ātman in the highest level of reality, the Ānandamayakośa.

This idea brings up the second point which we must discuss regarding manifest Brahman as the source of dissolution, namely the purpose of creation. In contexts presenting the creation stories, two reasons for creation have been mentioned, "desire for offspring" and "fear". In presenting the Kośa analysis, however, the *Taittirīya*[3] gives another reason "if that bliss were not present in the ether of the heart, who then could live; who could breathe? For it is he that fills all with bliss". Thus the created world is said to be maintained by and headed towards

1. See Ś.B. on *C.U.* 3.14.1.
2. Deussen, *loc. cit.* p. 183 ff.
3. *T.U.* 2.7.

ānanda-bliss. In what way is ānanda a "reason" for creation? It seems that if we are to view Brahman as the source and goal of the created world then there could not be ultimately a becoming something that has not been—as Deussen correctly observes.[1] In other words it is essential that Brahman be not only the perfection towards which creation heads but also he "be" that is not just as an ideal pattern with no existence; but he must be the ground of existence. Paradoxically this obviates any novel or real becoming. The pattern for the self's becoming must be laid in Brahman's nature itself. It would seem, then, that if development cannot be novel or new, then development must have some other purpose. The only purpose hinted at in our texts is ānanda or bliss. Aurobindo makes some issue of this in *Life Divine* whereby he speaks of it in terms of "Līlā".[2]

> "If delight of existence be the secret of creation cannot it be regarded as the reason or atleast one reason of this apparently, paradoxical and contrary Līlā?"

The treatment of the manifest Brahman, then, was not uniform throughout our texts. Early interest seemed cast in cosmological terms largely asking the question, "whence came all this perceived?" Interest in how it was sustained led to a shift from cosmological Interest to metaphysical psychology evident in the abrupt change to Yājñavalkya's philosophy in the *Bṛhadāraṇyaka Upaniṣad.* Here the prime question was "Where does it go?". Thus while one element is cosmologically oriented the other is eschatologically inclined and it is the latter interest which survived in the later Upaniṣads we are in this context considering. It can be concluded, however, that the Upaniṣads on the whole favour a real creation either by involution or creation of substrata and evolution. Brahman "preserves the world" in two ways; either actively as the core or soul of all multiplicity which follows from the Involution theory, or Brahman is the witness and support of existence linked through the heart cavity. Brahman is the source of dissolution of the individual in the sense that he is the goal, the fulfillment of the self. In the discussion of Brahman as the source of dissolution,

1. Deussen *loc. cit.* p. 355.
2. Aurobindo, *Life Divine* (American Edition), pp. 368-70.

it was also found that the monistic eschatological interest did not need a triune manifest Brahman, and as we shall now see it is because ātman-Brahman for them is unmanifest.

C. *The Unmanifest Brahman*: The discussion of the manifest Brahman overlapped with what is considered the unmanifest Brahman at two points. First in discussing Brahman as Sat it was clear that Brahman as the creator before creation was not-being in the sense that it was one, undivided, and without multiple activity. This point will be discussed here in the unmanifest Brahman in considering the first principle. Another place in our previous discussion at which the unmanifest Brahman appeared was in the monistic view of the Brahman, as discussed in presenting Yājñavalkya's philosophy. There we found no interest in a cosmology only Soteriology and eschatology. This point shall be further discussed in terms of the negative character of Brahman. One further aspect which shall concern us is the various anticipations of the later Sacchidānanda concept, and in what sense this may apply to the unmanifest Brahman.

If the manifest Brahman is that aspect of Brahman active in the Universe, whether directly as the core or soul of its existence or merely as support and witness, then the question naturally arises as to the nature of the creator as he is in himself before creation; that is to say what is the nature of the first principle, what is Brahman apart from the created multiplicity?

In the last section, in discussing " Sat", the conclusion was reached that " Sat" meant a "functioning Unity" and was represented by the predication of a greater participation in being by man than by the rock. Thus while the rock may be more homogeneous in its "Unity" clearly the man's heterogeneity accounts for his diverse abilities and yet greater functioning unity or purposive behaviour. This interpretation of 'Sat' does not cover all the passages and indeed perhaps only the *Chāndogya* passage[1], which has been already quoted "Before this was a mere state of being (Sat), one only, without a second."

1. *C.U.* 6.2.1.

Thus in speaking of being as a "functioning whole", it would be contrasted with becoming and represent what we might qualify as absolute being. In the last case, the *Chāndogya* passages quoted above, 'being' would rather be contrasted with 'not-being' and represent empirical created being. It must be carefully recognized then, that the Upanishads when referring to Asat are not holding to a void or nihil as a first principle. As a matter of fact from the logic of negative categories asat does not tell us anything about unmanifest Brahman. It is like trying to contrast apples with non-apples. We are not contrasting apples with nothing or a void, but something that has not the property of apple. This is not really informative because we might be referring to fountain pens, cars or oceans. Perhaps this problem is what led the author of the above *Chāndogya* passage to use Sat rather than Asat for the unmanifest Brahman. If the Asat passages do not inform us, then we must consider the passages using 'Sat' in the sense of absolute being as more important since it throws a light both on the manifest and unmanifest Brahman. One observation immediately arises from this; that is, the Unmanifest Brahman when considered as the first principle is "unmanifest" only in contrast with what is manifest. Moreover the manifest cannot be something other than the unmanifest, this would set up a dualism and open the concept of Brahman to criticism by something analogous to Aristotle's Second man argument against Plato's theory of ideas.[1] Whatever the position of the manifest to unmanifest, then, there cannot be two Brahmans only one differing in aspect or perspective. This conclusion is supported by the very word most often used in the Upaniṣads for creation 'Sṛṣṭi' from 'Sṛj' which basically means to emit or to pour forth.[2] This illustrates what was claimed above regarding manifest Brahman, namely that there can be no "new" or novel becoming and here it is also the case since Brahman must be that "being" which is the ground and perfection of all becoming or empirical being.

Unmanifest Brahman when viewed in terms of the first principle and cosmology seems, then, to be a "being" one without

1. See Aristotle, *Mataphysics*. 1.I; XIII 4.
2. See Bloomfield, *Vedic Concordance*.

a second, in the sense of being a homogeneous unity yet that in which all the forms of the multifold creation are latent. Moreover from our previous discussion we can see that were the unmanifest to "change", i.e., become limited to the multifold forms, then we would be open again to second man arguments i.e. there would always be a being beyond this limitation. The Unmanifest Brahman must in some sense, then, lie behind creation. The Upaniṣads offer much description of this unmanifest Brahman as "He who is the hearing behind the hearing, the mind of the mind, life of the life"[1] or as in *Taittirīya*[2] "I am the maker of their Unity (the Unity of food and consumer of food) I am the first born of the true (Sat). Before the Gods I was the midst of immortality". Behind the Ṛta of the manifest, then, is hidden the Unmanifest just as in the microcosm Ātman is the hidden guide of Puruṣa's activity. Unmanifest Brahman stands behind as guide (first born of Ṛta) for the macrocosm as well.

This is but one view of Brahman as unmanifest, that involved in passages occupied or supporting the various creation stories. There is another more important treatment in the Upaniṣads. Those passages dealing with Metaphysical psychology—the major emphasis after *Bṛhadāraṇyaka* and *Chāndogya*—seem often to speak of Brahman in negative terms or neti-neti. Such passages as the following illustrate this negative path.[3]

> "He, however (the Brahman), is not so, not so. He is incomprehensible; for he is not comprehended, indestructible for he is not destroyed; unaffected for nothing affects him; he is not fottered, he is not disturbed, he suffers no harm."

These psychological inquiries, then, claim self is Brahman; and the latter is neti-neti not any object of experience, something ineffable and indefinable. The inquirer is left with a transcendent Absolute in the generic sense of not being relative or phenomenal. The language of negation is quite difficult to properly evaluate; and this matter shall occupy our attention in the conclusions when all aspects of our study have been consider-

1. See *Kena Up.* 1.1,2.
2. *T.U.* 3.10.
3. *B.U.* 4.24, 4.5.15, 2.3.6, 3.9.26.

ed. It is sufficient to recognize here when negative categories are used they are essentially saying "Brahman is non-qualified or nirguṇa" as *Bṛhadāraṇyaka Upaniṣad*[1] says. "There is no other definition beyond this, that is not so (na-iti, na-iti). Although some scholars have tried to make a positive statement of na-iti,[2] Bādarāyaṇa[3] and Gauḍapāda[4] ; both substantiate the negative interpretation. Deussen[5] sums up the nirguṇa Brahman passages well when he says: "No characterization of him (Brahman)" therefore, is possible otherwise than by the denial to him of all empirical attributes, definitions and relations—neti, neti". This conclusion was precisely that which marks the first change in the Upaniṣads from the cosmological speculation of the early chapters of the *Bṛhadāraṇyaka* to Yājñavalkya's philosophy with its preoccupation with soteriological matters. This interest seems to start from the immediacy of change, desire, and misery[6] which, according to Yājñavalkya, require plurality of objects and subjects[7]. If this were all that formed their experience the monist would most likely expose the Lokāyata doctrine; but as a matter of fact they contrast this condition with the above unity of Brahman as Yājñavalkya does in teaching Maitreyī Saying:

> "As a piece of salt, when thrown into water, is dissolved into mere water and none is capable of perviewing it (although still having the taste of salt) ; behold the great being (Mahat) which is infinite, independent and mere insight (Vijñāna)...Springing forth together with these elements (the individual) is destroyed when they are destroyed. After departing, there is no consciousness (of particularity)".[8]

1. *B.U.* 23.6.
2. Hillebrandt, *Deutsche literature* (1891) also Deussen, *loc. cit*, p. 149.
3. *Brahma Sūtras* 3.2.22.
4. *Kārikā* 3.24.
5. Deussen, *loc.cit*, p. 156.
6. *B.U.* 3.4.2; 3.5.1.
7. *B.U.* 4.5.15.
8. *B.U.* 2.4.12.

This contrast is indeed just that we have encountered all along as the monism found in all the texts. We must now ask ourselves just how, starting from such particularity, can it be said of Brahman that he excludes, as a Unity "all plurality and therefore all proximity in space, all *succession in time* all interdependence as cause and effect, and all position as subject and object". In other words how can Brahman be Svaguṇa Veśika. Also from whence came this knowledge, negative sounding though it be? The answer to the second question clearly is that through insight (Vijñāna), the Brahman is "known" in a special sense. Still we are not told, just how one who has not this insight is even to suspect something in opposition to his experience which ultimately will negate it. Not much can be obtained from the Upaniṣads in answer; but for Śaṅkara it seems that this is the place of Śruti—revelation; and indeed the *Chāndogya*[1] passage telling of the blind-folded man requiring directions from one who knows, might well point this out—the Guru who has realized Brahman guiding the individual to this unfoldment. The answer sheds light on a possible answer to the first question. Since monistic passages are almost exclusively soteriologically preoccupied, then the student does not ask such ultimate questions as just wherefrom have these Saṁsāras had their origin and for what purpose; rather he is led like the blind-folded man returned to sight, "back home", but he may never know how he got there.

In conclusion, we can see, that the unmanifest Brahman in its Nirguṇa expression arises from the contrast of the experience of multiplicity by Puruṣa to a state of absolute consciousness which is antithetical to the relative changing consciousness. Brahman takes on just this contrast as being a Unity which rejects the plurality and which is only characterized as "neti-neti".

The last problem to be considered in relation to the unmanifest Brahman is finding to what extent the various anticipations of the later Sat-Chit-Ānanda (Sacchidānanda) apply to the Unmanifest Brahman. This problem seems to come up originally in the Upaniṣads in Yājñavalkya's philosophy, at

1. *C.U.* 6.14.

the close of his session at Janaka's court, where he says "Brahman is Vijñānam and Ānandam".[1] Also in the following sections there is the reduction of six symbols to six aspects of Brahman : Prajñā, Priya, Satyam, Anantam, Ānandam, Sthita.[2] The closer expression in the *Taittirīya*[3] we have already quoted as Satyam, Jñānam and Anantam.

Bṛh (3.9.28)	*Bṛh*	(4.1)	*Taitt* (2.1)	*Ma*
	Satyam	Sthita	Satyam	A
Vijñānam	Prajña	Priya	Jñānam	U
Ānandam	Ānanda	Ānanda	Anantam	M

Whatever be the actual wording we see that the Upaniṣads had a concept of three aspects of Brahman, Satyam (being reality), Vijñāna-Jñāna (consciousness, thought, the later cit) and ānandam (bliss, infinity). We have already considered Sat in the Unmanifest sense and found it to be absolute being as distinguished from becoming or empirical being (Asat is used in texts). In the case of the consciousness element we see Jñānam contrasted to Vijñāna, i.e., while the manifest Brahman is expressed in created multiplicity which one becomes aware of through discursive thought Jñāna, the Unmanifest is expressed and "known" only through Vijñāna or insight—immediate illumination—and Jñāna thereby becomes that which keeps consciousness bound to empirical modes of thought. The bliss or infinity aspect seems to have little to link it with the Unmanifest Brahman. Deussen's remarks[4] on the import of Sat-Cit-Ānanda is hardly well taken. The "bliss" (is) the negation of all suffering, as this exists in deep dreamless sleep". While it is true ānanda is associated with dreamless sleep, as we have discussed and as *Bṛhadāraṇyaka Upaniṣad*[5] associates them its value is not to be associated with the frequent descriptions in the *Bṛhadāraṇyaka*[6] or *Chāndogya*[7] where it is said "The Self (Ātman)

1. *B.U.* 3.9.28.
2. *Ibid*, 4.1.
3. *T.U.* 2.6.
4. Deussen, *loc. cit*, p. 142.
5. *B.U.* 2.1.19.
6. *B.U.* 3.4.21; 3.7.23; 3.5.1.
7. *C.U.* 8.1.5; 8.7.1.

the sinless, free from old age, free from death, free from suffering, without hunger and thirst". Rather as the *Taittirīya* and the *Kaṭha*[1] view Ānanda, as a calculus of blisses. Ānanda is to be associated with the concept of Bliss, joy, immensity (Bhūmā,) infinity (Anantam) which are positive. Thus what is contrasted as the bliss of man (viewed in Bṛhadāraṇyaka as negative categories, death, disease, etc.) and the bliss of Brahman may be only a negative comparison by virtue of the same sort of contrast between the ego-consciousness and the consciousness of Brahman which we have found all along conditioning the Monistic elements of the Upaniṣads, but here contrasting ānanda with pain, suffering etc. The ānanda element in the triune view of Brahman, then presents difficulties for Unmanifest Brahman viewed monistically as nirguṇa; the later monistic writers can only view it negatively. Even in the monism of the Upaniṣads, then, Bliss, infinity etc. is more likely the state wherein "one has no consciousness of outer or inner"[2] as has one who dallies a beloved wife. It is just at this point, however, that we shall see the need of a further concept of Brahman beyond the manifest, which the Upaniṣads do supply in the transcedent Brahman. We see this need when realising that the various occurrences of Ānandam in the Upaniṣads usually are associated either by contrast or completion with the manifest, but not always wholly negating the latter.

D. Problems with the Concept of Brahman :

1. The Problem of knowing Brahman : Thus far two aspects of Brahman have been considered—the manifest and unmanifest—along with their relation to each other. Two main difficulties were encountered, the nature of the unmanifest, and how Brahman as self relates to ordinary experience. Both might well be treated under one heading—the problem of knowing Brahman.

What is usually translated knowledge and ignorance has many terms in Sanskrit with subtle shades of meaning—vidyā,

1. *T.U.* 2.1; see also *Kaṭha Up*. 6.3.
2. *B.U.* 4.3.33.
3. *T.U.* 2.8.

jñāna, prajñā, vijñāna. In western thought, at present more popularly *deontological*, the one word "mind" usually is considered the term applicable to the source of the many different words above *i.e.*, knowledge, wisdom, insight or intuition. Indeed the Upaniṣads occasionally so use manas[1], but the above terms do contain the ontological distinction considered in the Puruṣa chapter, and roughly corresponding to the Kośa Analysis. Thus 'Vidyā' usually connotes "knowledge" more in the sense of "sense knowledge" (occasionally, however, vidyā is used to cover all senses of knowledge not immediate). Jñāna is usually wisdom acquired from other sources, such as smṛti, śruti, etc. and having less reliance on sense areas of mind and more on intuitive faculties, albeit vicariously obtained from sages, scriptures, etc. Vijñāna has the quality of immediate and direct insight into the nature of that known. Now from these three levels we can see Vijñāna stands apart from the other two. Thus when a man is fixing a machine he has sense knowledge of all the parts (vidyā) and wisdom of the working and nature of the machine (jñāna) but until he actually handles the machine and solves the problem of its malfunction he does not have insight (vijñāna) into its malfunction. He may ponder over and examine the machine any length of time; but only when finally a flash of insight comes, can he see exactly the cause of the malfunction in the context of the working of the whole machine. Vijñāna, then, is not "knowledge" in the same sense nor acquired in the same way as jñāna or vidyā.

If these distinctions are kept in mind then when the Upaniṣads say "Brahman is unknowable"[2], it cannot be asked "then how do we know that there is such a thing as Brahman, how do we know 'Brahman' is not an empty noise like 'unicorn' ?" Rather 'unknowable' here would seem to mean that Brahman cannot be realized by vidyā or jñāna, is not just acquired, but—also in some way "given". In other words, unlike Vidyā or Jñāna which is to be had solely by our effort, Vijñāna seems not

1. *B.U.* 1.4.7, 1.5.3; *C.U.* 3.14.2; cf. also Deussen, loc. cit, 271 f.

2. *Muṇḍaka Up.* 1.1.5; 3.1.7; *C.U.* 6.8-16; *B.U.* 2.3.26; 3.8.11; 3.9.26; 4.2.24; *Kaṭha Up.* 6.9 and others.

to come by effort alone; but after preparation through effort, there is a peculiar giveness about the insight. In the Upaniṣads, as in most religious literature, this is the element of "Grace" such as in *Kaṭha*[1]. "The Ātman reveals its own truth"[2]. Vijñāna then has two elements, the preparation or the effort and the given or grace, the revealed. In terms of our "knowing" Brahman, then, the Upaniṣads ate unanimous in saying Vijñāna is the only way Brahman can be realized.

Where there is difference of opinion is the nature of the effort, because here there is involved metaphysical differences. What must be asked is "if Brahman is a reality, and if Vijñāna is the way of realizing this Brahman, then, can there be conflicting Vijñāna's of Brahman ?" Simply put, can the *Chāndogya* which emphasizes Brahman's manifest aspect and the *Bṛhadāraṇyaka* which emphasizes his nirguṇa (unmanifest) aspect, both be an insight or Vijñāna into his nature ?

It is in answer to this question that we must reassess the two paths, immediate monism and ultimate monism, to be found in the Upaniṣads and also the two Brāhmaṇas. It would seem that sense experience in its permanence and coherence is not to be dismissed as illusory as the transitory and incoherent dream state might so be dismissed. Moreover, there seems to be something in perceived nature which appears to have an order and purpose about it. In addition there are those who claim to have an insight into this order (Ṛta) and force (Śakti) active in nature. Thus we might say active and manifold nature is one pole of our experience of Brahman, that which has been termed manifest Brahman. In another and extended sense the Unmanifest Brahman is also a pole of our experience. Reflection and meditation, when one withdraws attention from the senses, bring a sense of permanency and homogeneity which in comparison to the sense reports seems to have a greater priority on reality. This is common to many metaphysical outlooks notably to Paremenides and the Eliatics in Greece. In our texts Yājñavalkya, the earliest proponent, claims such an insight into an unmanifest nirguṇa Brahman. Can these two

1. *Kaṭha Up.* 1.2.23.
2. *Muṇḍaka Up.* 3.2.3,4,

actually be equally valid poles of our experience ? Two objections immediately arise from considering those two Brahmans equally valid poles of our experience. The more simply theistic elements in the Upaniṣads,[1] would accept neither as poles of experience and contrast ordinary sense experience, as experience of self, with Brahman as Īśvara or God. Such dualism, then, saves him from the apparent contradiction to our experience of Brahman as self. The monist would not reject the experience of manifest Brahman as a dream or illusory experience, but as Yājñavalkya seems to do make it really only experience of the nirguṇa Brahman, no matter what it may seem to the individual. Both seem not to appreciate the fact that in the texts both poles are to be found positively put forth; and also to be found in terms of experience of different states of consciousness through which the individual ranges in waking dream and deep sleep. The passages emphasising neti-neti and so nirguṇa Brahman have already been considered. There are also passages which emphasise iti-iti,[2] notably Prajāpati's teaching to Indra in the *Chāndogya*. There we see a growth through the various stages of first taking self solely through the senses up to recognizing its transcendent character. What is important is that this positive approach proceeds not by negation of each previous step but by inclusion, recognizing something hidden in and transcending the former concept. This, of course, is also the purport of the Kośa analysis in *Taittirīya*. Thus while the iti-iti path leads us originally to the experience of manifest Brahman—that self immanent and active in nature successive application of it to the different levels of consciousness between sense experience and the homogeneous reflective state, results in a sense of self which is not simply neti-neti or nirguṇa, homogeneous and non-active; but another sense of Brahman or self which is hidden in the others and in a sense inclusive of them.

We may conclude then that the realization or insight, (vijñāna) of Brahman as self is not independent of the effort of the individual towards that insight. Thus by neti-neti one pole is negated, the manifest; and as a result one has vijñāna of a

1. See especially *Kena* and *Aitareya Upanishads*.
2. *T.U.* 2, also *C.U.* 7,8.

nirguṇa, homogeneous permanent Brahman. Through iti-iti or affirmation one obtains insight into the manifest Brahman active in the world. While these insights seem contradictory, they are asserted by the texts and by reflection to be poles of our experience. The *Chāndogya* teachings of Prajāpati to Indra and the *Taittirīya* seemed to lead to different results, whereby the self was seen to be hidden in each of the various levels of consciousness and yet transcendent of them, in other words a Brahman that included both poles of experience. This can be seen simply by recognizing the neti-neti process to conclude the effort for Vijñāna by rejection of multiple-active consciousness, just as iti-iti alone limits experience to the manifold-active pole of experience; but according to the less monistic school of thought, by growth, by overflowing of each level of consciousness, the awareness gradually resides in a consciousness inclusive of both poles, just as the child grows to adulthood not by negation by each new experience but by expansion to see the same experience in light of an expanded awareness.

2. *Ātman, the Fourth State and the Transcendental Brahman* :

If we see that "knowing Brahman" is a special sense of knowing in which the path used to prepare for the insight in some way colors the whole insight into Brahman itself, then we see yet another interpretation of Brahman, one inclusive of and transcendent to both the manifest and unmanifest Brahman so far considered. Indeed there are many indications in the Upaniṣads that Parabrahman is neither of the above two. Three different points indicate this. The Upaniṣadic insistence that Brahman is beyond thought, the predication of contradictory qualities of Brahman, and direct assertions and various analogies to the effect that Parabrahman is beyond manifest—unmanifest distinctions.

We can see now that when it is said that "Brahman is beyond thought"[1] a new sense comes to light, namely whatever pole of experience the thought is representative of, Brahman transcends it in an inclusive way, i.e., he overflows the thought. It is in this sense that thought is a hindrance to liberation because it can never empty the whole meaning of Brahman. This use of "Brahman is beyond thought", then differs from the neti-neti

1. Muṇḍaka Up. 3.1.7.

sense illustrated by Deussen's remark[1] that "Ātman as knowing subject is itself always unknowable"; it differs in that realisation of Brahman does not exclude discursive thought but merely overflows it.

In terms of language this same point is made often in the Upaniṣads not by using negative predicates or positive predicates but using them both together as contradictory predicates; such as the following :

> "He moves, he does not move, he is far and also near, he is within all, he is out of this all." (Īśa 5).
>
> "Sitting it goes afar; sleeping, it goes everywhere. Who else, therefore, save myself, is able to comprehend the God who rejoices and not rejoices" (Kaṭha 2.21).
>
> "They think the fourth (turīya) him, whose knowledge are not internal objects nor external, nor both, who has not wisdom self-gathered, who is not intelligent and not unintelligent, who is invisible, imperceptible, unseizable, incapable of proof, beyond thought, not to be defined, the essence of the knowledge of the self, in whom all the spheres have ceased, who is tranquil, blissful and without duality". (Māṇḍūkya 7).[2]

From these quotations we see an entirely new language enter our discussions. The unmanifest Brahman was most completely expressed by negative predicates "Brahman is not this, etc." The manifest Brahman was expressed usually in terms of positive predicates. Here we have both, Deussen takes this as merely the "poetic style" in denying Brahman all empirical predicates; in other words another way of asserting neti-neti. Śaṅkara seems likewise to negate one pole and use the positive assertion merely to emphasize the negative one.[3] Both seem to have overlooked a more obvious meaning, namely that while Brahman cannot be limited to empirical predicates (positive qualities) nevertheless he cannot also be denied of them as

1. See Deussen, *loc. cit.* p. 79f.

2. Cf. *Īśa Up.* which takes up this transcendental Brahman, also *Muṇḍaka U.* 3.1.7; *Kaṭha Up.* 2.21. 10-15; *B.U.* 3.8.11,5.1.1.

3. See Ś.B. on above contradictory statements; and esspecially *B.U.* 3.8. 2.4.6.

this would itself constitute a limitation which a Supreme concept of Brahman is trying to avoid. Thus it would be more in line with the nature of contradictory predicates to ascribe an "aufgehoben" in the Hegelian sense and infer that the Upaniṣads were trying to convey something which transcended ordinary language distinctions. This conclusion is supported by Aurobindo in *Life Divine* where he says[1]—

> "It (Brahman) is describable neither by our negations neti-neti—for we cannot limit it by saying it is not this, it is not that—nor by our affirmations, for we cannot fix it by saying it is this, it is that, iti-iti and yet, thought in this way unknowable to us, it is not altogether and in every way unknowable".

The Brahman hinted at through these contradictory predicates is that Brahman which overflows thought and transcends both the manifest and unmanifest in an inclusive way.

The third way in which a transcendental parabrahman is indicated in the Upaniṣads is through various direct assertions and analogies. For instance, in the *Kaṭha*[2] after claiming objects to be higher than the senses and mind higher than objects, they pass through higher steps till it is said "Higher than the Mahat (the Universal Ātman) is the unmanifested, higher than the unmanifested, the self (transcendental Brahman of our usage), higher than the self is naught. This is the last limit and the highest goal". Also in *Muṇḍaka*[3] it is said that Brahman is "greater than the great immutable one". While 'immutable one' may refer to the Universal Ātman in this context, it seems that in view of the passages which predicate contradictory qualities to this Brahman and say he is without origin, life. *etc.* the transcendental Brahman is referred to. There is then some direct assertion that the parabrahman is beyond qualities and this duality includes distinctions between manifest and unmanifest. Perhaps even more directly some analogies point to a Brahman that has

1. Aurobin do, *Life Divine* (American Edition), p.992.; also Radhakrishnan takes the same position—see *Indian Philos*. Vol. I, p. 122f.
2. *Kaṭha Up*. 1.3.10, 11;
3. *Muṇḍaka Up*. 2.1.2,

manifested all creation yet remains unchanged transcending this manifestation, and yet is not unmanifest in the sense of excluding the manifest. Thus the *Kaṭha*[1] claims "Even as one fire has entered into the world but it shapes itself to the forms it meets, there is one spirit within all creatures, but it shapes itself to form and form, it is likewise outside these". The *Praśna*[2] however, seems to state more obviously that the trans-Brahman by analogy after presenting a discussion on creation says that the self is without parts "yet is the self in which the sixteen parts abide as spokes in the nave of the wheel", and in the next passage it identifies this self as "parabrahman."

There can be little doubt, then, that neither the manifest nor unmanifest Brahman is unequivocally, the parabrahman in the Upaniṣads; indeed there is no unanimity in this conclusion, but we have found from several passages that something other than the above two is often the conclusion. We found this from the problem of knowing Brahman, various direct assertions and analogies and most clearly the language. Neither solely positive predicates nor only negative predicates are used to describe the parabrahman, but contradictory ones. This observation shall follow us through even the next part; and the conclusions on such language will be dealt with fully in the general conclusions. It is sufficient here to recognize that by using both a positive and a negative predicate, the text is claiming that parabrahman can be described by such qualities but not defined or limited to them by virtue of also negating the quality i.e., Parabrahman is also described as being beyond qualities. Perhaps the most important point to be recognized is that by using contradictory predicates the text is clearly attempting to convey something not to be found in the meaning of the words alone but trying to use the language of evocation to quote W.T. Stace[3], trying to key in an experience, or at least the effort necessary for an eventual vijñāna. Thus we might conclude that experience is the center of the Upaniṣads' attempt to talk of Brahman; and further when negative or positive predicates are used one may fall into the error of infer-

1. *Kaṭha Up.* 2.5.9-15.
2. *P.U.* 6.5.8.
3. W.T. Stace, *Time and Eternity*, Ch. VI.

ring the predicates used in reference to Brahman convey meaning as words. When contradictory predicates are used no such mistake can occur and it is obvious the predicates are used merely to evoke a response in the reader which is beyond language's ability to convey in meaning.

In spite of this inherent unknowability and inexpressibility of the parabrahman, it is apparent that the passages talking of the parabrahman do not reject cosmological problems nor soteriological ones. Rather the parabrahman is viewed as the source and foundation for all created multiplicity, permeating all creatures as their "inner guide", yet not being exhausted in this manifest activity, nor indeed being so bifurcated into two Brahmans manifest and an unmanifest behind it. Perhaps the only analogy, of those above, which brings most clearly a conviction is the *Māṇḍūkya* passage quoted above, namely that the two Brahmans are really one organic whole. Just as the letters A and U are made into one organic whole by the letter "M". "OM" which results is not composed of the letters, A, U and M as "parts" in the sense of parts of an extensive magnitude, but in this case more analogous to an intensive magnitude in which the parts are not so separable. Just as *Māṇḍūkya* claims, then, Parabrahman is an organic whole like 'OM' and is indeed found to have aspects manifest and unmanifest but to break Parabrahman down into manifest and unmanifest is to cease talking of Parabrahman. Just like breaking OM down into A U and M one ceases to have OM; even though 'OM' may have the property 'A' and the properties 'U' and 'M', so in the case of Parabrahman it has the property of being manifest and also being unmanifest but not being limited or bound by them since both the unmanifest and manifest is "in" the nature of the parabrahman not *vice-versa*. This then is the most complete sense of Brahman and of self to be found in the Upaniṣads. At best, however, it has only an intuitive appeal.

E. Conclusions—Brahman as a Concept Of Self:

Brahman is the most general sense of self to be found in the Upaniṣads. Its use seems to include both the microcosm and the macrocosm as well as multiplicity and universality. Thus while Ātman, although transpersonal in its most generic sense is, nevertheless, reached through the microcosm of Puruṣa; manifest Brahman which is indeed also this transpersonal universal self, is reached on the other hand from the more generic standpoint of both macrocosm and microcosm.

In the texts of the Upaniṣads we found four separate views of Brahman. One, the manifest Brahman, corresponded largely to the transpersonal Ātman, another was the unmanifest Brahman viewed as nirguṇa, the third viewed the unmanifest as standing in conjunction with the manifest (considered in the chapter as the Unmanifest first principle); yet another transcended both distinctions. Before passing on to the next chapter to draw the conclusions to our study of the Upaniṣads, let us briefly sum up these views of Brahman, each a conclusion in itself as to the nature of self.

1. *The Manifest Brahman and Pantheism* :

Some portions of the Upaniṣads carry on the pantheism found in the earlier portions of the Veda. These texts occur in three contexts. On the one hand the manifest Brahman is Īśvara to Puruṣa, and on the other is the transcendental Brahman in its more personal and immanent aspect; also some Upaniṣads such as the *Chāndogya* seem to concentrate largely on the manifest Brahman and here it is a conclusion as to the "nature of Brahman", although admittedly it is difficult sometimes to distinguish the manifest from the transcendental Brahman.

One almost infallible guide to finding manifest Brahman passages is the language used. In the case of the manifest, positive predicates are used of Brahman. This implies then that if language is a mirror of waking reality, then the manifest Brahman is that state in which one finds the ultimate reality an active and dynamic principle uniting the otherwise manifold and divergent universe. The positive qualities, relations etc. are just those aspects of the manifest which makes it a being, a functioning unity, the goal of all phenomenal becoming.

In this role Brahman can be treated as having three natures — the creator, the preserver and the destroyer. Conclusions regarding Brahman were influenced by the different theories of creation and how Brahman stood to creation, such as the creation being successive covers of cloaks which Brahman has taken on and through which he is active. This is the involution and the Kośa analysis. The other theory was the creation of a substratum having all the potentials of Brahman and so created from "his own nature". From this substratum an evolution brings out all manifold creation. In the former view Brahman is most intimately the Universe, the sole actor and participant in the manifold becoming. The latter makes the Universe a reflection of the nature of Brahman but only linked to him through the substratum and Brahman's subsequent animation of creation. This, then, is the manifest as creator and preserver. In the Upaniṣads Brahman as the source of dissolution is largely only the source of dissolution for individuals, only vague and unsure reference being made to any dissolution of the Universe as a whole. Moreover the particular view of creation taken colors not only the aspect as preserver but even more the aspect as source of dissolution. Thus there seems to be two theories of soteriological action implied by the creation myths. One is that the individual reaches salvation by negation or rejection of that which is not Brahman; and that other involves a growth or unfoldment.

There are two views of the manifest Brahman, then, in one case Brahman is Īśvara or God to which the Puruṣa is a reflection. This seems largely a projection of personality by puruṣa into what seems to be not self; and so Brahman thereby becomes the cosmic personality underlying creation, the divine father. This point has also been treated under the discussion of Ātman. This view of the manifest Brahman is a reflection of the theism also to be found in some of the mantras and Brāhmaṇas of the Vedas.

The manifest is also the Universal self, the goal of all becoming. This is Brahman as the archetype for all manifestation and also its support. This sense of Manifest Brahman is found largely in two texts, the first in those texts where the Universal self is the conclusion as to the nature of Brahman. In the second case the manifest is the one pole of experience which is used to evoke an integral response, along with the experience of the unmanifest.

Certain problems arise from the three roles of manifest Brahman and the manner or contexts in which it is discussed.

First we can see that manifest Brahman is not in clear juxtaposition with the unmanifest because no unequivocal case of cosmic pralaya has been found. The unmanifest appears only in consideration of the first principles or as nirguṇa, both in the same contexts as the manifest. One is left with a doubt, therefore, as to just how far the manifest extends, is it merely the world which the senses bring us, or does it include all the numberless worlds which the earlier more symbolic material spoke of as Pitṛloka, Devaloka and Brahmaloka. Those contexts in which the unmanifest Brahman is the conclusion as to the nature of Brahman seem often to use the unmanifest in such a way as to merely be in opposition with the senses. By and large the manifest is used, however, not in such a metaphysical sense as to bring up its relation to the unmanifest. The manifest Brahman mostly serves as the Upaniṣadic pantheism, and serves also as a link between the Vedic pantheism and theism, and their later expression.

The place of the manifest Brahman as a concept of self, then, is largely one of standing for the cosmic sense of self, the one universal being which is found in the fervor of the Bhakti, the identity of the pantheist, and the God of the theist. But also there is its position as an aspect of the parabrahman, here an intermediate step in unfoldment of self of the individual, whereby the one cosmic self is realized yet the play of individuality does not cease. This is what Aurobindo seems to be putting forth as Sacchidānanda and overmind[1] and what Dasgupta[2] speaks of when saying the Upaniṣads teach "idealism of dynamic pantheism" not absolute idealism.

2. *The Unmanifest Brahman and Immediate Monism* :

The unmanifest Brahman appears in two areas of discourse, first as the first principle, the Brahman before creation; and second as the nirguṇa Brahman. Various terms are used for Brahman as the first principle such as 'death',[3] 'non-being'[4] or Ātman[5]. As was brought out in summarizing Manifest

1. See *Life Divine* (American Edition) p. 133f., 290f.
2. See Dasgupta, *Indian Idealism*, p. 67f, also p. 50.
3. *B.U.* 1.4.10.
4. *C.U.* 3.19.1; also *T.U.* 2.7.
5. *B.U.* 1.4.1; 1.4.17.

Brahman, the unmanifest is not clearly separated from the Manifest in most of the Upaniṣads. The occurrence of positive terms for the first principle shows that the unmanifest in this sense is not simply viewed as a non-entity, rather perhaps as Svaguṇāveśika—void of internal differentiation.[1]

Where this view of the unmanifest differs from the nirguṇa view is that in some way the first principle from this homogeneity emitted all this heterogeneity, whereas the unmanifest viewed by the monists is simply spoken of as nirguṇa and contrasted with all qualities, no consideration of creation or a first principle being given. By and large then, the most important treatment in the Upaniṣads for later Indian Philosophy is the Unmanifest Brahman by the Monists.

The language used by the Monist in talking of the Unmanifest is exclusively negative predication; Brahman is "neti-neti". Through this language an experience of complete withdrawal from sensory and divided consciousness is the aim. Along with this withdrawal from the relative to the absolute by virtue of using negative predicates, the Unmanifest becomes limited from and opposed to the relative or empirical. The significance of this language, then, is two-fold: one the implications of the language in describing Brahman, and the other its implications for the Sādhanā to attain that realization.

Upaniṣadic monism, culminating in the concept of the nirguṇa Brahman stands also as a link between the monistic passages of the Vedas[2] and Advaita as a philosophical school. In the general conclusions we shall briefly try to find the sources of difference between this earlier monism and later advaita. In the Upaniṣads it is conspicuous in occupying the major portion of the earliest Upaniṣad, the *Bṛhadāraṇyaka*.

The place of the unmanifest Brahman as a concept of self is in offering an absolute sense of self, one not limited by all the imperfections of personality, a sense of self that is as the first principle was also described-Svaguṇāveśika—void of internal

1. See *Ś.B.* on *B.U.* 1.2.1.

2. *Ṛgveda* X. 114, most of such passages seem to be found in the 10th Maṇḍala. See Discussion, Radhakrishnan *Indian Philosophy*, I. 92-99.

differentiation. An analogy is used in the text by equating this sense of self to deep sleep where no sense of duality is had, purely a homogeneous awareness. This absolute self of the Monist is familiar in many philosophies and indeed, as was mentioned above, carries through from the Veda to modern Darśanas. This absolute self is in contrast to the sense of identity felt in the pantheism of the manifest Brahman. Both feel a unitary self, in the latter case, however, this unity is found active in the multiplicity of creation, whereas in the former case the awareness of the absolute self does not permit "consciousness of particulars"[1] These two views, then, are conclusions of different schools in the Upaniṣadic thought : One going on to a Parabrahman, the other considering the nirguṇa to be the Parabrahman.

2. *Transcendental Brahman—Ultimate Monism and Pantheism*:

The third view and metaphysically the conclusion of the Upaniṣads on the nature of Brahman, is that which infers an inclusive absolute, both the manifest and unmanifest as aspects of its nature. Perhaps such a transcendental Brahman is the origin for the lack of clear distinction between the unmanifest and the manifest, we have found in our discussion above. The first principle, the Unmanifest Brahman, sought for was one which would reconcile both its unmanifest homogeneous nature and the manifest, heterogeneous. Later Dārśanic literature attacked this problem on the more generic level of causation; but even there the clarity was not found, as we shall see in our final conclusions. The Upaniṣad's solution is a Brahman which is at once both manifest and unmanifest, yet transcendental, an organic whole for which the two are aspects.

Many texts searching for a concept of Brahman beyond the manifest Brahman--Ātman, as was recognized in our discussion, often used negative predicates yet employing a positive assertion at end, such as[2].

> "Invisible, incomprehensible, without genealogy, colorless, without eyes or ear, without hands or feet, Eternal,

1. *B.U.* 2.4.
2. *Muṇḍaka Up.* 1.1.5.

pervading all and over all, scarce knowledge, that unchanging one whom the wise regard as "beings' womb".

Clearly the positive assertion takes the latter negative statements out of the realm of the nirguṇa Brahman. Most commonly, however, directly contradictory predicates were used, which is the only method to convey the experience otherwise inexpressible in ordinary language. The "aufgehoben" or synthesis of the contradictory terms paves the way for vijñāna or insight into this Brahman which at once is inclusive of both poles of experience, the saguṇa or experience of multiple active self, and the nirguṇa or absolute self.

As a concept of self it represents the ultimate goal of the Sādhanā, the Paramārtha. Yet at the same time it is the inner guide, the pure subject, "the knower of the known, which cannot be known". It is, in other words, both the transcendental unity of appreciation and the thing in itself according to Kant's philosophy. Since it is an "ultimate" concept of self, in spite of its synthesis of the otherwise divergent manifest and unmanifest Brahman, it is easy to ignore for one of those latter concepts more directly accessible to our immediate experience.

CHAPTER V

CONCLUSIONS

A. *Summary: The Four Concepts Of Self.*

Four concepts of self can be found in the Upaniṣads, each a conclusion of various schools of thought. The first is the Puruṣa as immediate egocentric self and Īśvara as God the cosmic non-self. The second concept is the manifest Brahman-Ātman as universal Self. The third is the Unmanifest Brahman as supreme self. Lastly transcendental Brahman as inclusive self.

1. *The Puruṣa—Immediate egocentric self.*

From the early symbolic material most of the concepts of self have arisen as more philosophical interpretations of what is in the mantras veiled under various cosmological and theological symbols. One reaction to all this material is that largely of the Brāhmaṇas. The various deities and Brahman are Gods or God to be worshipped and propitiated by rituals, sacrifices and religious observances. The self in this case, then, is looked upon as that most immediate sense of self to be had in superficial observation of our day-to-day experience. Here selves are conceived after the pattern of objects, being separable, self contained entities. Various organs have macrocosmic equivalents in the deities to which the functions of these organs return on dissolution of the body. The individual is linked in other ways to the environment, through works such as the begetting of offspring, maintenance of household, wives, gifts to Brāhmaṇas etc, all of which are duties. Rewards for these duties are "conquest" of the various "worlds", the Pitṛloka or the Devaloka.

It seems that there is never a growth out of these atomistic personalities; and like the dualism of Madhva there are irreducible souls and Īśvara[1]. Worship, propitiation, etc. can be our only posture since the gulf between the two is unbridgeable.

1. See Madhva Bhāṣya on *B.U.*, Maitreyī Portion, also *Īśa Up.*

The texts supporting such a view are to be found throughou the Upaniṣads, and are conspicuous by their theistic tone. Brahman is spoken of purely in devotional terms. The *Aitareya* and *Kena Upaniṣads* are largely centered around this view.

This, then, is the bedrock of the concept of self. The other concepts to be found in the Upaniṣads freely draw and depend upon this concept as an analysis of immediate self. We found that the guṇa theory, for instanc e, had its origin in such analysis of Puruṣa. The kośa analysis and various sensory analyses also provided starting material for the other concepts of self; a link to immediate experience so to speak.

2. *The Manifest Brahman—Ātman—Universal Self and Pantheism.*

From out of the above material, along with the rich symbolic suggestions of the Mantras, arises the first of three fundamentally different senses of self. Here the self may immediately be what common sense recognises it to be, a spiritual atom, but not ultimately and basically. The Upaniṣads, then, are more concerned with what is the basic and ultimate meaning of self, and are content to start from the above immediate view merely as a self in some way, through some cause, limited severely from its real potentialities.

The first of these three concepts of self is the manifest Brahman-Ātman as a unitary cosmic self, a transpersonal being permeating all creation, and towards which all creation is progressing. This we have dealt with in the conclusions of the last chapter. The realization of this state would seem to imply that one's awareness was centered in the heart-lotus and individuality would in this state be felt only as a momentary play of the cosmic self, only felt against the background of the cosmic self. As an implication from this view, it can be seen that individuality is not rejected wholly; and rather the Puruṣa serves as the seed or nucleus for the full expression of Ātman. This was termed the dipolar nature of the Ātman in our discussions.

The texts so discussing the manifest Brahman can almost invariably be recognised by their use of positive categories saying Brahman is the hearing of the hearer, etc. This by implication suggests a real link between Brahman and the quality predicated. It is then not so much the particular predicate ascribed to Brahman, as all positive predicates could be so predicated and yet not be exhausting of his nature—he is the infinite and inexhaustible universal self.

This concept is found in many Upaniṣads as the conclusion as to the nature of self; for instance it is largely the conclusion of the *Chāndogya*[1]. It does not seem, however, as important as a conclusion as the unmanifest and transcendent concepts between which most of the later Upaniṣads waver.

This concept of self is also to be found embryonically in the pantheism of the mantras of the Vedas. In these early symbolic passages the many cosmic deities, all aspects of the one cosmic principle variously termed Agni, Prajāpati, etc., is the source material along with the Puruṣa or egocentric elements for the Upaniṣadic treatment of manifest Brahman. The validity of this conclusion strikes even the casual reader in the many references to the Gāyatrī, to Prajāpati and the many analogies of Agni used by the Upaniṣads to convey this concept. The Upaniṣadic view in turn seems to have influenced to some degree the later Bhakti cults with their strong pantheistic leanings; and indeed Rāmānuja may also have drawn on this concept of self in the Upaniṣads.

3. *The Unmanifest Brahman* : *Immediate Monism* : *The Absolute Self* : *Monistic Idealism* :

Not all the Upaniṣads accepted without question the Puruṣa as the basis for self. Instead of using this concept positively, the monism of the Upaniṣads viewed self in direct contrast to this first concept. The egocentric self is the "ignorance" which clouds the awareness of the real or unmanifest, unitary self. The manifest Brahman discussed above, would find the Puruṣa open to the same objection insofar as it takes the egocentric self and the manifold creation finally. Since this is the case, the monistic passages are conspicuous in the Upaniṣhads for their preoccupation with psychology rather than cosmology. Thus the only analogy for the unmanifest in our ordinary experience is that of deep sleep, which is the rejection

1. See Chapters VII and VIII.

of the waking state's mobility and heterogeneity. This swing to psychology had the immense advantage of bringing the study of self out of the cosmological and theological sources of early and pre-Upaniṣadic thought. In so rejecting the ego and cosmology, however, no link to man's immediate awareness could be made. Therefore only through "knowledge" could this other absolute self be realised. The path to this consciousness which is self absorbed, self sufficient, and void of all action in the universe, parallels the path taken daily in passing from waking to dream and finally a complete rejection of all thought, ideas and mental activity to fall into the deep sleep state. Sannyāsa and meditation are the main tools.

In consonance with the concept of nirguṇa or absolute self and the Sādhana used to approach it, the language used is almost invariably one of negative categories, the rejection of all phenomenal activity on the part of the witness. Again as in the manifest Brahman it is not the particular negative predicate used, as indeed all negative predicates could be used; it is only a method of emptying the mind of all links between this sense of self and the mobile diverse consciousness of the world to which the immobile self has no corresponding ultimate existence.

The unmanifest Brahman forms one of the two great conclusions as to the true nature of self to be found in the Upaniṣads. Yājñavalkya's philosophy in the *Bṛhadāraṇyaka Upaniṣad* stands out in sharp contrast from all the rest of the material in the Upaniṣad for its preoccupation with Soteriology as against the cosmology of the earlier chapters. His formulation of the monist doctrine seems to have little change right through to the *Muṇḍaka* Upaniṣad and even to Gaudapāda's *Kārikā* on the *Māṇḍūkya*. There is little doubt of a monistic tradition even in the Vedas, however, and indeed Max Müller's "henotheism" is really such a monism. (Collected works Volume VI page 21 passim). The proponents of monism, however, claim sole orthodoxy for their system as found in later Vedānta Darśana. From Yājñavalkya's monism there is little doubt that they can claim textual support even though perhaps not a claim to sole orthodoxy.

4. *The transcendental Brahman : Inclusive self, Panentheism and Ultimate Monism*

The Monism of the Upaniṣads is not exclusively of a negative character. Another view of self seems at least numerically by the number of passages, to be more often the conclusion. This view attempts a synthesis between both of the apparently conflicting aspects of the manifest and unmanifest Brahmans. The key note of this view is expressed in *Life Divine*[1] by Aurobindo as : "The real self is the eternal who is obviously capable of both the mobility in time and the immobility basing time—simultaneously, otherwise they could not both exist, nor could one exist and the other create seemings". In other words there is the feeling that both the experience of the mobile multiple world and the immobile self absorbed state are poles of our experience and the latter is not to be given ontological preference merely because of its apparently greater logical consistency. Like the manifest Brahman, here the ego or immediate self is the basis, the raw material for a growth and expansion to cover the consciousness both of the "immutable one and the mutable many in one eternal all relating, all uniting self knowledge". The self which is here viewed is precisely that one we shall find in the *Gītā* (X. 42) when Kṛṣṇa after describing his "divine glories" says "But what is the knowledge of all these details to thee O Arjuna ? Having pervaded this whole universe with one aspect (ekāṁśena) of myself, I remain". This is the God—godhead of *panentheism.* One can see that it is not simply the pantheism whereby the description of such divine glories (positive qualities) brings insight into ultimate self, but combines also the feeling that only one aspect (aṁśa) of self is to be so found in the mobile, multiple world, the whole is yet transcendent.

The difficulty with such attempts at a synthetic view is that it is attempting a transcendence of all immediately graspable concepts in our experience. It is, in other words, that complete self which "ever eludes us by always proceeding on in front of us". When by human nature the burden of proof is usually upon one

1. p. 454.

asserting a link between two factors, or claiming a concept to be had only by insight or Vijñāna, the inclusive self suffers from its critics simply by not being for "narrow legalistic minds with their defensible position" which Plato describes of those whose criterion is logical consistency in the *Theatetus*[1]. One can see that all the latter three ultimate concepts of self are conclusions of the Upaniṣads on the nature of Brahman, the reality—the real self. The manifest and the unmanifest Brahman are precisely these more defensible positions.

Nevertheless the Upaniṣads bravely throw aside the safer position of monism and pantheism in some passages and boldly hint at a *panentheism*. Such conclusions are found throughout the Upaniṣads and can be recognised in two ways, by the language and by the Sādhana advocated. The first criteria of recognition of course, is the language of contradictory predicates whereby assertion of both categories, that of the monists and that of the pantheist is made in one statement. The Sādhana is that for instance found particularly in the *Taittirīya* also in *Chāndogya* 8, where step by step one is led to accept more and more ontologically complete expressions of Brahman. In the *Taittirīya*, for instance, first the material (Annakośa) then vital (Prāṇa) and mental (Manaḥkośa), etc., till final reaching the bliss (Ānanda) in the heart-lotus, and also reaching the fourth or turīya state which seems to be viewed as infusing all the other three states and is this experience beyond language, beyond the shifting ego and hence is this inclusive self searched for. It is important to realise that this self does not necessarily eternally elude us in our pursuit as some such synthetic attempts conceive it (cf. Kant's idea of the moral ideal never being reached in *Critique of Practical Reason*).

Panentheism has always been a view which finds sporadic expression by philosophers now and then with little organised backing. Indeed the monism of the Vedic Mantras in some cases seems to be of this *Panentheistic* variety rather than the more purely immediate Monism of the Upaniṣads[2]. On the other hand the inherent logical appeal of immediate monism in

1. Plato, *Theatetus*, 176.

2. We might see this in Müller's "Henotheism" which Radhakrishnan also uses (*Indian Philosophy*, Volume I, p. 89 ff.)

the Upaniṣads, coupled with later natural cultural developments, has developed tremendous organised support both in the form of Buddhism and Advaita Vedānta. This ultimate monism seems almost to have died out after Buddhism, being closely approximated only by Vallabha and recent times by Aurobindo.

The reason for this lack of appeal, then, rests in its position as a concept of self. It is a concept which can be "understood" only by insight, which indeed is not wholly achieved by effort, and requires a growth or unfoldment to be "reached". This implies little hope of "immediate liberation" which the other views hold in their eschatology. It does, however, represent the ultimate concept and goal of self, and also stands as the metaphysical conclusions of the Upaniṣads on self.

B. *Critical Evaluation of the Four Concepts* :

In order to properly assess these concepts of self it will be first necessary to recall the discussion in the introduction regarding the language of the Upaniṣads. There it was remarked that the style was almost aphoristic and is to be looked upon as poetic expressions of the philosophical and religious experience. The use of myth, allegory and symbolism has been well borne out in our discussions. While such language enriches the Upaniṣads, just as myth and allegory enriched the Platonic dialogues, at the same time it prevents any clear and rational or logical analysis. In order to properly appraise the conclusions of the Upaniṣads on the nature of self, we must first ascertain that all four concepts are conclusions which the Upaniṣads actually put forth. Thereupon the application of the criteria of coherence and completeness can be made. Finally comparison can be made with other inquiries into the nature of self in order to see just to what extent the concepts of self in the Upaniṣads are the experience of others.

First it is evident that the first concept is put forth as a concept of self, both from the obvious realization of experience and of the metaphysical outlook of the Brahman as inherited by the Upaniṣads. In this latter case we concluded that the egocentric self was truly its conclusions as to the nature of self;

and at this point the Upaniṣads overlapped the latter portions of the Vedas. We might say that the language of these portions seems to extract the meaning from the Vedic ritualistic symbolism. Insofar as theism is the preoccupation with most such passages, then the first concept of self is not just the building material, the starting point for the others, but actually represents one conclusion as to the nature of self. Thus the *Aitareya* and *Kena* largely are written in this style of language and with this theism. Chronologically these two Upaniṣads are posterior to the *Bṛhadāraṇayaka, Chāndogya and Taittirīya* which form the earliest outline of the other three concepts. Therefore theism and this concept of self is a conclusion put forth just as in the Mantras and in the later theism of the Dārśanic period.

Taking both the manifest and unmanifest together, it is readily evident on two scores that each of these are actually conclusions as to the nature of self. The one is that the difference in language is mutually exclusive, such that two different schools of thought are implied; and second that in style of language not only are symbols used but language used itself is symbolic; that is, whether negative or positive predicates are used, both are not trying to convey meaning directly through their statements by virtue of the reference of the predicates to objects for which they stand. Rather since any predicate can be used, it is evident that in both cases avocation of some experience which is not ordinarily conveyed in language is being attempted. Both views, then, insofar as they each use a distinctive style of language and since their language represents a reaching out beyond the language level of experience, then both represent conclusion as to the nature of self made by different schools of thought.

The same applies to the fourth concept of self. The use of both of the above styles of language in the same context, contradictory predicates, indicates that an ineffable experience of a different sort is striven for. Moreover, its position as an attempted synthesis of the above two, places it both as a conclusion and the conclusion of the Upaniṣadic concept of self.

It immediately appears evident from this discussion that not all four concepts are logically of the same order even though they may be conclusive experiences as to the nature of self.

Thus the egocentric sense of self is least "complete". Most obviously because not all experiences of self can fit into this concept. For instance altruism in ethics and the aesthetic experience can hardly be fully appreciated by the egocentric view of self even though there are numerous proponents of this who do so attempt to fit all experience into ego-consciousness. Fortunately psychology and parapsychology show that all of us are not so limited, not just a few who experience broader horizons.

The manifest Brahman is more complete as a concept of self because it is not so exclusive of the poetic, aesthetic and moral expressions of self. While these experiences of self may not be the normal, nevertheless, the concept of self is not to be judged by simple statistical normalcy.

The unmanifest Brahman although standing in opposition to the manifest, does offer a more complete sense of self. This can be seen simply in the language used. Negative predicates do not reduce Brahman to a void but merely to a self absorbed, self sufficient being which logically and metaphysically can act as the foundation for the manifest appearance. It is this dependence of the manifest upon an unconditional source for all this conditioned world, that places the unmanifest more complete as a concept of self than the former concept. This is to say simply that the unmanifest self explains a broader cross-section of our experience of self and its expression, albeit even if explaining the manifest inadequately. The manifest self in the Upaniṣads, at best, carried only a hazy notion of the Unmanifest as first principle and almost no appreciation of the immobile, self absorbed areas of experience.

The most complete concept of self in the Upaniṣads is quite clearly the fourth concept. It explains the broadest area of the experience and expression of self, not only in each one of us, but also exceptional cases of sages and saints. At the same time it accepts the experience of withdrawal into immobility and self-sufficiency and also the extension into manifest or mobile active and conditioned consciousness without reducing one to the other.

The four concepts, then, form an ascending order of completeness in explaining the phenomena and states of consciousness ascribed to self. The Purusha is first, manifest, unmanifest and transcendental Brahman as the highest level of self. The picture is not quite so simple when considering their internal coherence. This factor of coherence we remember prevented our taking elements not applicable in an attempt to obtain a complete intuition. This is to say "a-ā" forms the most complete concept but lacks completely in coherence. The trouble in the case of our present analysis is just that, that as the concept becomes more complete it seems to lose coherence. When we search behind the concept of coherence, we are using however, we find an ambiguity, i.e., of logical coherence and psychological coherence; i.e.; by reason coherent and by experience coherent. The former being what was applied above. The difficulty with our scheme of analysis, then, is that it requires a decision. Is reason the criterion or experience in a broad sense of the word, to be used. Recalling the very reason for adopting these criteria, we see that it rests upon an assumption that the language of the Upaniṣads appeals to the intuition and not directly to reason; and this in turn assumes that there are different sources of knowledge. In this case we are forced to assume this by the very subject matter and the nature of the language in the texts.

While logically the manifest and transcendent Brahman are most obviously incoherent, we note that the latter seems also psychologically incoherent since the unmanifest and manifest are not directly poles of our experience but themselves metaphysical concepts derived directly or indirectly from cosmological and theological speculation. As a result there is little basis of relating the two elements of each concept psychologically or logically. The former, the manifest, is more coherent than the transcendental and less so than the egocentric and unmanifest views.

Thus in conclusion of the coherence of our concepts we can say that logically the concepts fit into two categories;

(1) The Puruṣa and the Unmanifest coherent because of their "homogeneity".

(2) The manifest and transcendent incoherent because of their bipolar character and the obvious contradiction

between the one and the many and the manifest and Unmanifest.

This logical coherence in the present case, due to the nature of the subject matter, is to be rejected in favour of psychological coherence. In this case we have the (1) category above unaltered; but (2) is changed. The manifest is actually more coherent with our bipolar experience of a witness and support to action and an active changing consciousness; the transcendental on the other hand has little basis in our experience with which to heal an obvious opposition between the manifest and Unmanifest, except to note, that the manifest metaphysically requires an unmanifest creator.

The first concept of self is obviously acceptable to all on the basis of immediate experience. For this reason the egocentric sense of self is the concept first accepted by self analysis. The fact that the other three concepts are not solely the conclusions of the Upaniṣads but represent larger area of thought can be seen from the above summary of our conclusions, i.e., the very terms 'Pantheism', 'Monism' and 'Panentheism' indicate that certain elements of the philosophical experience lead one to make such conclusions. For instance Deussen, steeped as he was in Kant and neo-Kantian idealism, at many places read Kant through Śaṅkara into the Upaniṣads.[1] There is indeed some similarity between Kant's transcendental unity of apperception and its unknown ability and the unknowableness of the Nirguṇa Brahman as Deussen observes.[2] Whitehead also comes to conclusions rejecting egocentric self in favour of an almost identical transcendental self in formulating his concepts of immortality and God.[3] Thus philosophy does have the job, in treating the concept of self, not merely to adopt as modern psychology does the statistically normal experience of self but to try to make sense out of the abnormal and supranormal too. Modern psychic research par excellence shows us that all three of the last concepts are actually the experiences of some people and subliminally the possible experience of all. There is little doubt, then, that all four concepts are actually concepts which

1. See Deussen, *Philos. of Up.* p. 40 ff., also Radhakrishnan *loc. cit*, p. 191.
2. Deussen, *loc. cit.*, p. 45 f., p. 75.
3. Cf. *Process and Reality*, Part I, Chapter III, Sect. I, also Part V especially is this true of his four step process in the perfection of actuality.

legitimately fall under what must be taken as self even though common sense would make reality a broader concept than self on the basis that reality "is" while the self still is becoming. Other philosophical systems and psychic research, then, parallel the conclusions of the Upaniṣads as to the concept of self; and point to the conclusion that egocentric self is only the surface consciousness; and many subliminal aspects, to be explained only in terms of the other three concepts, actually play a part in the experience of self.

Indeed this broader sense of self which the Upaniṣads put forth, perhaps, is the appeal for such philosophers as Schopenhauer when he said, "The Upaniṣads have been the solace of my life and they shall be the solace of my death[1]". The vast interest in the Upaniṣads shown by such authors as David Thoreau and Emerson, and in our own time the many translations into all languages is some indication that the concepts of self in the Upaniṣads are to a large extent the expressions of experiences common to all men.

C. *Critical Reflections On The Concept Of Self In The Upaniṣads.*

From the discussions on self, especially Brahman, it is possible to evaluate to what degree the concepts actually developed as one passes from the apparently earliest *Bṛhadāraṇyaka* to the latest *Māṇḍūkya*. Thus while all Upaniṣads seem to have some material of the first concept, such as the earlier chapters of the *Bṛhadāraṇyaka*, as one progresses chronologically, a greater diversity is found till in the *Kaṭha*, *Muṇḍaka* and *Praśna* for example, it is difficult to assign any one concept to it. Thus, as was observed in section A, the *Bṛhadāraṇyaka* is largely monistic, the *Chāndogya* largely concluding the manifest Brahman, and the *Taittirīya* and *Īśa* the transcendental. While scholars give rough chronological orders to these four Upaniṣads we have suggested Vedic origins for all four concepts and thus in the Upaniṣads they merely represent their first appearance as philosophical concepts.

Even though we cannot find any chronological development of these concepts from each other, it is possible to recognise

1. Schopenhauer, *Parerga und Paralipomena* II 185.

both a shift in interest from cosmology to psychology and an increasing attempt to bring all the reaches of the psychological experiences so uncovered into a synthetic concept of self. The Īśa and *Māṇḍūkya* represent such an attempt to consider the entire breadth of the psychology and so the later Upaniṣads are a more structured attempt to develop the concept of self through analysis of the waking, sleep, and dream states. This also marks a break with the cosmo-theology of Vedas, and more truly striking out on what may be termed a more philosophical path.

We can see, then, that the Upaniṣads were left with a problem, now to reconcile the manifest Brahman-Ātman and its multiple offspring with the unmanifest Brahman. Various attempts were made even from the earliest the *Bṛhadāraṇyaka* in the forms of allegories and mantras. This was, however, difficult when cast against a cosmo-theological background, as for instance, Yājñavalkya in the court of Janaka answering to the questions of the priests. We have then conclusions ranging from the acceptance of Manifest Brahman-Ātman and the multiple self by Satyakāma when instructed by the fires, etc. to the idealism of Yājñavalkya and the Unmanifest. Already, then, the germs of later systems have been laid. Other than this distinction of change to psychology from cosmology, which is qualitative, i.e., one of degree of emphasis and not a sharp change, no chronological development of the concept of self can be realised. Metaphysical development, of course, is observed in the Upaniṣads which put the most complete concept of self as the synthetic attempts; and this is to be found in the *Māṇḍūkya* and *Īśa* which are by the table of p. (7) in the last and middle positions both well after the *Bṛhadāraṇyaka*, *Chāndogya*, *Taittirīya*, *etc.*

Another problem which arises from the above is to what degree is there continuity and unity of purpose in the Upaniṣads, i.e., do the Upaniṣads teach any one doctrine which is the "śruti?" One way, this might be answered, is to see just how philosophers both ancient and modern, writing on the Upaniṣads, have viewed them. It is apparent from the many quotations in our discussions from the Bhāṣyas of Śaṅkara and Gauḍapāda—the oldest direct commentaries on the Upaniṣads we have—that these two philosophers and Advaita Vedānta conclude that the Upaniṣads teach unmanifest Brahman as a concept of self. In fact Śaṅkara's idea[1] that the Mahāvākya (the dominent thread) is "tattvamasi" (that art thou, the Brahman is the Ātman) and Brahman is one without a second (ekamevādvitīyam), the latter which was given in the Upaniṣads in context of a discussion of the Creator before creation, is just this elevation of one of the Upaniṣadic conclusions on self to the sole teachings. The two sciences of the *Muṇḍaka* are thereby taken Universally, making all passages not teaching Unmanifest Brahman (here the first and second concepts) for weak minds, i.e., the lesser science. While there are many supporters for this view, ancient and modern; and certainly much evidence of such teaching in the Upaniṣads can be cited, nevertheless we are not obliged to agree that either this concept is the "dominant passage" or what one may call "the teachings of the Upaniṣads". Dasgupta, Radha-Krishnan and Ranade all agree on this point[2] in spite of the fact that most of them are otherwise followers of Śaṅkara. Directly opposed to this advaita view are the conclusions of Madhva and Rāmānuja. Madhva in his commentary on the *Īśa Upaniṣad*, for instance, seems not to appreciate the continuity of the verses. Taking the first two as dictums for Vedic works (rituals and sacrifices) he takes the rest of the Upaniṣad as discussing Brahman which for him is indeed not soul or self. Dualism, of course, can be found, especially in the passages treating egocentric self, and indeed it is these passages that are Madhva's conclusions[3].

Rāmānuja though not commenting on the Upaniṣads directly, can be expected to follow roughly the pantheism of the manifest Brahman. That this is true, we shall have more occasion to see in the next part on the *Gītā* and the final conclusions.

The modern philosophers seem to fall into roughly two groups, those supporting 'Śaṅkara and those interpreting the

1. Śaṅkara : *Gītā Bhāṣya*, 9. 1, also Ś.B. on *B.U.* 17 especially also on *Brahma sūtras*, III 3.1.

2. Dasgupta, *Indian Idealism*, *p.* 7 f, 50, Radhakrishnan, *loc. cit.*, vol. I., p.139 ff.

3. See Madhva's Bhāṣya on *Kaṭha* Up. 4, and *Īśa* for illustration of this failure to appreciate monism.

teachings as "mystical idealism" and usually taking the fourth or second concept of self. In the former group are Deussen and Gough. The many quotations of Deussen[1] have proved this well. Gough[2] also supports Śaṅkara in the conclusions as to what the Upaniṣads taught. In the second group are Ranade[3], Dasgupta,[4] and Radhakrishnan[5] all agreed that the Upaniṣads teach "mystical idealism" to use a term of Dasgupta rather than an "absolute" or "rational idealism", as claimed by Śaṅkara. The philosophers of this category seem more agreed on the difficulties of assigning a "teaching" on self to the Upaniṣads, than those of the first group. Most modern philosophers writing on the Upaniṣads would fall either into the one group or the other, for example Aurobindo would fall into the latter and R. Garbe and most western scholars would come under the first group.

It is apparent from this that the answer to our question "to what degree is there continuity and unity of purpose in the Upaniṣads?" is answered by the philosophers themselves that the Upaniṣads seem not to have conveyed a unity of purpose and indeed from both the Upaniṣads and the Bhāṣyas it is difficult to find agreement throughout complete Upaniṣads.

Not only have the Upaniṣads conveyed different thoughts to different philosophers, and so may be said not to have a complete unity of purpose but also from our investigations it is apparent that the four concepts of self represent divergent interests in the Upaniṣads. We may conclude, then, that the Upaniṣads do not teach only "one doctrine" and indeed this is also obvious from the realization that the Upaniṣads are largely a collection of the teachings of quasi-historical sages; and not only can we say that these sages were of different times and different schools of thought, but also many Upaniṣads have not necessarily been of a single authorship. (The Bṛhadāraṇyaka and Chāndogya are notable examples.) In one sense, how-

1. See especially pp. 130, 133, 134, 139ff. 168.
2. Gough in his *Philosophy of the Upanishads*, Preface.
3. Ranade, *loc. cit.*
4. Dasgupta, *loc. cit.*
5. Radhakrishnan, *loc. cit*, Vol. I, p. 139ff, cf. also Keith, *Religion and Philosophy of the Veda and Upaniṣads*, pp. 507-10.

ever, it may be said that there is unity of purpose in the Upaniṣads and that they teach one doctrine. The psycho-philosophical approach (termed metaphysical psychology in our discussions) of some Upaniṣads may be said to sum up the other concepts insofar as they seek to elaborate what has been called the inclusive self or the fourth concept, which is an attempt to solve the manifest-unmanifest problem. This is the only way in which the Upaniṣads may be said to teach a single doctrine of self; and this sense is a metaphysical one, i.e. only applicable to the reader viewing the Upaniṣads as a whole, as a body of philosophical literature. But this is a metaphysical statement of the reader and actually constitutes only a part of the activity of the Upaniṣadic interests on self which have been here classified under four headings. The sages themselves, then, although having a unity of purpose—seeing the nature of Brahman—showed little continuity or unity of purpose in their conclusions, except insofar as in this metaphysical sense, i.e., may be said to include the other attempts in the more complete concepts of self.

Holding in mind the four classifications under which the teachings on self in the Upaniṣads have been classed and the above recognition that there never has been complete unanimity of purpose except in the search for Brahman itself, if we hold these in mind then we can see reasons and bases for the formation of the Darśanas. This will be even clearer after considering the *Gītā*; here, however, we shall merely take cognizance of the Upaniṣadic bases for the formation of the three—Sāṅkhya-Yoga-Vedānta. It is apparent that the fourth concept held the others together only for a few people who were favourably disposed towards such synthetic attempts. The Darśanas can be seen in this light as percipitations and bifurcations of the Upaniṣadic teachings made in order to attain some sort of logical clarity. This point can be better seen when we recall the conclusions of the second chapter on the Upaniṣadic origin of much of the Sāṅkhyan metaphysics. So against Deussen and Śaṅkara we must maintain that Sāṅkhya does have Upaniṣadic support as a definite conclusion on their teachings regarding self. In the crystallization of the Sāṅkhyan system the substratum-evolution theory was the cosmological conclusions accepted.

This is in consonance with the overall realistic interest which the entire Sāṅkhyan system seems to reflect (see Radhakrishnan, I.P., p.II 249ff. for support of this conclusion). As remarked in the discussion (see above) it is but a short step to reject the creation of prāṇa and rayi or Puruṣa and Prakṛti by Brahman as elements embryonically having the potential for the entire evolutionary structure of the universe. Thereby what are in some way the emissions of Brahman as "seeds" for the evolution of the world are absolutized into a simple dualistic realism. Sāṅkhya, however, seems not satisfied with this simple dualism, it also attempts to apply the eschatological interests of the Upaniṣadic monism and thereby makes a Puruṣa (in the Upaniṣads Prāṇa or life stuff or force) inactive in its true nature. This cosmological dualism and eschatological monism cannot be so combined in a realistic framework without vitiating its entire metaphysics; and indeed Puruṣa almost becomes useless to Sāṅkhyan metaphysics in trying to adopt the Upaniṣads' cosmology of Prāṇa and rayi and the Monistic eschatology of liberation to an immobile self-absorbed Brahman. In Sāṅkhya the rejection of Brahman withers up the self absorption to a meaningless abstraction. We might conclude that Sāṅkhya is the logical product of taking only the first concept of self and trying to view all the teachings of the Upaniṣads from this standpoint of the multiple, egocentric position of self; the simple realism so found shows that even logical consistency cannot be had from such a basis. Materialistic monism or pluralism is the only consistent realism possible from such an analysis of Puruṣa as we have found in Chapter II or at least with the addition of the traditional Vedic views of Svarga. The very fact that Sāṅkhya does not so adopt this more consistent realism is proof that it is an āstika system in its roots and interests and does not stand in rejection of the Vedas as some have hypothesized (Radhakrishnan *loc. cit.*, II. 25).

Vedānta in all its later forms seems to adopt the Kośa analysis as its psycho-cosmological conclusions. Advaita is then easily possible by setting up a metaphysical and epistomological conclusion as to causality—the Vivartavāda of Śaṅkara. The Kośas by this view of causality, then, merely became Adhyāsa upon the nirguṇa Brahman-Ātman. This doctrine of Adhyāsa itself takes on the same appearance of an attempt to collapse the teachings of the Upaniṣad into one logically consistent metaphysics. The doctrine of adhyāsa could conceivably have no place in a nirguṇa Brahman; for a self absorbed absolute is inconceivable in the role of a self riddling itself through superimpositions upon its nature. This criticism is precisely Aurobindo's criticism in *Life Divine* (p. 413-16). Also the fact that Bādarāyaṇa's *Brahma-Sūtras*, which is the founding work in Vedānta Darśana, have been interpreted by the four Ācāryas each according to his own views, shows that insofar as the *Brahma-Sūtra* is the summary of the Upaniṣads there is no way to collapse it into a logically complete metaphysics.

Yoga perhaps is the only one of the three that comes close to preserving the atmosphere of the Upaniṣads. Insofar as it itself eschews an attempt to set up a logically complete metaphysics it thereby preserves the interest in philosophical psychology so preoccupying in the Upaniṣads and throws over logical consistency for psychological consistency which were the conclusions we have come to also in analysing the Upaniṣadic teachings as one. Also the fact that Yoga as a sādhana is freely used by Vedānta as well as Sāṅkhya is also indicative of its different status from these others.

We can conclude, then, that experience was given a much higher place than logic or metaphysics in the Upaniṣads and the concepts of self, with the exception of the first, all are really a Sādhana, a pointing out of the path to exploration of deeper levels of self and not metaphysical systems to be simply intellectually interpreted.

PART II

THE CONCEPT OF SELF IN THE BHAGAVADGĪTĀ

CHAPTER I

INTRODUCTION

Historical Introduction

A. *The Gītā as a work of literature*

Any attempt to understand the *Gītā* as a philosophical synthesis must first appreciate its place as a work of literature; for only against this background will the full import of its position as a work in early Vedānta be realised.

The *Bhagavad Gītā* forms a part of the *Bhīṣma Parva* of the *Mahābhārata*. The plot of the *Mahābhārata* leads up to a great war at the Kurukṣetra. It is just as the armies are drawn up for battle that the *Gītā*, although carrying the thread of the plot, seems to be an interlude which has little place in the plot itself. It is so to speak a philosophic interlude whereupon the air charged with the impending violence of battle is held suspended while a synthesis of early Vedāntic doctrine is given. Nevertheless, the work is presented in response to the sudden gloom of Arjuna when faced with the task of slaying near relations; and this, indeed, is the link of the *Gītā* to the bulk of the narrative.

The *Gītā* is not the only philosophical interlude in the *Mahābhārata*. There are three others, the *Mokṣa Dharma*, *Sanatsujātīya* and the *Anu Gītā*. These others, however, are dwarfed in comparison to the poetic and philosophical insight of the *Gītā*. In addition to these interludes, the philosophical import of the epic itself, as well as the expression of Dharma which the author takes every opportunity to expound, both show the epic definitely as more than the simple aesthetic import. Its impress upon the mind of the reader, moreover, seems to be the same as Homer's epic on the mind of the Greek. In the latter case it was not only the aesthetic guide book for the Greek but in addition, as shown in Plato's Dialogues, was upheld as a philosophical and religious rule book. This combined aesthetic and philosophical appeal, then, marks the epic style in general.

In trying to assess the place of the *Gītā* within the *Mahābhārata*, scholars seem divided. Western scholars in general, Garbe[1], Otto[2], Hill[3] and Hopkins[4] seem to agree that it is an insertion into the *Mahābhārata* at a later date and solely for the devotional and philosophical purposes of the Kṛṣṇa-Vāsudeva cult. Although there is great disagreement as to the teachings of the original *Gītā*, most of these scholars have agreed that the *Gītā* was originally a part of the Epic, but in a vastly changed and much simpler and shorter form. Some like Keith[5] and Farquhar[6] view the original *Gītā* as a late Upaniṣad after *Śvetāśvatara* (the word Upaniṣad is, in fact, used by the *Gītā* in reference to its own teachings). Garbe[7], moreover, thinks the original *Gītā* to be a Sāṅkhya-Yoga treatise, a view which is now generally disregarded. Hopkins[8] regards the work as "at present a Kṛṣṇite version of an older Viṣṇuite poem; and this in turn was at first an unsectarian work, perhaps a late Upaniṣad". Holtzmann[9] considers it a remodelling of an old pantheistic poem by the followers of Viṣṇu. Rudolf Otto, on the other hand, regards the original *Gītā* as "a splendid epic fragment that did not include any doctrinal literature".[10] The variety of these suggestions breathe sheer speculation; however, for purposes of our work it will be necessary to affix both date and origin as possible.

In assessing its origin, we also have to consider the fact that the *Mahābhārata* is a reworking of an older work, the *Bhārata* to which there are references in the *Mahābhārata* itself[11], and this in turn is linked by tradition to an older work, *Jaya*. The fact that the *Mahābhārata* is a reworking of the *Bhārata* does not necessarily indicate that either the *Gītā* was a reworking of an

1. Garbe, *Indian Antiquary* XLVII (1918) Sect 36, esp., p. 5.
2. Otto, *The Original Gītā*, (Turner transl.) p. 132 ff.
3. Hill, W. P. *Bhagavad-Gītā*, introduction to his transl., p. 18ff.
4. Hopkins, *J.R.A.S.* (1905), pp. 384-9.
5. Keith, *JRAS.* (1905), pp. 547-50.
6. Farquhar, *Outlines of the Religious literature of India* (1928), Sect. 95.
7. Garbe, R, *loc.cit.*, p. 26, esp. p. 5.
8. Hopkins, *Religions of India* (1908), p. 389.
9. Holtzmann, see Garbe, *loc. cit.*, p. 2.
10. Otto, R., *loc. cit.*, pp. 12, 14.
11. See *Mahābhārata* 1. 1., *Passim* and Radhakrishnan, *loc. cit.*, I, p. 479.

old epic poem of the *Bhārata* or even that the *Gītā* was in the *Bhārata*. What is evident is that the *Mahābhārata*, as it now stands, is not simply an epic in the sense of the term as normally used by the above scholars. Even in portions most directly connected with the plot there is ample indication of its philosophical bent. Moreover, there are references to the *Gītā* in the *Mahābhārata*[1] itself. In objection to the above critics who would make the *Gītā* a working over by a Vedāntin of the 2nd Century[2], the language used is uniformly archaic and indeed most inferences that the *Gītā* is of heterogeneous origin stem from the belief that the diverse philosophical elements of the *Gītā* are only loosely strung together. We shall shortly see the error in this view-point when we undertake to examine the *Gītā*, not as a work of literature but as a philosophical treatise. At the moment, from the literary and philological point of view, we can at least say that the *Gītā*, one of four major treatises in the *Mahābhārata* exhibits a dominantly philosophical character. These four are not necessarily out of place or variant in style within the overall context of the *Mahābhārata*. It is virtually impossible to tell whether and in what form the *Gītā* could have been in the *Bhārata*. By references to the *Gītā* in the Epic and by the *Gītā's* subtle interweaving of its teachings against the background of the narrative itself one is led to view the *Gītā* as an integral part of the *Mahābhārata* whatever its supposed place, if any, in the *Bhārata*. The uniformity of language with the rest of the epic also supports its integrality[3]. Whether then, the *Mahābhārata* is a more philosophical reworking of the *Bhārata*, or whether it merely amplifies the older narrative, the *Gītā*, from the purely literary and philological point of view, should be considered an integral part of the *Mahābhārata*. This assumption is supported by Radhakrishnan[4], Dasgupta[5] and Telang[6]. Our only problem then is whether the form we have is the

1. Ādiparva 2. 69; 1. 179; 2. 247.
2. Garbe, *loc. cit.*
3. Tilak, *Gītā Rahasya*, appendix, also Telang *Sacred Books of the East*, VIII, introduction to Gītā, discuss this point philologically.
4. Radhakrishnan, *loc. cit.* I.523-4.
5. Dasgupta, *History of Indian Philosophy*. II. 549-52.
6. Telang, *loc, cit.*

original of the *Mahābhārata.* The absence of any variations except the minor variations of the Kashmir rescension would seem to indicate little change in form in the *Gītā.* This point will be made clearer when considering the philosophical character of the *Gītā,* since, if there is any indication of philosophical homogeneity, for our purposes this would be of more importance than chronological or stylistic homogeneity.

In assessing the date of the original *Gītā,* we must admit complete failure, both for the above reason as to the original character itself and also because of the doubt surrounding the *Bhārata.* Therefore we can only obtain some approximate date when the *Bhagavad Gītā* in its extant form is first referred to. This will be based, of course, upon the assumption that it is a fundamental part of the *Mahābhārata* and therefore, homogeneous with it.

The one reference to the *Brahma-Sūtras* in the *Gītā*[1] and also references in the *Brahma-Sūtras* to the *Gītā*[2] are often used to indicate its coincident authorship. This, however, is based upon the assumption that the *Brahma-Sūtras* referred to are Bādarāyaṇa's or even that a philosophical work at all is referred to. This has been questioned by Radhakrishnan[3] and Dasgupta.[4] If the *Brahma-Sūtras* were referred to, it would place its date only roughly before Buddha. According to Garbe's theory, the Sāṅkhya-Yoga cult was fixed into the Vedic tradition about 300 B.C.; yet the original *Gītā* dates 200 B.C. and the Vedāntic reworking 200 A.D., according to Garbe.[5] Through philological considerations Telang places it before the 3rd Century B.C. Bhandarkar[6] also thinks the *Gītā* is prior to 4th century B.C. by similar considerations. Radhakrishnan[7] finds possible reference to

1. 13.4.
2. 2.3.45, 4.2.21. The word 'Smṛti' is used which does not at all unequivocally refer to the *Gītā.* We have only the concurrence of the Ācāryas on its reference to the Gītā.
3. Radhakrishnan, *loc. cit.*, I. 524.
4. Dasgupta, *loc. cit.* II. 549.
5. Garbe *loc. cit.*
6. Bhandarkar, *Vaishnavism, Shaivism and Minor Religious Systems*, p. 13.
7. Radhakrishnan, *loc. cit.*, I 524.

the *Gītā* in *Karṇabhāra* of Bhāsa (2-4 A.D. or 2nd B.C.) and *Pitṛmedha Sūtras* and *Gṛhya Sūtras* (2.22 B. 49.24). Bodhāyana is placed by Radhakrishnan as around 4th-5th Century B.C. Radhakrishnan's date is not conclusive, however, because it is not known whether the above works echo the *Gītā* or *vice-versa* at least from philological and internal references. The consensus of opinion seems to place it around 300 B.C.

Before treating the *Gītā*'s philosophical character, we must illuminate its philosophical structure by a rough sketch of the plot itself. The *Gītā*, although appearing as a philosophical dialogue is, nevertheless, a part of the epic in plot and literary appeal. Its dramatic effect is well calculated; and upon examination has the utmost importance for its philosophical teachings. The setting of the *Gītā* has two great armies drawn up ready for battle. This is a battle of kinsmen where one member of the family fights another. Arjuna represents not just the warrior captain of the Pāṇḍava army but the average enlightened and inquiring individual. When he sees so many kinsmen and gurus drawn up ready to fight his army, Arjuna is suddenly overtaken with grave doubts about the propriety of such a family slaughter. Being a sensitive and ethical individual, he refuses to start such a holocaust and gives up saying he would rather become a beggar. Kṛṣṇa, his charioteer, the incarnation of God, remonstrates him for his weakness and exhorts him to be 'manly' and fight. Such exhortation serves only to further bewilder Arjuna and bring his 'surrender' (II.7) to Kṛṣṇa as a disciple seeking understanding on his problem. The *Gītā* as a philosophical work, then, begins with this 'surrender', the first chapter and few verses of the second serve to set this stage and the circumstances for Kṛṣṇa's teachings. The *Gītā* ends as a philosophical work with Kṛṣṇa's remark "abandoning all dharmas, come into Me alone for shelter" (18.66). Thus we see that we have here the trappings for an intense drama, of universal appeal, eliciting the bankruptcy of man's learned ethical code in the face of a duty of slaying friends, teachers and relatives. In such a tense moment, all action is stilled while Kṛṣṇa shows that Arjuna's rejection "Slaying these sons of Dhṛtarāṣṭra, what pleasure can be ours?" (1.36) is really a rejection not from proper motives, but confusion through ego-centricism. After his complete bankruptcy and surrender to Kṛṣṇa as Guru, Arjuna is not merely told what to do, nor is he offered the choice between action and inaction; instead, he is offered the choice of various postures to an action which has been thrust upon him. This one point, the climax of the *Gītā* as a piece of literature, is most significant not only in its dramatic appeal but also in its philosophical import. At this climax Arjuna was offered a choice of different ways he could face the actions which were placed before him. (see 18.58-60,63). Thus the *Gītā* has the duty to describe all these possible postures to action.

Both, western scholars such as Garbe and Otto and the Indian Ācāryas have overlooked the *Gītā's* aesthetic nature in their evaluation of the philosophical teachings. What has not been appreciated is the literary vehicle through which the *Gītā*'s philosophy is taught; although we may recognise the *Gītā* as a philosophical synthesis, the facts of the plot must also be recognised. Since Arjuna is offered a choice of actions, the *Gītā* has the duty, as a piece of literature, to complete the plot by describing these choices. Thus in one sense, namely, the sense in which the *Gītā* is a drama, it is not a synthesis but an exposition of the various paths open to a warrior about to face a battle which is the crisis of his nation. This is not to say that the *Gītā* as a drama cannot show preferences for which mode of action might be preferable, indeed it does; and it is at this point that the *Gītā* as a philosophical synthesis enters the drama. Krishna tries to show an integral path as the culmination of the many choices. When Garbe and Otto and others criticise the *Gītā* as being a loosely knit agglomeration of Sāṅkhya, Yoga and Vedānta, seemingly out of context in the *Mahābhārata*, perhaps they don't fully appreciate that the *Gītā* is a piece of quite successful didactic literature, a drama used as the vehicle for a synthesis of often divergent philosophical systems. The *Gītā* then has the duty to treat each choice in addition to expounding its own conclusion. This is a point often overlooked. Śaṅkara, for instance, has the firm belief that the *Gītā* teaches only one doctrine and that is Advaita. Had Śaṅkara realized the above point, many of the other paths which are inimical to Advaita, and so explained away, could have taken their rightful place. Also it is evident that the basis for Garbe, Otto and the others in their speculations as to the original *Gītā*, namely, the heterogeneity vitiating the philosophical synthesis, actually is not supported in the light of the dual import of the *Gītā*—its literary appeal and philosophical duty.

In addition, the very success which the *Gītā* has in subtly interweaving the philosophical teachings and the drama may have some implications on the problem treated above, i.e., whether the *Gītā* was an insert or not. We can conclude, then, that the *Gītā*, even if it is an insert into the *Mahābhārata*, is quite adroitly interwoven with the thread of the narrative and has considerable dramatic appeal in itself. Furthermore, its language is roughly uniform with the rest of the narrative and may be tentatively assigned to around 300 B.C.

2. The *Gītā* as a philosophical synthesis

We have seen above that many scholars consider the *Gītā* to have a heterogeneous origin. Let us investigate some of these criticisms in order to shed light on the nature and value of the *Gītā*'s philosophical synthesis. Garbe[1] claims that the *Gītā* is a poem of the Bhāgavata sect in which there is preached Kṛṣṇaism based philosophically on Sāṅkhya-Yoga, while Vedānta is taught in the additions and revisions. What Garbe seems to be referring to is the discussion of some of the *Gītā*'s doctrines under the heading of 'Yoga', 'Sāṅkhya' and 'Vedānta'. Indeed it seems also that the dates he gives rest largely upon this supposed heterogeneity. Otto follows the same line of thought, differing considerably on what the 'original *Gītā*' taught; but there is agreement with Garbe in considering the *Gītā* as systematically oriented rather than Upaniṣadically oriented. With little exception one finds the idea in Western scholarship of the *Gītā* as a synthesis of the Darśanas. If this were in fact the case, then the *Gītā* would be both heterogeneous and failing in its supposed synthesis. Although no certain conclusion can be reached, we shall try to show rather that the *Gītā* draws much more heavily on the Upaniṣads and along with the Upaniṣads may represent the early stages in the precipitation of the Darśanas. The first link between the *Gītā* and

1. Garbe, *Indian Antiquary*, XLVIII (1918) Suppl., p. 5.

the Upanișads is the closing of the chapters; the word 'Upanișatsu' the locative plural indicating the *Gītā* is considered popularly as being an Upanișad. Also, we have seen the word 'Yoga' used roughly in the way that Patañjali later used it and also in the *Kațha Upanișad*[1] from which the *Gītā* borrowed also two other passages (II.19,20). In the case of the word 'Sāṅkhya' there is a reason to believe that Sāṅkhya had earlier counterparts which most probably preceded the *Gītā*; nevertheless, this earlier system cannot be necessarily equated with the later system formed by Kapila. Therefore, in spite of the fact that Kapila's name is used (X.26) we cannot tell whether it was the founder of Sāṅkhya's name or even that if it were, that Sāṅkhya was a formulated system[2] in its present sense at the time of the *Gītā*'s composition. In fact the date 300 B.C., if correct, would make such a darśanic reference unlikely, in the case of both Sāṅkhya and Yoga. It seems then that Sāṅkhya in the *Gītā* would be drawn more from the Upanișads where we found it in a remarkably developed form. Moreover, we find the *Gītā* rejecting the Sāṅkhyan metaphysics of Purușa, precisely where we found the Upanișadic Sāṅkhya so differing in using Prāṇa instead of Purușa. Vedānta is a much easier term to assess than either Sāṅkhya or Yoga. The word literally implies the end or culmination of the Veda; and this term was later appropriated like 'Yoga' for darśanic use. From the less technical Upanișadic use[3] certainly its doctrines are found to a large extent as an element in the Upanișads. Although there is a reference in the *Gītā* apparently to the *Brahma Sūtra* and vice-versa, we cannot be sure, as stated earlier that Bādarāyaṇa was implied in the *Gītā*'s reference. The specific passage "Ṛșis have sung (of the Kșetrajña) in manifold ways, in many various chants, and in decisive Brahma Sūtra verses full of reasonings," (XIII 4) makes such a general reference to *Brahma Sūtra* that it might simply be an adjective describing 'words' not a specific reference to the treatise of that name. Whatever the meaning it is a fair conclusion that at least the *darśana* as interpreted in the Ācārya's time is not to be found. We may safely

1. See *Kațha Upanișad*, 2. 18, 19.
2. Radhakrishnan, *loc. cit.*, I.528, supports this.
3. *Kațha Upanișad* 6.11,18; 2.12, *T.U.* 2.4. *Śvetāśvatara Up.* 2.11; 6.13.

conclude, then, that the *Gītā* draws heavily upon the Upaniṣads; its teachings under Sāṅkhya, Yoga and Vedānta being quite parallel to those of the Upaniṣads studied in the first part. It is to be realised then, that the *Gītā* represents a stage in the perception of the *darśanas* when the three schools—Yoga, Sāṅkhya and Vedānta—became self-conscious of themselves as different approaches to the one Early Vedāntic problem of reality-self. Yet if the *Gītā* is pre-darśanic, then, the so-called synthesis of the divergent *darśanas* takes on a new light. Sāṅkhya had not yet become atheistic and changed from the Upaniṣadic theism, nor had Yoga adopted its negative tone of Cittavṛttirodha, but was still the Sādhana to realization of Brahma-self. Indeed the Vedānta mentioned in the *Gītā* is hardly that of the *Darśanas*, rather a safer conclusion is that the *Gītā* represents a pre-darśanic statement of what were already rather divergent concepts of self in the Upaniṣads, in terms of Sāṅkhya, Yoga and Vedānta elements as found in the Upaniṣads.

The *Gītā*'s synthesis is achieved by the addition of another element not wholly foreign to the Upaniṣads but indeed not there developed in its Bhāgavata form found in the *Gītā*. This is the element of Bhakti which so personalizes the concept of the absolute that the description of self in the *Gītā* becomes clear and definite avoiding the intuitive limitations concerning the concepts of self found in the Upaniṣads, e.g., in the *Muṇḍaka* and *Īśa*. It was Kṛṣṇa-Vāsudeva, the beloved of his devotees who gives a distinctive mark to the Bhāgavata Cult and the *Gītā*. In respect to the Bhakti and its Bhāgavata origin most scholars at this point are agreed. *Cf.* Garbe[1], Otto[2], Dasgupta[3] and Tilak[4], all of whom credit the *Gītā*'s philosophical synthesis largely to this Bhakti element.

If we take all these factors into mind, viz.,

1. The *Gītā* as a work of literature and as a philosophical synthesis
2. The Upaniṣadic leanings of the *Gītā*

1. Garbe, *loc. cit.*
2. Otto, *loc. cit.*
3. Dasgupta, *loc. cit.*, II.545, *ad passim.*
4. Tilak, *loc. cit.*, XXV.

3. The addition of the Bhāgavata element of Bhakti,

then we can see that the *Gītā* loses much of the heterogeneity of origin and teachings which some scholars claim, and rather becomes the last stage in the precipitation of the darśanas, the final self-conscious attempt to hold together the divergent concepts of self explored in the previous chapter above. In the consequences of this conclusion our interest in the *Gītā* takes on new light.

B. *Our Interest in the Gītā*

From a consideration of the Gītā's plot, it is evident that Arjuna's problem is one of *adhyātma vidyā*. That is his doubts, fears, etc. are not the result of anything unexpected or changed in the environment but rather the bankruptcy of his old concept of self and its consequent roles with the environment. The *Gītā*, *par excellence*, then considers our problem of the concept of self.

In spite of the fact that factors in the environment have not necessarily changed in producing the gloom of Arjuna, yet when Kṛṣṇa shows Arjuna new concepts of self, even the picture of reality changes right along with it. Therefore in order to adequately assess the concept of self it will be necessary as in the Upaniṣads to consider Bramha and Ātman as well as Puruṣa.

Moreover, there is another aspect to our interest. Through the study of the concept of self, much of the rest of the metaphysics, epistemology and even ethics can be evaluated in terms of completeness in explaining various aspects of our experience; and also in its cogency in making order of what would otherwise be conflicting tendencies. Also through a study of the concept of self a more fundamental level is reached in the consideration of the *Gītā* than merely investigating the Mārgas, even though the latter seem to occupy more of the *Gītā*'s attention. Most studies of the *Gītā* are satisfied in treating mainly of the Mārgas. Therefore, perhaps in unfolding the *Gītā*'s concept of self we will be in possession of a more definite way to evaluate the *Gītā's* philosophical homogeneity.

C. *Linguistic Difficulties and Solution*

Much of what was said in the General Introduction as to the language difficulties in the texts chosen for study will apply *ipso facto* to the *Gītā*. The problem might even here as in the Upaniṣads be stated as the study of the meaning of the words 'Puruṣa, Ātman' and 'Brahman'; but the *Gītā's* language is more systematic using adjectives for the single term 'Puruṣa', in talking of self, rather than a looseknit combination of all three terms.

The *Gītā* too is given in an inspirational language which is hinted at in Kṛṣṇa's answer to Arjuna's plea in the *Anu Gītā*[1] for Kṛṣṇa to teach him again the *Bhagavad Gītā*. Kṛṣṇa says, "I cannot again attain that same state of Yoga." The language, therefore, is seen to be largely descriptive and definitely authoritative. "Kṛṣṇa does not think he could be in error."[2] "The problem of self is not, then, a problem for the *Gītā*. The teachings are in response to Arjuna's doubts and fears, and not simply an argumentative treatise. The teacher claims to be a divine incarnation in other words, and merely describing what Arjuna cannot see with his mortal vision.

In consequence of this inspirational and descriptive language many Sanskrit terms baffle the reader unless it can be taken in the context of the whole metaphysical teachings of the *Gītā*. This only illustrates that the *Gītā* like the Upaniṣads uses a very plastic language, giving new interpretations and even metaphorical meaning to some terms. Six terms should be briefly considered to illustrate this : 'Aṁśa', 'Māyā', 'Yoga', Sāṅkhya, and Nirvāṇa. First to consider 'Aṁśa' which is normally translated 'portion' or 'fragment', it is plain that these two English terms can at best be metaphorical; two main contexts use 'aṁśa' (X. 42) (XV. 7) in the same sense referring to an aṁśa of the Puruṣottama which became the creation. Were we to take the term literally we would have a fragmentary absolute which merely sent one fragment into creation. Perhaps what is implied is 'aspect' rather than 'fragment', just as in the conclusions to our previous discussion of the problem the difference between intensity and extension was brought out. This latter difference is that which precisely applies here. An aṁśa under this hypothesis is more akin to an intensive

1. *Anu Gītā* 1.10-12. See *S.B.E.*, VIII., P. 230.
2. Radhakrishnan, *loc. cit.*, Vol. I 522.

magnitude like temperature rather than an extensive magnitude like an audience, or a straight line; the latter can have fragments, the former only "degrees". 'Māyā', with one exception, (XVIII. 61) is clearly not to be translated by illusion or appearance, its darśanic use, but by "power" or "force". Simple scanning of the passages which use it make this apparent[1]. 'Yoga' seems to have many uses in the *Gītā*; first its main use[2] is as 'mind poise' which is that use found in *Kaṭha Upaniṣad* and also in the later darśana; second as Karma (usually Karma-Yoga) or work, practice as compared to Sāṅkhya or knowledge; thirdly it is used in its etymological sense ($\sqrt{}$Yuj—to yoke) as merger with the supreme Puruṣha. 'Sāṅkhya' likewise has a specific meaning in the *Gītā*, perhaps most clearly shown by III. 3, where it is used in the sense of "Yoga by Knowledge". Elements which were part and parcel of the later Sāṅkhya are discussed in the *Gītā* but significantly not titled Sāṅkhya.

The last term, 'Nirvāṇa' likewise is used in a sense quite different from its Buddhist connotation. 'Brahmanirvāṇa' is actually the term and its etymological meaning is nirvāṇam from root Vā—to blow out or extinguish; in this sense extinction of suffering or satisfaction is not here implied. Rather it seems to be used more as the Bliss of dissolution in Brahman."[3] These few terms are just a sample of many others which shall come up in our investigation. They illustrate the free and almost poetic use of language common to it and the Upaniṣads.

One other series of words which are of importance are those terms of worship such as 'Bhakti'. These terms nearly all have a built in dualism (worshipper-worshipped) which would seem at first glance to be foreign to the *Gītā's* metaphysics. These words must be kept in mind lest one conclude a rigid theism from the *Gītā*. Thus Śaṅkara for instance, seems to have missed the entire value of Bhakti in the *Gītā* by relegating it to a lower science. Madhva taking the concepts at face value concludes a dualism which has no place for the various expressions of monism also to be found. Parallel to this problem of devotional words is the

1. *Cf.* VII. 15, XVIII.61; VII. 14.
2. See chapter VI.
3. Cf. Dasgupta, *loc. cit.*, II. 450, for support of this conclusion.

problem of 'I' and 'me' and such possessive pronouns used in the *Gītā* by Kṛṣṇa referring to himself. At the moment it shall suffice merely to point out these two sets of difficulties. Later we shall have occasion to evaluate more precisely their meaning and value to the *Gītā*'s teachings.

D. *Methodology*

In order to develop critically the *Gītā's* concept of self we shall have the two-fold duty of both being sensitive to the use of language discussed above, and at the same time develop all the ramifications of the *Gītā's* concept of self.

Before deciding upon a scheme of analysis, it will be necessary to recall many points so far made in this introductory chapter. First the technique of presentation of the *Gītā's* teachings is dialectic, i.e., a dialogue between Kṛṣṇa and Arjuna. This dialogue, however, has a professedly dual intent. On the one hand, it has the literary aspect, to teach Arjuna the various ways of facing actions that lay before him; and on the other hand it has the professed reteaching of the ancient Yoga fallen into corruption and disuse (cf. 4.2, 3). In the solving of Arjuna's dilemma and the reteaching of the ancient yoga through him, we find this dual appeal already discussed, the aesthetical and the philosophical synthesis. The *Gītā's* own teachings are subtly woven into the descriptions of the various paths, yet standing out unmistakenly as an integral path. The unification of these two appeals is in the very conclusion when Kṛṣṇa tells Arjuna "having reflected on it fully, act as thou wishest". (18.63). In other words by our identification with Arjuna as the enlightened devotee we too are led to "choose".

Our interest, here of course, will be the *Gītā's* self appraisal as reteaching the original Yoga. The *Gītā* then is going back to the Upaniṣads, and represents both an Upaniṣadic synthesis, much like the later *Māṇḍūkya* and *Īśa*, as well as a step along the line from the Upaniṣads to the ultimate splitting of the early Vedānta into the three darśanas—Sāṅkhya-Yoga-Vedānta.

In addition to these points, our approach must be sensitive to the *Gītā's* context, i.e., its continuity and discontinuity. For example, II. 14 says, "The unreal hath no being; the real never ceaseth to be,.." Śaṅkara in *Ś.B.* takes this as support for his Vivarta-Vāda and so treats it out of context as a separate verse. Actually the two preceding verses and the following vitiate his interpretation. It is said in these verses "contacts of matter...giving cold, heat, pleasure and pain, they come and go impermanent.. "(II.14)". The man whom these torment not... balanced in pleasure and pain, steadfast, he is fitted for immortality." (II.15). Our verse then is not supporting Śaṅkara's view of the world but merely saying that the unreal—the 'contacts of matter' are only mental impressions : they do not have and can never have real existence. This is supported by reference to pain and pleasure in the next two verses, a more general comparison between the indestructible one (who has pervaded or spread out all this) and the finite bodies; yet the same idea of the real never coming into being is not here repeated or hinted at. Instead the *Gītā* presents the contradictory position of a multiplicity of finite bodies and the indestructible embodied one. We see then that context must be carefully preserved so that the interpretation does not immediately contradict the context in which it is set.

By way of evaluation, the remarks in the General Introduction as to the nature of the language of our texts and the need for criteria to fit the level of language rather than simple logical criteria, resulted in two criteria "coherence" and "completeness". Such criteria will be used again here in the *Gītā*, since the language is largely similar to that of the Upaniṣads. In using such categories to bring out the intuitive value, we might avoid the pitfalls into which Garbe and Otto have fallen, as has been discussed above. Both have found the *Gītā* to be heterogeneous. Their scheme of analysis, then, did not fit the level of language, and was like making an analysis of the Bible in terms of Kant's categories or Russell's logic.

Since the *Gītā* seems to differ little in describing the self, except at the higher level of Puruṣa (as Brahman), then we can analyse self by using its own terms of Prakṛti and Puruṣa as elements. Moreover, these two categories arise also out of the two criteria of analysis since Prakṛti and Puruṣa represent different levels of completeness and coherence in the concept of self. The following scheme is proposed :-

I—The Self as Prakṛti :

a. The two-fold Prakṛti
b. Prakṛti and the individual
c. Prakṛti and the Guṇas
d. Guṇas and the individual
e. Manas and Indriyas
f. Buddhi and Jñāna
g. Vijñāna
h. Dharma in the light of Prakṛti

II—Self as Puruṣa :

a. The Kṣara Puruṣa
b. The Akṣara (Kūṭastha)
c. The Avyakta
d. The Puruṣottama
e. The Vibhūti and the Avatāra

Using the above outline, organized on internal categories we will develop the *Gītā's* concept of self, in this way we will not bias our analysis with a self imposed and perhaps inapplicable set of categories of our own. It is to be noted in criticism of the above scheme, however, that such elements of analysis as Buddhi, Vijñāna, and Jñāna have no clear place wholly in either Puruṣa or Prakṛti. Indeed that is also a problem in later Sāṅkhya. This does not injure our analysis, however, since the parā and aparā Prakṛti which Kṛṣṇa speaks of (VII.4-6) simply are not parts to be separated but two overlapping aspects which cannot be wholly divided in a facile manner. In short it shows that Prakṛti is not wholly unintelligent and Puruṣa not wholly inactive as Sāṅkhya so took it. The Vibhūti and the *avatāra* we shall see are the *Gītā's* additions by means of the concept of Bhakti to the Upaniṣadic teachings in an attempt to reconcile monism and theism. We shall have occasion to see just how successfully this has been done.

Another aspect to our analysis will be required. In the *Gītā* as in the Upaniṣads we shall see that the concept of self arrived at is not independent of the method used in reaching it. Therefore the *adhyātma vidyā* which is the main focus of the *Gītā* on self will be considered, to show in what degree the *Gītā* teaches one concept of self, and how the various concepts found in the Upaniṣads are meted into a single concept. Again in this part of the analysis, internal categories will be used, because they offer both the best classification and the best way to bring out any possible variants in the teachings regarding self realization. These categories are the following :—

I—The Path of Karma

a. Lower Path

b. The Higher Path

II—The Path of Jñāna

III—The Path of Bhakti

IV—Attempts at an Integral Path.

If these are the criteria for analysis let us set about first to investigate prakṛti which is the foundation for the concept of self in the *Gītā*.

CHAPTER II

THE DESCRIPTION OF SELF

A—Prakṛti

'Prakṛti is a word with many uses. Its etymology implies Prakṛti is "that which is pre-supposed", "putting before". In this sense it is opposite to Vikṛti or "derivative form". Hence it means original form, natural form, nature, disposition etc. The *Gītā* often uses it in this general sense implying nature or constitution or form. What will at first concern us here, is its derivative technical use as Sāṅkhya so used it, as 'matter'. In this use it seems to parallel the Upaniṣadic use of 'annam.'

What is unique to the *Gītā* is the use of 'Prakṛti' in a much broader sense than either Sāṅkhya or the Upaniṣads used it. It is to be noted that there are passages highly Sāṅkhyan in character (cf. 13.29, 14.19), but when considered, in its context and against the background of the *Gītā*'s whole teaching, we find a far different meaning than the apparent Sāṅkhyan one. In the *Bṛhadāraṇyaka*, we remember, the Sāṅkhya was anticipated in the two substrata of Prāṇa and Rayi. In the *Gītā*, however, these two fall under Prakṛti and the other element Puruṣa clearly has a different ontological status and is not a substratum.

The broadest division of reality—self in the *Gītā*, then, is Puruṣa-Prakṛti. These two encompass all three terms 'Puruṣa', 'Ātman' and 'Brahman' which was discussed in the Upaniṣad portion. In the principles Puruṣa and Prakṛti we do not simply have a dualism, rather there is overlapping between the two and on the level of akṣara or immutable Puruṣa, Prakṛti and Puruṣa are joined to a large degree. We may say, simply, that Prakṛti applies primarily to the mutable. The Puruṣa, therefore, goes beyond this and yet extends into the Prakṛti and *vice-versa*.

With this much introduction, let us consider the 'Prakṛti' fully. Prakṛti is divided into 2 aspects Parāprakṛti and Aparāprakṛti. The following table lists the analysis of the two components :—

Kṣetra and Vikāras (III.5)	Aparāprakṛti (VII.5)	Parāprakṛti (VII. 8-10)	Kṣetrajña (XIII.16)
Earth) Water) Fire) Air) Ether) 5 gross elements	Earth) Water) Fire) Air) Ether) 5 gross and/or subtle elements	Pure fragrance in Earth The rapidity in waters The brilliance in fire Life in all beings The sound in Ether	
Mind (Manas) 10 indriyas and 5 pastures.	Mind (Manas)		
Reason (Buddhi)	Reason (Buddhi)		
Egoism (ahaṁkāra)	Egoism (ahaṁkāra)	The reason of one reason endowed rājasa, tāmasa, sāttvika are all in one not in them. The jivabhūta (VII. 5) or life element by which the universe is supported.	
Desire-aversion			
Organism intelligence firmness			Not divided amid beings and yet seated distributively. That is to be known as the supporter of beings, he devours and he generates.

Kṣetra and Vikāras (III. 5)	Aparāprakṛti (VII. 5)	Parāprakṛti (VII. 8-10)	Kṣetrajña (XIII. 16)
		Know that to be the womb of all beings. I am the source of the forthgoing of the whole universe and likewise the place of its dissolving (VII. 6).	

From this table it is apparent that Aparāprakṛti is roughly that view of Prakṛti of which is propounded Sāṅkhya. This principle is given a more descriptive title of Kṣetra to which it corresponds. If the *Gītā* were to stop here, however, the Sāṅkhya analysis of a primordial, unintelligent, active prakṛti would be the result. The *Gītā's* singular contribution is the addition of a second or higher nature, Parāprakṛti. Thus Prakṛti has been divinized; for we at once recognize, the novel fact that Parāprakṛti is an aspect of the Supreme, the Puruṣottama, not just the life element as it was at first defined. Were the Parāprakṛti to be this last, the life element, then there would be an inevitable contrast between the active aparāprakṛti and an immutable parāprakṛti, the life element, compelling action but not itself active, just the contract made by Sāṅkhya. That this is not the case, is shown by the quotation from VII. 6 in the table and in the next two verses where one is led in an unmistakable context to the "1" or Puruṣottama. This same conclusion as to context and meaning of Parāprakṛti is reached by Aurobindo in *Essays on the Gītā*[1]. The rest of the seventh chapter of the *Gītā* goes on to relate the parāprakṛti to the aparā, the subject for the next section, Self as Puruṣa. Its value in the present discussion is its nature as Prakṛti, i.e., Kṛṣṇa has called this "Eternal seed of all beings" (VII.10) as Prakṛti not Puruṣa. This brings one to the conclusion, perplexing at first, that Prakṛti is not only the lower primordial "matter" or "nature" and Puruṣa the consequent "Spirit" or "Self" but rather Prakṛti is ultimately "my nature" (Parāprakṛtir me). In other words for the *Gītā* it seems that Prakṛti and Puruṣa overlap in a most novel way. Prakṛti seems to be the supreme's "primordial pole" to use a term of A.N. Whitehead, i.e., the Puruṣottama as he is in manifestation and supporting manifestation and indeed in the next section we shall find that when 'Puruṣa' is used the unmanifest aspect or that inner support and guide is implied. If this is what the *Gītā* intends by Prakṛti, we immediately recognise that Puruṣa and Prakṛti if they are to be translated by spirit and matter, must be understood somewhat in a spinozistic sense as attri-

1. (American Edition) P. 237.

butes of God each being on a logical par with one another, and not translating Prakṛti only as annam or material stuff and Puruṣa as Jīva Ātman or soul, as is occasionally used in the Upaniṣads.

If this is the sense in which Prakṛti is found in the *Gītā,* let us consider primarily the lower or aparāprakṛti in this section, the self in its limited sense as an individual, active and endowed with a limited ego-consciousness. Indeed our discussion must overlap the higher nature at a few places; and it is now, perhaps evident why manas, buddhi, jñāna and Vijñāna were placed in the discussion about Prakṛti in the outlines of our discussion in the introductory chapter, even though a complete separation from Puruṣa is not possible.

Let us proceed, then, first to find out what is Prakṛti in its lowest sense and how it is related to the individual. The *Gītā* unlike the Upaniṣads does not deal elaborately with the body and the senses. The above table is the sole analysis of the sort given in the *Gītā*. A very brief reference, however, to the nine-gated city is made (V.13) implying that the feeling of agency in action arises in the city itself. Also we are told in the second chapter (XVIII.20) that the body is finite and perishable compared with the self which is immutable and eternal. Thus far it would seem that some sort of body-soul dualism were intended. This is not the case, however, and in order to fully appreciate the individual from the view point of Prakṛti one must first inquire into Prakṛti itself.

Like the Sāṅkhya and the Upaniṣads, the *Gītā* gives, in addition to the above analysis of Prakṛti in terms of its elements, yet another analysis. This is the Guṇa theory. While in the Upaniṣads the Guṇa theory had mainly a cosmological significance, and in Sāṅkhya has been more fully developed, yet it seems that it remained for the *Gītā* to elaborate this into a metaphysical and ethical theory. Indeed if we can appreciate fully the Guṇa theory, the whole *Gītā* will become clear as relates to self, on this lower level. While the above Sāṅkhya analysis of the various elements of Prakṛti may reveal more the structure and extent of Prakṛti, the guṇa theory undoubtedly reveals its essence, and this essence is action. One must distinguish, as the *Gītā* does (XIII. 19 and XIII. 5) between the guṇas or qualities and the vikāras or modifications. The latter were the last members on the list of the Kṣetra, pleasure, pain, desire and aversion, etc., and represent what Aurobindo calls[1], "Deformation in the field," i.e., the change of a cosmic quality in existence into a limited function of it in the body by taste, for example, pleasure and pain from ānanda. Guṇas on the other hand are really the essential properties of matter itself "matter born" as the *Gītā* terms it (cf. XIV.20). Actions of Prakṛti are classified just as in the Upaniṣadic[2] and Sāṅkhyan tripartite division. The three Sattva, Rajas and tamas are viewed as the essential attributes of all things manifested in Prakṛti; like the Upaniṣadic description, these three are always present in an organism (cf. XIV.5, 10); and one of the three will prevail. This does not seem to be always a permanent arrangement and the same entity may show prevalence of different qualities at various times (XIII.5). This fluid character is a marked step over the Upaniṣads for whom these three constituents, while being likewise in different proportions, were more a mark of its nature and not so subject to variance. Even the *Sāṅkhya-Kārikā* (VIII, XV & XVI, XVIII) does not seem to have quite this feeling for the changing nature of the entity which the Guṇas make up. The reason for this seems to be, as mentioned above, that the interest of the *Gītā* is not cosmological at this point but primarily metaphysical and ethical, and so as an entity's action so the quality which predominates, which are listed as follows:—

> "When the wisdom-light streameth forth from all the gates of this body, then it may be known that intelligence (Sattva) is increased."
>
> "Greed, outgoing energy, undertaking of actions, restlessness, envious desire—These are born of the increase of mobility (Rajas)."
>
> "Darkness, stagnation and heedlessness and also delusion — These are born of the increase of inertia (tamas)".

1. Aurobindo, *Essays on the Gītā* (American Edition), p. 371.
2. *C.U.* 6.4; the red-white-black anticipation of the guṇa theory.

These three apply no matter what the entity may be; and indeed it is said (XVIII. 40) "There is not an entity, either on earth or again in heaven among the Gods, that is free from these qualities, born of matter."

Before passing to consider in more detail the nature of the Guṇas from the standpoint of the individual, one point must be considered; viz., action and the guṇas in respect to the whole range of Prakṛti. It is clearly stated that the guṇas are the doors of all action (III.27,28) ; and only confusion makes it seem that Puruṣa is the agent. The *Gītā* then says rightly that everything in aparāprakṛti is "bound helplessly to the Guṇas" (III.5) This much we can clearly understand from the above discussion; but a problem arises when Kṛṣṇa as the Puruṣottama speaks in the early chapters (*cf.* III. 22-25) saying, "These worlds would fall into ruin, If I did not perform action." A first hand reading of this passage would lead the reader to predicate the guṇas also to parāprakṛti and to the Puruṣottama itself. Actually we must carefully distinguish between action and desire, want, delusion, etc. This is precisely the distinction we found Yājñavalkya in the *Bṛhadāraṇyaka Upaniṣad* failing to make, and indeed all monists[1]. The very next verse from the above quotation gives some insight into this distinction : (III. 25). "As the ignorant act from attachment to action so should the wise act without attachment (asaktaḥ) desiring the welfare of the world (Lokasaṁgraha)." Thus it seems that Kṛṣṇa is saying that the essence of these worlds (all manifestation) is action; and unless action were performed all would become a chaos, fall to ruin; and moreover action can be done from two standpoints, either from ignorance bound to the three Guṇas in which case we have action in aparāprakṛti, or without attachment, through understanding of the nature of the guṇas and Prakṛti itself, in which case we have the supporting action or dynamism of the parāprakṛti. This point sheds much light on the Upaniṣad's attempts to find the basis of ignorance keeping man bound to the three states. Indeed it shall have an important part in all our consideration of the *Gītā's* concept of self.

1. See Ś.B. on *B.U.* 2.4.14; *cf.* also Ś.B. on IV. 32.

The point has already been made that all entities in this world and heaven are subject to the guṇas. If this is the case, not only is the individual subject to the guṇas according to his "own nature" (svabhāva) but also all other objects and persons he engages in action will be part of such an interplay with one or the other of the guṇas predominating. At the moment let us restrict our attention to the individual. It is important to understand the peculiar position of the individual as jīva, partaking of both Puruṣa and Prakṛti, i.e., of both natures of the Absolute. In the *Gītā* it is put as Prakṛti being the womb, Puruṣa as the seed of all creatures (XIII. 26, XIV. 3-5, 18). One might imply from these two sides to man's nature that the binding character of the guṇas was only insofar as his awareness was limited to the extreme sense of individuality which egocentric consciousness brings. In this case, as the *Gītā* says, he thinks, "I am the doer". The whole problem of the guṇas' import to the individual is even further complicated however. Were we to stop merely with an organism active and the self inactive, we would stop with the Sāṅkhyan analysis. Indeed some passages of the *Gītā* seem to support this Sāṅkhyan view[1]. However if the passages are not taken as "The teachings of the *Gītā*" then one would have to assert that in the total context of the teachings about self, either the self inactive merely refers to inactivity in respect of the guṇa activity, or the self referred to was avyakta Puruṣa. Rather there is another sense of activity as has been shown above in the remarks on Puruṣottama being active. Therefore the guṇas seem not to merely divide activity from inactivity, in the self, but refer to a dominion between modes of activity. Perhaps an analogy to modern psychology might bring out a possible meaning here. When one initially conceives an action and wills to do it, it seems that there is an abrupt break between this mental activity preparatory to the act and all the neuro-muscular activity in carrying the will out. This is a little explored area in psychology and its difficulties of comprehension have led to such theories as behaviorism which claims that the mental activity preparatory to action is actually unconscious muscular movement which excites a derivative

1. See chapters III and IV.

impression in the brain. This seems just about what the *Gītā* is saying, *i.e.*, the guṇas represent in aparāprakṛti a closed system, the origin of the activity and the consequents are all to be found in the lower Prakṛti just as in behaviorism unconscious muscular activity was its origin, not a mental image or its willing in the mind. Other forms of psychology refute behaviorism's exhaustiveness in explaining activity and claim that there are actually two orders in explaining actions, i.e., a mental image and will which in the brain is translated to neural impulses to the muscles; and we are aware only of the beginning and the ending of the process. The *Gītā* likewise is analogously not claiming that the guṇas fully represent a closed system but that there is a higher order of activity of the parāprakṛti beyond the guṇas. So long as we are unaware of this higher Prakṛti, we are like the behaviorist's man driven by the unconscious muscular activity for which the mental images are merely anciliary. The man traiguṇyātīta, the one who has "become aware of the guṇas and their functions",[1] performs action without attachment, i.e., subjecting the activities to the controlling influence of dharma, from the mental image which is a true source of activity, yet not active as the consequent guṇa activity. We can see, therefore, that the *Gītā*, if the above analogy holds, appears not to be making the contrast between active Prakṛti and inactive Puruṣa, but making them only the source and consequence of the entire link in the chain of activity. Moreover, when the *Gītā* says not to disturb the foolish who are "bound to the qualities", (III. 29) it may be saying that until one becomes aware of the parāprakṛti as the true source of all activity and that the actions of the guṇas represent merely the semi automatic, unintelligent carrying out of this activity into the body (IV. 21) and lower prakṛti or Kṣetra (field), until that time the guṇas themselves will determine his actions. This is the state wherein the modifications of the Kṣetra are the main activity of the self-pleasure, pain, desire, aversion etc. In this sense, by comparison, the self is truly actionless (XIII. 29, XIII. 19).

If this completed the picture of the guṇas and the individual, then we would be left with having, a lower nature in which the

1. See III. 28 *ad passim*.

then we would be left with having, a lower nature in which the guṇas are at work or "the senses move among the objects of the senses" (V.9), and a higher nature which may or may not be the mainspring of action depending upon whether the individual has escaped bondage and confusion in the guṇas. One might infer from this that objects of sense largely determine whether the individual is sāttvic, tāmasic or rājasic. We have not said much about the individual. The picture, however, of the individual in relation to the guṇas is rounded out by significant passages stating that the duties of caste are arranged "according to the guṇas born of their own nature (Svabhāva)." (VIII. 41). This concept of "Svabhāva" supplies the missing link. Although the *Gītā* does not discuss non-human levels of individuality to any extent, one is almost led to infer a pan-psychism in which one's own nature, in line with one or the other guṇa, acts as the inner drive leading the individual in all his actions either to the sāttvic, rājasic or tāmasic elements in the objects met with. The *Gītā* does not seem to develop this point further ; but if we anticipate the Puruṣa section we can see that if the *Gītā* holds eschatologically to the theory of Saṁsāras and rebirth till liberation or Mokṣa, then an individual evolution is implied which would bring in the pan-psychism which was in doubt above. This Svabhāva, then would represent the level of evolution towards the higher nature which the individual had reached, and seems to be much like Leibnitz's store of possibilities in the monad which expresses as actualities only a portion of them. Moreover, since not all individuals have progressed to the same level, we are left with a range of expressions in actions, arrangeable according to the guṇas and called caste duty (Varṇadharma). The individual is born with a congenital duty (Svadharma) which the *Gītā* definitely insists upon rather than the duty of another caste. Whether this is support for the rigid caste distinctions or whether congenital duty means not so much which family you were born into but rather your svabhāva which appears to be inborn, whichever is intended, no conclusion could be reached. There is little doubt, however, that svabhāva, and its derivative svadharma is the core of the *Gītā*'s teaching on the guṇas and the individual, and the answer to the above inadequacy about inner drives of the objects. We can see, far from the objects of the sense determining the individual's nature rather even if he is still under the sway of the guṇas "his own nature" leads him in the direction of one of the three qualities in all objects; in food, for example, either to the pure, delicious, bland food supporting energy and vigour which is the sāttvic food (XVII. 8), the hot, pungent, bitter, saline, dry and burning which result in pain and sickness (XVII. 9), or the stale, flat, putrid, the leavings, this is the unclean food of the tāmasic persons (XVII.10). The various descriptions of the threefold division of man sāttvic, rājasic and tāmasic given in the 17th chapter, then, is really an expression also of the caste characteristics.

In conclusion, then, the guṇas are not only the essential character of the lower nature (aparāprakṛti) but also play an important role in the case of the individual. In both cases the guṇas are arranged in an ontological order from tamas—rajas to Sattva in an increasing order of expression of the parāprakṛti in the action. In the case of the individual, the Svabhāva, which represents the inner drive towards one or the other of the three, led to Varṇadharma or caste duty. This seemed to imply an individual evolution towards eventual expression of activity in the parāprakṛti.

In the light of this explanation the passages claiming that the guṇas were the doers of all action and the self was actionless were reconciled with those claiming activity for the puruṣottama and extolling naiṣkarmya karma. The difference was seen to lie in the guṇas being the consequent part of activity and the dynamism of the parāprakṛti was the source. The *Gītā* sums this up by saying (V.II) : "Yogīs, having abandoned attachment, perform action only by the body, by mind, by reason, and even by senses for the purification of the self (ātmaśuddhaye)". This is the turning of the play of the guṇas to direction under the higher faculties expressing more the parāprakṛti.

Before passing on to consider these higher faculties manas, buddhi, jñānas which reflect more the higher nature, let us consider briefly one point which will be later required in discussion of Puruṣa and Puruṣottama, i.e., Prakṛti, the guṇas and causation. Full consideration of the problem of causation will be beyond the scope of present work. What we must ask ourselves here is just what are the mainsprings of the purposeful action of the individual ? How does the *Gītā* distinguish the various causes for his activity ? In a significant passage the *Gītā* puts forth a basis of explanation "Matter (Prakṛti) is called the cause of effect, instrument and agent, and the soul Puruṣa is said to be the cause, in regard to the experience of pleasure and pain". In terms of our above discussion of Prakṛti it is evident that the *Gītā* is saying here that since the lower Prakṛti is eternal (XIII.19) and also the lower nature of the Puruṣottama then the material and efficient cause of acts rests in the guṇas of lower Prakṛti while the Vikāras of the Kṣetra—pleasure, pain, etc.—are caused by the Puruṣa through the form of the higher nature, and this cause is basically a confusion or ignorance. In other words the problem of bondage in the *Gītā* is not that the proximity of Puruṣa with the play of the guṇas results in bondage as in Sāṅkhya; because in the *Gītā* the Prakṛti is the lower nature of the Puruṣottama and eternally a part of his activity (XIII. 19,24), not either as a disturbance of some primordial unmanifest homogeneous state of Prakṛti as for Sāṅkhya. Therefore, in the *Gītā*, the cause for the individual's bondage is due to confusion of the whole range of Prakṛti with the lower Prakṛti solely. It is, a condensation of something much broader into the narrow reaches of the guṇa activity. This is the Vikāras mentioned above, a transformation or "deformation" as Aurobindo puts it, in which a quality of the higher nature such as ānanda is understood only through the guṇa activity making it pleasure and pain etc. As a conclusion from this, the removal of ignorance is not pralaya, the withdrawal of Puruṣa's support as in Sāṅkhya, but a broadening of the understanding of the nature of activity and its causal bases, leaving the "guṇas to play among themselves" (III.28, XIV.23) ; and then merely supplying the formal and final causation through the support of the higher Prakṛti. In terms of our above psychological analogy to muscular activity it would be like leaving the nerve and muscules to do their own job and only directing that activity according to some form and purpose. By that analogy then Behaviorism is precisely that condensation of all causal activity solely into the modes of guṇa activity. The *Gītā* reaches this conclusion when in the middle of the 18th chapter it deals with the five Sāṅkhya causes for the accomplishment of all action—(1) body or seat of action, (2) the agent, (3) instruments, (4) the many kinds of efforts and (5) Providence. Finally reaching the conclusion "The man of perverse mind who, on account of his untrained understanding, looks upon himself as the sole agent, he does not see truly". This point has much significance for the whole view of Prakṛti in the *Gītā*. It is saying, then, that from the standpoint of causes of activity, apart from the individual confusion of them that the Puruṣottama is the sole agent[1]; moreover, it is also saying that lower Prakṛti is the instrument and the energies for action, through the body as the seat of action and the various vital forces. The "daivam" or providence seems to be the formal cause, the pattern of becoming found as the higher nature. These five causes find their meeting place in the individual who indeed has a higher purpose than the mere witness of the Sāṅkhyas, given in the *Gītā* the role of instrument to the Puruṣottama. Closing the doors on this instrumentality, consequently, is the Ahaṅkāra referred to in the *Gītā*,[2] whereby one becomes the sole agent and all the five causes of activity are limited to the play of the guṇas and sense mind to the consciousness of the individual.

Thus far we have considered Prakṛti only in a general way as relates to the individual. There are other terms which represent a more specific modification of Prakṛti and is more intimately to be considered the individual's lower nature. These terms are 'Indriyas', 'Manas', 'Buddhi' and 'Jñāna' and represent a few of the various instruments mentioned in the above discussion of the causes of activity. When we consider the individual in the *Gītā* we note that it has already been found that the lower Prakṛti alone is not sufficient, and that Puruṣa enters the picture even when considering these simpler aspects. It is in considering the sense faculties and mind that this becomes most apparent. These faculties then are not simply evolutes of Prakṛti, but are the result of "The seed of Puruṣa in the womb of the Prakṛti". (XIII. 26, XIV. 3,4). They are if you wish the moulding of the lower Prakṛti according to purposes of the higher Prakṛti (VII. 5, 6). Even in the above arrangement

1. See III.24,27; XIV.19; XVIII. 13, 16, 18.
2. III. 27; XVI. 18; XVIII. 56, 57, 59.

of the faculties, this can be seen. From Manas to Jñāna one approaches a greater reflection of higher Prakṛti into these workings of the lower (see III.42 also XIV).

Let us proceed then to consider them in order: first Indriyas and Manas. There are two passages which give some clue as to the number of the senses the *Gītā* conceived. One mentions 10 and the Manas (XIII), the other only 5 and the mind (XIV). Since we found that the Upaniṣads already conceived of the ten Indriyas, it is most reasonable that the *Gītā* was aware of their enumeration and distinction into Karma and Jñānendriyas. The Manas is pretty clearly the more restricted use of the term as inner sense organ. It is what might be called the sense mind. The senses and manas clearly bring only awareness of the manifest state of gross objects (as might be inferred from II. 26-28).

The *Gītā* also puts forth a theory basic to its view of bondage, that "affection and aversion for objects of sense abide in the senses". (III.34). Thus the sense of touch has an aversion for objects too hot or too cold but an affection for objects properly warm. This affection and aversion, while in its simplest cases may be the normal action of guṇas, the *Gītā* claims at least that when the senses and sense mind are allowed to be the seat for such likes and dislikes, that "the excited senses of even a wise man, though he be striving, impetuously carry away his mind"; (II.60) and a straight path to destruction is thereby outlined (II. 62, 63). The sense mind in this condition is either tāmasic—absorbs self in the routine, blindly follows natural impulses, or rājasic—following desires and passions originating both internally and externally, or sāttvic—is the instrument of reason seeking harmony among multiplicity brought by the senses. This concept of affection and aversion being built in the senses by their nature and the nature of the guṇas is of utmost significance in pointing out that hierarchy mentioned above of the senses, manas, buddhi and Jñāna; in other words the senses and the sense-mind must be put under control of the buddhi or reason in which case the sense mind becomes sāttvic. Also in passages exhorting this control such as "whose senses are all completely restrained from objects of sense, of him understanding is well poised" (II.68), we find clue to the concept of Ahaṅkāra and possibly even Māyā of Śaṅkara. Thus the restraint of the senses from the object do not imply a withdrawal from sensory activity as it did for Yājñavalkya in the *Bṛhadāraṇyaka Upaniṣad*[1], but rather implies removing the affection and aversion from its imposition upon reason. This is the first step in the above discussed expansion of the source of activity out of the confinement to solely the guṇas[2], since the senses and their objects are wholly within the play of the guṇas. Thus Ahaṅkāra according to the *Gītā*, is the limitation of the causes for activity wholly within the senses and sense-mind; and when the senses are restrained from this function of desire and aversion which they have usurped, we are not suddenly transported away from a consciousness of particularity and liberated, but rather the desires are transformed into the purposeful guidance of the higher faculties. This point is important; for we find Yājñavalkya and indeed Śaṅkara both conceiving action as having solely desire as its root sense. Moreover, this desire is conceived as having its root in the subject object distinction common to the senses and manas[3], whereas the *Gītā* would make desire and aversion ultimately rest in the Puruṣottama, perhaps as described in the devic and asuric sections in the 16th chapter. Thus the *Gītā*, metaphysically speaking, would distinguish Ahaṅkāra and Māyā[4], the former having its seat in the senses and the mind, the latter is "Mama Māyā" (VII.14). Monism seems to be collapsing these two into one concept, Māyā; in other words monism such as in Śaṅkara's claims that the illusion of the multiple phenomenal world is sublated; or the guṇas actually cease when the nirguṇa Brahman is recognized to be the only reality. This is saying that the personal causes for illusion or distortion of reality (ahaṅkāra) are the cosmic causes for illusion or distortion upon the Nirguṇa Brahman (Māyā). The *Gītā* on the other hand carefully distinguishes Ahaṅkāra from Māyā by showing Māyā to be the creative power of the Puruṣottama; and when Ahaṅkāra is sublated you only have the Jīvanmukta, the man who is conscious of the universal self as the support, the

1. See *B.U.* 2.4.14 *ad passim.*
2. See p. 153.
3. See *B.U. loc. cit.* and Ś.B.
4. *Cf.* XVIII. 16; XVI.18; VII. 14; especially III. 27.

ground for the play of the multiple phenomenal world, not a dropping of all phenomenality; this last of which is a function of the Puruṣottama, not like ahaṅkāra resting on the misuse of the manas.

The senses, then, are wholly within the play of the guṇas, and an ordinary man is the seat of affection and aversion in acts and so is three-fold according to whether the play is tāmasic, rājasic or sāttvic. When this affection and aversion is removed, then the senses and the sense mind are subsumed under direction of the reason; and then the *Gītā* claims that "that which is night of all beings, for the disciplined man is time of waking.." In other words affection and aversion cloud the understanding as to the true 'nature of things', and this true nature of things the *Gītā* is claiming to be often counter to affection and aversion.

So far in our consideration of Prakṛti and the individual we have seen that the body must be under control of the senses and the senses under the mind. Now we see that the sense mind has a higher control in reason or the understanding (Buddhi). Let us proceed to examine the faculty of Buddhi or understanding.

In the Sāṅkhya, Buddhi is the first evolute from Prakṛti and is associated with Mahat[1]. Used by the *Gītā* referring to the individual it is the last stage. Vācaspati Miśra in his commentary on the *Sāṅkhya Kārikā* (23) says, "every man uses first his external senses, then he considers with the Manas, then he refers the various objects to his ego (Ahaṅkāra) and lastly he decides what to do with his buddhi". This order and specially the use of 'buddhi' is largely adopted also by the *Gitā.* For the entire range of the mind; then we have two terms 'manas' and 'buddhi' that is used. Much as in the Kośa analysis of the Taittirīya and other Upaniṣads,[2] 'Manas' is used instead of 'Buddhi', in this same broad sense. Judging from contexts and the fact that it is always used in the singular, it covers what is broadly intended by 'mind'. Under its headings fall intellect, determinate reason ("Vikalpa" in the Up.) will, and insight. Therefore in our present discussion we shall consider its function as an organ of knowledge and wisdom first, along with its

1. *Sāṅkhya-Kārikā* XXII, XXIII.
2. *C.U.* 7, *Muṇḍaka Up.*

relation to the guṇas. After this we shall consider its two higher functions—Jñāna and Vijñāna.

Perhaps the best term to translate 'Buddhi' is by 'intelligent will' which is the term Aurobindo uses[1], i.e., "that discriminating and deciding mind which determines both the direction and use of our thoughts and the direction and use of our acts, intelligence, judgement, perceptive choice and aim are all included in its functioning". We see the interesting fact that the *Gītā* does not wholly separate volitional and intellectual processes much as with the Greeks such as Plato. In Manas and the senses we find a built-in affection and aversion, which unless subsumed under Buddhi, led the individual to utter chaos. In Buddhi, then, there is also this volitional element and it is intimately associated with reason or intelligence. In the *Gītā* then, as in the Upaniṣads we cannot expect to find an elaborate metaphysics constructed quite apart from experience or references to reality. What metaphysical structure there is, is intimately associated with experience, the experience of Arjuna and Kṛṣṇa. This is demonstrated in the two-fold breakdown of the buddhi into "determinate reason" (Vyavasāya) which is one pointed, and the "many branched and endless" thoughts of the irresolute (II.41). This division is clearly a conative one; for discursive ideas and perceptions we do not condemn only the discursiveness of aims and desires. Buddhi, then, has a broad extension; on the one hand it is an intelligence reaching to and involved in Manas (associated with the seizing of the objects by the senses, the lusts, desires and impulsions); and on the other hand it is the intelligence, one pointedly reachin inward and upward towards the Puruṣa. When the last case is also the controlling seat of judgement, the entire individual is thereby focussed, the senses under the mind, and the mind under this determinate reason, Buddhi. From this we can conclude that Buddhi is the mediator between the lower nature, the senses of the individual, and the higher nature the life element and the akṣara Puruṣa. While it has this mediating function, nevertheless, it should not be forgotten that it still is of the nature of lower Prakṛti, the highest stage of aparāprakṛti.

1. *Essays on the Gītā*, p. 86.

This is illustrated by the fact that the buddhi is three-fold, either Sāttvic, Rājasic or Tāmasic.

XVIII.30 Sāttvic—"That which knoweth activity (Pravṛtti) and abstinence (Nivṛtti), what ought to be done and what ought not to be done, fear and fearlessness, bondage and liberation".

XVIII.31 Rājasic—"That by which one understandeth amiss right and wrong, also what ought and ought not to be done".

XVIII.32 Tāmasic—"That which enwrapped in darkness, thinketh wrong to be right, and seeth all things perverted".

If this be the nature of the Buddhi let us see just what its major functions constitute. The first, Vijñāna, may seem familiar to us from the Upaniṣad portion of our discussion where it stood for insight supposed to be comprehensive. Actually, however, from the scanty references to Vijñāna (XIII. 18, XVIII.42, VI.8, III.41) it seems rather that the contrary is meant in the *Gītā* by Vijñāna—discursive logical knowledge. Śaṅkara (III.41, VI.8) translates Vijñāna as "anubhava, personal experience, of things so taught through Jñāna". Rāmānuja (III.41, VI.8, esp. VII.2) takes Vijñāna as 'ātma-viveka' or discriminatory knowledge of the self. Radhakrishnan[1] takes Vijñāna to be logical knowledge. Aurobindo[2] takes Vijñāna as related to Mahat, as 'infinite idea' ideative capacity of universal energy. While any view might be implied from the scanty references and almost no context, the very scarcity of references compared to Jñāna makes Radhakrishnan's interpretation the preferred one. Vijñāna then is the Sāttvic function bringing about the 'knowledge of both activity and abstinence, what ought and ought not to be done', etc. Better in terms of our discussion of Prakṛti it may be the discriminative knowledge of the Field and knower of the field (XIII.24).

Standing over against this function of buddhi, the discriminating function, Jñāna is more clearly an essential knowledge. In

1. *Bhagavad Gītā*, III. 41.
2. *Essays on Gītā*, pp. 329-81.

terms of the two-fold reaching of Buddhi, Jñāna is the reaching up towards Puruṣa, an essential self knowledge (V.16, IX. 1). The truth of our differentiation between Jñāna and Vijñāna can be seen in such passages as the following which use Jñāna in the sense of the Parāvidyā or highest knowledge: "I will again declare the supreme knowledge (Jñānamuttamam), the highest of all knowings, which having known, all the sages have gone hence to the highest perfection". If, as we have established, buddhi has this mediating function, then it follows that Vijñāna is the discursive reaching out towards lower Prakṛti bringing a discursive yet comprehensive knowledge of Prakṛti; and over against this stands Jñāna which we can now see as a reaching towards Puruṣa, an essential knowledge. Aurobindo describes it[1] as "The light by which we grow into our true being", which he contrasts with intellectual (scientific or psychological) knowledge. The *Gītā* seems to lay a basis for Jñāna, Jñeya and Parijñātā (XVIII.18). These divisions, to a large extent, define the limits of this function of buddhi. The following tables (on pp. 160, 161) of the divisions illustrate this.

From these two tables interesting conclusions can be reached. First in the triad of Jñāna—Karma, Kartā, it is apparent that Jñāna here is roughly what was described under the buddhi as the variations according to the guṇas[2]. Moreover, it is apparent from the table that the rājasa knowledge as well as the tāmasa, although resembling Vijñāna in being a discursive knowledge, actually is to be distinguished, in that Vijñāna as a sāttvika function of buddhi is a reaching out from the Sāttvika Buddhi, not clouding of the Buddhi. Thus the Sāttvika wisdom is the finding of unity in diversity which seems to be the reflection of the Aparāprakṛti into the Parā or lower Prakṛti.[3] The tāmasic is the contradictory of this, the fixing upon a single unit of the diversity and taking it as the whole, a following of misplaced generality in logic. The Rājasa wisdom is the contrary of the Sāttvika, a diversity without unity. These three levels clearly mark an ascent out of the multiplicity and activity of the lower Prakṛti till in the

1. *Essays on the Gītā*. p. 182.
2. See p. 158.
3. See Ś.B. XIV. 6, 18, 22 also Rāmānuja Bhāṣya *Ibid*, Madhva seems to have no place for this metaphysical structure in his system.

Kṣetra (*XIII*.5.6)

5 elements Ahaṅkāra
Buddhi
The Unmanifest
10 senses
Manas
objects of sense

Jñāna (*XIII*. 7-11)

1) Humility, (2) Unpretentiousness (3) Harmlessness, (4) Forgiveness, (5) rectitude.
6) Service of the guru,
7) Purity, (8) Steadfastness. (9) Self-control,
10) Unattachment, (11) Absence of self identification with son, wife or house;
12) Constant balance of mind in wished-for and unwished-for events,
13) Unflincing devotion to me by Yoga.
14) without other object.
15) Resort to sequestered place.
16) Absence of enjoyment in company of men.
17) Consistency in wisdom of self.
18) Understanding of the object of essential wisdom.

Jñeya (*XIII*. 12-17)

1. That which be known
2. The beginning eternal supreme Brahma.
3. Can be called neither being nor non-being.
4. All enveloping in world.
5. Shining with all sense faculties , without any senses.
6. Unattached supporting all.
7. Free from qualities enjoying qualities.
8. Without within all beings.
9. Immovable and movable by its
10. Subtlety imperceptible.
11. Near and far away.
12. Not divided amid beings and yet seated distributively.
13. Denotes and generates all
14. light of all lights beyond darkness.
15. Jñāna, Jñeya, by Jñana to be reached.
16. Seated in hearts of all.

Jñāna (*XIII.* 20)	*Karma* (*XIII.*23-35)	*Kartā* (*XIII.*3.26-28)
Sāttvic : That by which the seer sees one indestructible Being in all beings, inseparable in the separated.	An action which is ordained done by one not desirous of fruit, devoid of all attachment without love or hate.	Liberated from attachment, not egotistic, endued with firmness and confidence, unchanged, by success or failure.
Rājasic : That knowledge which regardeth the manifold existence of different kinds in all beings as separate.	An action done by one longing for fulfilment of desires, or with much effort.	Impassioned, desiring to obtain the fruit of actions greedy, harmful, impure, moved by joy and sorrow, discordant, vulgar, stubborn, deceitful, malicious,
Tāmasic : Clingeth to each one thing as if it were the whole, without reason, without grasping the reality, narrow.	Action undertaken from delusion without regard to capacity and consequences, loss and injury to others.	Indolent, despairful, procrastinating.

Sāttvika you have the purest reflection of the higher nature by reflection of the unitary Akṣara-Puruṣa and Parāprakṛti into the diversity of the guṇas. Vijñāna and Jñāna in the Sāttvika level of buddhi can better be distinguished by the second triad the field (kṣetra), Jñāna, and the object of wisdom (Jñeya). Vijñāna is that function of buddhi which perceives the difference between the field and the knower of the field, referred to in the *Gītā* as the "Jñānacakṣu", the eye of wisdom. In other words this is the discrimination necessary as the first step out of the confusion of the sense mind, limiting the causes of activity solely to the guṇas[1]; and in general what is meant by logic or scientific knowledge as Radhakrishnan[2] so uses it.

Jñāna on the other hand is best represented by three qualities of Jñāna in the above table, "constant balance of mind in wished for and unwished for events", and "understanding the object of essential wisdom and consistency in the wisdom of self". Thus we see that all wisdom must culminate in this Sāttvika "balance of mind". This as we can see is the door to higher Prakṛti which was discussed above as "the expansion of the source of activity out of the confinement to the guṇas".[3] In addition Jñāna is shown to be the "constant understanding of self". This self, the Jñeya of the above table, is the Puruṣottama. This view of Jñāna supports Aurobindo's use as "the reaching towards Puruṣa"[4]. Radhakrishnan in one place[5] translates Jñāna as "spiritual wisdom" but in general is not clear on this higher function of the buddhi.

It must be clearly remembered that Jñāna—knowledge or wisdom—is not simply an intellectual or cognitive knowledge. It has an inextricable element of affection or feeling, a conative reference[6]. Therefore, when we ask ourselves just what is the place of Jñāna in reference to the individual in Prakṛti, it becomes apparent that the various qualities of the Jñānī in the first table above[7] spring from the earlier description of the

1. See p. 152 *ad passim.*
2. Radhakrishnan, *Bhagvad Gītā,* III.41.
3. See p. 155-156.
4. *Essays on Gītā,* Arya Pub. House, P. 299; *cf.* chap. XX.
5. *Loc. cit.,* III. 41.
6. See p. 157 f.
7. See p. 160 f.

agency of action. In other words the whole problem of Arjuna in the *Gītā* is that he feels that in being the agent of the act of slaying his relatives and revered elders, he is committing a heinous crime. Kṛṣṇa's teachings again and again bring in the idea that "he—who owing to untrained reason—looketh on himself alone as the actor, he, of perverted intelligence verily seeth not". If this is the case, then Jñāna is not only a knowledge of the Puruṣa but a reaching towards the Puruṣa. It is in this combined conative-cognitive reference, that we are to take the second chapter's attempt to show Arjuna that his "self" is unborn (II.20), unmanifest (II.25) yet dwelling in the body (II.18). Jñāna in this sense is an attempt to actively center the consciousness in this more expanded sense of self which is otherwise beyond the present awareness of self. One aspect of Jñāna, then, is an active change in self awareness to a realization of immortality (see XIII.2). The highest state of Jñāna, however, is more often characterized by such terms as unattachment (as asaktabuddhi or vairāgya), or controlling the self by firmness (XVIII.49). These seem to be summed up under another term also commonly used, "equality" (V.19), also "harmonized" (Yuktaḥ). This concept of "harmonized mind" and equality of outlook was seen as the essence of Sāttvika Jñāna[1]. The *Gītā's* description of the Jñāni, however, imperceptibly passes over from a Sāttvika Jñāna to a triguṇātīta Jñāna, a wisdom beyond the three qualities and hence beyond the lower Prakṛti. This can be seen by comparing Kṛṣṇa's answer to Arjuna's direct question as to the "marks of him who hath crossed over the three qualities" (14.21) with other descriptions of the highest state of Jñāna[2]. Kṛṣṇa in the former passage replies "He,—who hateth not light of knowledge nor outgoing energy, nor even desires caused by delusion, when present, nor longeth after them when absent" (XIV.22). The same is effectively said when summing up the Gītā's teachings in the 18th chapter saying, "Having cast aside egoism, violence, arrogance, lust, hate, covetousness, selfless and peaceful he is fit to become the eternal". (XVIII.53). Since the Sāttvika Jñāna is yet bound to the guṇas, according to the *Gītā* (XIV.6), by attachment to bliss (Sukha) and wisdom (Jñāna), then

1. See p. 158.
2. See chapters IV, V where 'Jñāna' is often so used.

there must be a difference between Sāttvika Jñāna and the above two passages, even though it can only be an implication from the rest of the Gītā's metaphysics. Moreover, even though Jñāna seems to blend from the Sāttvika stage into the triguṇātīta state, there should be an entire change in organ of knowledge used in the two cases. The former of course is still a function of buddhi which is as listed above as an evolute of lower Prakṛti[1]. The latter is left in an ambiguous state. Either the buddhi is used in this state as an instrument yet not bound by the qualities, or else there is a different organ of knowledge for the triguṇātīta state. Such terms as 'Ātmasaṁsthāna manaḥ' (self-seated mind) (IV.25) or Brahmavid Brahmaniṣṭhitaḥ (Brahma-knower seated in Brahman) (V.19,20) seem to call for the latter. Clearly the consciousness, however, cannot both be seated in Brahman or Ātman and yet limited to buddhi for its instrument of knowledge. The many emphases on the liberated self's serenity and inactivity would seem to call for a seat elsewhere as a basis of knowledge'. It is possible, however that buddhi yet has a part in the awareness of the liberated individual. The concept of the harmonized mind "which is central to the *Gītā*'s Yoga seems to imply action through the buddhi as an instrument but not there generated as with the man yet under sway of the guṇas. Moreover, since the lower Prakṛti is an eternal part of God's nature, the man passing beyond the modes of nature cannot, as in Sāṅkhya, drop the lower Prakṛti altogether. Such passages as "I do not anything, should think the harmonized one (Yuktaḥ) who knoweth the essence of things, while seeing, hearing, touching, smelling, eating, moving, sleeping, breathing" (V.8), seem to be saying, when taken in conjunction with the many passages speaking of liberation as becoming assimilated into the Brahman or the eternal, that the liberated man yet uses the Buddhi, manas and senses as instruments of the higher Prakṛti; but whether the lower Prakṛti is still formed into such instruments after death for the one assimilated to Brahma is a speculation which cannot in the context of the *Gītā* be made; and as a matter of fact such passages (IV.21, VII) as those claiming the senses, mind etc. are instruments "for the purification of self" leave

1. See p. 111.

unsaid what their place is after self is here purified". All that can be said is that the consciousness of self in the Jñānī who has passed beyond the qualities is centered beyond buddhi yet using the functionings of the buddhi as an instrument. The *Gītā* does not concern itself with the eschatological description of the consciousness of self; so that what ultimately is the position of lower Prakṛti to the higher after death in the individual assimilated to Brahman cannot be said. It is here that the basis for the various Ācārya's interpretation of the *Gītā's* teachings are made. The final state of absorption of the individual to Brahman is left just enough unsaid to give their many interpretations a basis. Just how many are justified in the light of the overall teachings of the *Gītā* we shall see later. We may conclude, then, that the highest level of aparāprakṛti, buddhi, blends in some yet unspecified manner into the Parāprakṛti through its highest function Jñāna. While yet embodied in lower Prakṛti, for the traiguṇyātīta, the buddhi, manas, etc. are used as instruments of the higher.

Before discussing Puruṣa, however, one point must be made to tie Prakṛti fully into the context of its use in the *Gītā*, that is dharma and Prakṛti. Dharma plays a central role in the *Gītā's* plot and it is for this reason that Prakṛti has been discussed in all its ramifications. Arjuna's initial rejection of the task of battle is couched in terms of what he believes to be a breach of dharma in slaying his relatives and teachers (I, II. 4,5). Kṛṣṇa immediately reproaches Arjuna for the unenlightened view of dharma and initially appeals to Arjuna's dharma as a warrior (II.31-32, 37). When Arjuna is not satisfied with this simple appeal, Kṛṣṇa then enters the basis of the dharma, svadharma (II. 33, 35), and the metaphysics we have so far discussed. From this discussion four basic principles leading to the understanding of dharma from the perspective of Prakṛti, arise—

(1) Prakṛti is the 'nature' of the Puruṣottama and has a lower and a higher aspect.

(2) The mark of the lower Prakṛti is incessant action classified under three modes tamas, rajas and sattva Guṇa.

(3) The Puruṣottama and certainly man who is cast in lower Prakṛti is obliged to action. Therefore the choice before Arjuna is not between action and inaction but merely how action will be done.

(4) After presenting the entire teachings, regarding the lower Prakṛti and leading to the higher Prakṛti, the real meaning of the various passages in the 2nd chapter emphasizing the self being unborn (II. 20), eternal (II. 18), etc. are seen. Simply put it is found that the seat of the self is in the Puruṣottama, in his higher nature and the lower Prakṛti are instruments for the self and merely its lowest extension.

It is to this core of self that we must now turn, the self as Puruṣa.

B. The self as Puruṣa

So far in our discussion we have had to use such words as lower and higher Prakṛti, Kṣetra and Kṣetrajña to distinguish two aspects of the nature of Puruṣottama. When discussing the lower Prakṛti or the Kṣetra it was possible to clearly distinguish Prakṛti and Puruṣa. We find, however, that when discussing Prakṛti as it relates to the individual that this Kṣetrajña (Akṣara-Puruṣa and higher Prakṛti) was inextricably interwoven and indeed the consciousness of self of the individual followed the stages of the eight fold Prakṛti and imperceptibly passed from Sāttvika Jñāna in the lower Prakṛti to triguṇātīta Jñāna in the higher Prakṛti. The import of this imperceptible transit from the lower to the higher nature as well as the blending of the Puruṣa and Prakṛti in the individual will be discussed fully later in considering the import of the Vibhūti. Suffice it here to recognize that the individual even within the three guṇas yet is a blending of Puruṣa and Prakṛti, Prakṛti as the womb and Puruṣa as the seed. We might suspect, then, that Puruṣa and Prakṛti are basically only descriptions of the individual, or the Puruṣottama from different perspectives and do not represent, themselves, dual elements in the world. This point is important to realise here, because before proceeding to consider Puruṣa fully we must recall the conclusion reached in the introductory portion of the last section as to the natures of Puruṣa and Prakṛti[1]. Essentially we found that the aparāprakṛti or lower nature was the stuff, the womb from which seed of life or Puruṣa brought forth the individual. The higher nature or Parāprakṛti came in many places as the 'life element' (The Jīvabhūtā) as it is put in the *Gītā* itself, "that by which the

1. See p. 141 f.

Universe is upheld". This higher nature is more clearly put in the fifteenth chapter as "An eternal portion of mine ownself" (XV.7). If this "eternal portion(aṁśa)of mine ownself" is the reaching out of Puruṣottama characteristic of Prakṛti, then we have cut across the normal distinction in Western philosophy between spirit or form and matter. Indeed this is the mark of the *Gītā* that it avoids the schism between Prakṛti and Puruṣa as Sāṅkhya makes it along this spirit-matter level of distinction[1]. Later Western Philosophers, such as Whitehead, in a similar way make matter and spirit not of ontologically different status but merely two poles of all life, without either one of which there would not be the concrete living being, only a metaphysical abstraction. So in the case of the *Gītā* there is this bipolar character to all living things.

If this is the relation of Puruṣa and Prakṛti and we now understand both levels of Prakṛti, then we must now ask ourselves just what is Puruṣa. From an inspection of the verses and context in which 'Puruṣa' and related terms occur in the *Gītā*, the following common characteristics of all these contexts arise.

(1) Puruṣa is the source of all beings and pervades all (IX.4), reached by harmonized mind(VIII.8,10) by unshaken devotion to him (VIII.22).

(2) Unborn lord yet seated in all bodies (II.18; VIII.4), seated in Prakṛti is the "supervisor or permitter, enjoyer, supporter, great lord and also the supreme self (Paramātmā); thus is styled in this body the supreme spirit" (XIII.22).

(3) Self (Ātman) actionless. Unmanifest, unthinkable, immutable he is called (II.25, II.21).

The diversity of these three principles are clearly to be described by different Puruṣas being referred to. Nevertheless, some common characteristics do appear; and from these we might infer that the Puruṣa is to be translated by such terms as spirit, godhead, being, seat of consciousness, or reality when compared to the Prakṛti as matter, becoming, appearance[2]. Each of the

1. See Guneon, *Man and His Destiny According to Vedānta*; for the same conclusions as to matter form being Prakṛti-Puruṣa in Sāṅkhya.

2. cf. Aurobindo, *Essays on Gītā* (American Edition), pp. 70,71; *Life Divine* (American Edition), pp. 316-18, also Radhakrishnan, *Bhagavad Gītā*, p. 332.

three ācāryas seem to take Puruṣa according to their metaphysical commitments and none really appreciate fully all three of the above meanings. Any of these terms by themselves express only one aspect of Puruṣa and it seems that the concept of Puruṣa in the *Gītā* lies closest to what A.N. Whitehead has termed "The consequent pole of God" as compared to the Prakṛti being the Primordial Pole[1]. In more familiar terms it is the Nivṛtti aspect of Puruṣottama as compared to the Pravṛtti; Prakṛti reaching out into active becoming and Puruṣa holding back in supporting being, and this is the distinction between Puruṣa and Prakṛti in the most general sense. Perhaps the one single word best translating Puruṣa is 'entelechy' as used by Driesch[2].

Since we have recognised in the above list of characteristics of Puruṣa different senses or levels of Puruṣa much like Prakṛti, it might be expected that the closer one approached the Puruṣottama this difference between Puruṣa and Prakṛti would grow less apparent. Indeed we shall see this in considering the Vibhūti later. At present our conclusions as to the levels of Puruṣa and Prakṛti in the *Gītā* might best be summarised in the following table which shall be our guide in considering the Puruṣa :

Kṣara Puruṣa — the individual — Lower Prakṛti
| |
Akṣara Puruṣa — Īśvara — Higher Prakṛti
or
Brahma
|
Puruṣottama

Puruṣa shall be considered, then, under three heads, the Kṣara, the Akṣara and the Uttama or Puruṣottama. Before doing so, however, let us relate all the terms denoting self to one or another of these three categories to facilitate our study. The following are the terms used : 'Ātman', 'Paramātman', 'Brahman,' 'Kṣetrajña', 'Kūṭastha,' 'he' or 'him,' and 'I' or 'me,' 'Parameśvara'. First Ātman seems to stand for self in a

1. Whitehead, A.N., *Process and Reality*, Part I, chap. III, cf. Northrop and Gross, Anthology, MacMillan (1953), pp. 699 f.
2. Driesch, H., *Man and the Universe*, pp. 81, 88.

universal sense such as in the following passage "...for by this thou wilt see all beings without exception in the self (Ātman) and thus in me..." (III.35). This does not exhaust the senses of 'Ātman' however and there are subtle plays on the term such as (VI.5,6,7, XIII.24.28) "Let him raise the self (Ātmānam) by the self (Ātmanā), and not let the self (ātmānam) become depressed; for verily is the self (ātmā) the friend of the self (ātmānam) and also is the self (ātman) the self's (ātmanaḥ) enemy." Likely two or three meaning of self, corresponding to the various levels of Puruṣa, are here intended. Therefore, we shall consider ātman passages according to context as falling in usually the Akṣara sense but having occasionally the Kṣara sense. The Kṣetrajña in the thirteenth chapter is not elaborately discussed but seems to be identified with the Akṣara-Puruṣa and ultimately Puruṣottama (see XIII.2). The Kūṭastha on the other hand is directly identified (XIII.26,34; XV. 16) with the Akṣara-Puruṣa. The Puruṣottama is occasionaly referred to as 'Paramātman' (see VI.7, XIII. 22,31. XV. 17; esp. III.22) or 'Parameśvara (XI.3; XIII.27). The terms 'Brahman' and 'Brahma' are to be found throughout the *Gītā* and seem to refer to Īśvara as the Cosmic Being.[1] The entire fifteenth chapter is devoted to setting up the three Puruṣas as a systematic way of explaining all these other terms expressing self. Lastly 'He' and 'Him' used so frequently in the second chapter (II. 20-30) seems to refer to Ātman in the sense as universal self. 'I' and 'me' are used by Kṛṣṇa here in the *Gītā* to refer to the Puruṣottama and occasionally specifically as the avatāra of the Puruṣottama. These three categories of Puruṣa must not be looked upon, however, as three distinct elements in a pluralism, otherwise the *Gītā's* doctrine of Puruṣa becomes openly contradictory by such passages as those in the fifteenth chapter (XV. 7-20; esp. VII.15) claiming the Puruṣottama immanent in all created multiplicity, and those passages elsewhere (VI. 29, 32) describing the Akṣara as seated in the heart of all beings, and even passages where Kṛṣṇa as the Puruṣottama identifies himself with this Ātman (see X.20).

1. These passages are too numerous to list completely (44) passages of Brahma and (compounds), cf. however XIII. 12, 30, XVIII. 50, VIII. 3, 13 for support of the Brahma being Īśvara.

Rather it is quite clear that we here have that monism which is not rigidly unitarian as is Yājñavalkya's teachings in *Bṛhadāraṇyaka Up.* and corresponds roughly to the trinitarian attempts of some of the later Upaniṣads such as Muṇḍaka and *Svetāśvatara,* and of course this is an argument for Rāmānuja's interpretation of the *Gītā* over the other two ācāryas. Puruṣa, then, in our discussion is to be taken as expressed in three levels of discourse Kṣara, Akṣara and Uttama. This sense of levels of discourse is necessary because it averts an otherwise unrecognised dualism were we to consider Kṣara-Puruṣa as a distinct entity from the other Puruṣas or even Prakṛti. It is precisely identification of Puruṣa and Prakṛti, in the Puruṣottama which is the important synthetic element in the *Gītā* as we shall see. Our consideration therefore must not only differentiate the three aspects of Puruṣa but also relate them to the corresponding aspect of Prakṛti. If all the above terms are now classified under one of the three heads, Kṣara, Akṣara and Puruṣottama, let us proceed to consider them.

The individual such as Arjuna, Bhīṣma etc. are described in terms of Prakṛti by the guṇa activity of the aparāprakṛti; and Kṣara Puruṣa is the Puruṣa associated with this lower Prakṛti. This is the Puruṣa as individual and multiple what might best be translated as souls. From the discussion of Prakṛti in the last section, we remember that so long as the self identified itself with the movements of Prakṛti, then just that far was the self changing its states (sattva—rajas—tamas) and even bound to rebirth[1]. This state of Kṣara-Puruṣa is that which we might recognise as bound and clouded by *Ahaṅkāra*. It is also found in the passage claiming the self as "the cause of pleasure and pain" (XII.20,21). The dehin or Arjuna, the individual, it is important to note, finally comes to bankruptcy in this identification of self with the lower Prakṛti; and the gloom of Arjuna over the task he faces is just this sort of bankruptcy. The recognition of this bankruptcy enables us to avoid the error of identifying the Kṣara Puruṣa and Jīvabhūta or Parāprakṛti, which it seems Radhakrishnan does[1]. By comparing the three ācāryas on this passage (VII. 5), we see that Śaṅkara mistakes

1. See pp. 148-152.

the parāprakṛti as the Ksetrajña of the 13th chapter and so as Puruṣa. There is no textual support for this identification as Kṛṣṇa is careful not to use 'Puruṣa' in this connection. Rāmānuja takes the passage in our sense as Prakṛti of Jīva and Prakṛti of God; but one in this mistake merely rephrases the Sāṅkhyan sharp dualism between Puruṣa and Prakṛti in different terms. True the higher nature is a supporter of the lower prakṛti; but to make it the personal supporter of the action, Kṣara Puruṣa, is to remove the divine impersonal sanction to the lower nature which Kṛṣṇa seems to be emphasising as higher nature[2] and perhaps analogous to the important concept of ṛta in the Vedas. This confusion is precisely the Sāṅkhya problem which the *Gītā* wishes to overcome. The Kṣara Puruṣa, then, is clearly the Sāṅkhya Puruṣa as it is associated with the guṇas of lower nature, as active, multiple and mutable. When the Puruṣa for Sāṅkhya releases this support and drops back into its own nature as multiple, inactive and self absorbed, the Prakṛti for it has no longer a hold since Puruṣa is its sanction and support. The higher prakṛti of the *Gītā* is just this impersonal, universal support, and so puruṣa is never 'isolated'.

From this Kṣara or soul, involved as it is in the actions of the lower nature, concentrated and lost in the waves of becoming, awareness of the Akṣara or immutable self is first brought forth in the *Gītā* by Kṛṣṇa in the second chapter in emphasizing the Puruṣa's immortality (II.12,13,17) and its indestructibility (II.18), such as the following verses :

> "These bodies of the embodied one, who is eternal, indestructible and boundless, are known as fruit... (II.18)"
>
> "He is not born, nor doth he die; nor having been ceaseth, He any more to be; unborn; perpetual, eternal and ancient, He is not slain when the body is slaughtered. (II.21)".

This last verse and the one immediately preceding it (II.19, 20) are shared with the *Kaṭhopaniṣad* and there, as in the *Gītā*, they mark the transition from the Kṣara-Puruṣa to the Akṣara

1. Radhakrishnan, *Bhagavad Gītā*, p. 25, VII.5.
2. Cf. chaps. VII, XIII; esp. VII.5, he uses 'Jīvabhūtam' not 'Jīva'.

Puruṣa or Ātman of the Upaniṣad. From these passages and others, the following characteristics of the Akṣara can be correlated :

1. It is universal, unitary and infinite (II.18).
2. It is to be described in negative terms— immutable (XII.3), inactive (XIII,29), unmanifest (XII.3), unchanging (XII.3).
3. Seems to be prior to and indifferent of the world of change (Kṣara-Puruṣa and Aparāprakṛti) (IX. 7,9,10).
4. It is all-pervading and seated in all beings (X.20).
5. It is unmanifest only in references to that which is manifest (cf. X.42; XV. 17).

It would seem that in the first three we have the avyakta or nirguṇa Brahman being described. Indeed there are passages making this identification (XII.1,3; VIII.20,21) and such as this :

> "They who worship the indestructive (akṣara) ineffable (anirdeśyam), unmanifested (avyakta), omnipresent and unthinkable, unchanging (Kūṭastha), immutable (acalam), eternal (dhruvam), restraining the senses, regarding everything equally in the welfare of all rejoicing, these also come to me." (XII.3,4).

This seems contrary to the last three which are a weaker form of unmanifest, almost including what we considered in the Upaniṣads as saguṇa Brahman. Our first observation, however, is that in the above-listed passages all the terms seem to be considered by the *Gītā* as referring to one Puruṣa and not many different ones as the contradictory character of the above list might indicate. Thus there is the identification of the Kūṭastha, avyakta and akṣara, etc. This is to say that the akṣara is viewed both as standing aloof from the manifest and yet also viewed as hidden in and supporter of the manifest activity. As we concluded in the Upaniṣads, then, the unmanifest or avyakta here is unmanifest only in relation to the manifest and indeed it seems that it is, according to the *Gītā*, also dissolved at "the destruction of all beings" (VIII.20). This unmanifest is not, then, wholly equivalent to the monistic unmanifest; for, although the *Gītā* says: "Verily there existed higher than that unmanifest another unmanifested Eternal, which during the destruction of all beings is not destroyed." (VIII.20) and "that unmanifested 'indestructible', it is called; it is named the highest path. They who reach it return not. This is my supreme abode." (VIII.21). The very next passage shows that this unmanifest is to be viewed as the Puruṣottama, and is a "trans-personal personality", and not merely an unmanifest impersonal absolute. This we shall consider further later. At the moment it is important to recognize merely that the akṣara is avyakta in the weaker sense given in the Upaniṣads—that which stands apart from the manifest—and yet in addition to this it is said as the kūṭastha to be seated hidden in and supporter of the manifest and relatively inactive (relative to guṇa activity). This is not only the nirguṇa Brahman, then, but also the saguṇa. Like the Ātman of the Upaniṣads it too then might be viewed as dipolar, one pole the unmanifest aloof from creation and another pole universal and pervading all creation as supporter and witness of manifest activity. One might, however, instead of this, attempt to infer that there is in addition to the Akṣara on avyakta Puruṣa (the akṣara being vyakta) this would give four Puruṣas and avoid this broad concept akṣara. True the above passages emphasising the avyakta are in the 11th chapter. Whereas the metaphysics of the three Puruṣas are given in the 15th but even the predication of the barest continuity to the *Gītā's* work would necessitate that the *Gītā* actually considers this unmanifest as the akṣara and even some of the passages quoted above in the 8th chapter seem to make this identification. It must be noted here, however, that in the 8th chapter these are a series of verses (VI. 18-21), most likely either later inserts or at least passages not fitting in with the rest of the *Gītā*[1]. This is not to say that these passages are out of context, indeed the idea that "the worlds upto Brahma are perishable lead naturally to this consideration of the unmanifest. It is just that the passages are obscure; and indeed (VIII.18) is contradictory to IX chapter, where Kṛṣṇa claims the Puruṣottama to be the creator. One finds the unmanifest only in VIII.18 as creator, elsewhere it is the Puruṣottama (IX.7,8). Whatever the reason for the obscurity and

1. See Garbe, *Indian Antiquary* XLVIII (1918), Supplement; he claims verses 20-28 are interpolated but this cuts right across the context of the difficult passages.

apparent jump in context we can safely reject these passages for our analysis, since they are subordinated in their contexts to the Puruṣottama and Brahman.

The *Gītā's* Akṣara, then, is both Sāṅkhya's Puruṣa inactive and self-absorbed after dissolution from Prakṛti (but is not multiple as Sāṅkhyan Puruṣa), and is also the Upaniṣadic, unmanifest Brahman in its weaker form. It is this Puruṣa, the akṣara, then, that is contrasted the Sāṅkhyan fashion[1] as inactive, witness and impersonal against the active Prakṛti. This, however, is only its negative formulation. In its positive expression it is associated with Parāprakṛti as the creator and supporter of all nature. It is important to recognise this positive formulation, for it is here that the basis of the schism between the nirguṇa and saguṇa Brahman found in the Upaniṣads is altered and healed by cutting across this manifest-unmanifest distinction and instead making it a contrast between kṣara or mutable and akṣara or immutable. Both of these are more clearly interdependent than the manifest and unmanifest distinction. The terms 'kṣara' and 'akṣara' themselves indicate this in making the distinction between the changing and unchanging. In this case you are not left with the gulf which the Upaniṣads put up between the nirguṇa and saguṇa Brahman which was only partially bridged over by the transcendental Brahman of the *Māṇḍūkya* and *Īśa Upaniṣad*; but we are given principles, themselves, which cannot be so separated as the cosmologically created manifest and unmanifest. In other words the changing and unchanging are primarily dependent as Kant[2], Plato[3] and many others in Western philosophy and nearly all Indian philosophy apart from Buddhism recognizes; in order to have change you must have an unchanging reference or substratum. Of course the one strongest point linking these two Puruṣas is the importance of the various concrete beings of which the Puruṣa and Prakṛti are the descriptions in perspective, e.g. Arjuna, the individual in the case of the aparāprakṛti and kṣara Puruṣa. In this formulation Arjuna or the individual does not stand in the same opposition to Īśvara as does the dialectic of akṣara to kṣara. Thus while the latter

1. See chapter IV, esp. 5.
2. *Critique of Pure Reason*, Smith translation, 212, 218.
3. *Theatetus* 184-186; also *Sophist*.

are clearly in opposition, the former Arjuna and Īśvara are not; and Īśvara is characterised as residing as witness and support (IV.6; XV.17) in the hearts of all beings and is "active" although in some different sense of the term than Guṇa activity (III.22-25). The embodiment of Puruṣa brings in also Prakṛti to the discussion; and so here although there is no opposition at best there is only the gulf between the lord and man.

In conclusion, then, we can say that the akṣara puruṣa has different formulations in different parts of the *Gītā* and in different contexts. At first (Chapters II, IV,V,VIII) it is described as impersonal witness and inactive and termed avyakta or unmanifest. The later formulation makes the akṣara seated in all beings yet universal, unitary and witness to all activity. In this last case akṣara is more the immutable witness to the mutable's activity, than being the unmanifest which is wholly outside of and negating the manifest. These two rather diverse treatments of the akṣara Puruṣa are clearly conceived by the *Gītā* as one immutable, inactive witness to the activity of the kṣara. The *Gītā* attempts in two ways two link this avyakta and akṣara; first in the 12th chapter it openly uses the two terms as synonyms (XII.3) along with both alternative formulations in the same Chapter (12, passim), secondly it talks of an Īśvara which seems to be the concrete expression of the self which akṣara and parāprakṛti both are perspectives. This is to say that the Īśvara seems to fill this role, being immanent in the world yet aloof and witness to all creation. This is what one formally conceives of as a personal God and indeed seems largely what Rāmānuja takes as the model of Brahman. Therefore, the two divergent formulations are held together in this case in one cosmic being. The reader, however, is yet left somewhat unconvinced and in doubt as to what degree actually these two akṣara and avyakta have in fact been successfully made one in this second case because of the *Gītā*'s reluctance in discussing eschatological matters. Thus the individual immersed in guṇa activity described as kṣara Puruṣa and aparāprakṛti; upon becoming traiguṇyātīta clearly passes into what can only be described as akṣara Puruṣa. Indeed although the reader may identify this state with the *Gītā*'s use elsewhere of the 'kūṭastha' (XV.16); yet in describing the traiguṇyātīta

(V.19-25) little reference is made which would aid the reader in conclusively deciding this and identifying the traiguṇyātīta fully with the cosmic akṣara. In addition little or nothing is said about the state after death except that the traiguṇyātīta is not reborn. In our present discussion the identification of these two formulations of the Puruṣa—avyakta and akṣara has been made on a basis of the metaphysics of the Puruṣa, which is much more complete than the sādhana relating to the concrete beings Arjuna, Īśvara, etc. limited as this latter is to Arjuna's immediate problems. We shall, however, take up this sādhana material in the next chapter. Here if we recognise only some textual support in considering the akṣara Puruṣa as the inactive witness, impersonal and unmanifest and yet seated hidden in all beings (the Kūṭastha), then our purpose would have been served; for we can see that the *Gītā* intended to contrast the mutable world of guṇa activity in which one found mutable, active souls (kṣara Puruṣa) with the immutable inactive witness world hidden in and from the activity of the former, and yet acting as its foundation.

Were this all of the *Gītā* we would be left not only with the open opposition between akṣara and kṣara Puruṣa, but even with the more subtle schism between the world of mutable individuals and the immutable world of Īśvara. Rather weak and long would be the bridge between these worlds; but because of the peculiar nature of prakṛti in the *Gītā* as "me prakṛtiḥ". These two Puruṣas are shown to be simultaneously characteristics of the one Puruṣottama; both worlds are merely aspects of the one world of the Puruṣottama; both Arjuna and Īśvara are instruments of the one Puruṣottama. However successful the opposition between these two realms of discourse is overcome, there is little doubt that the *Gītā* intends the Puruṣottama to be this healing agent to the divergency found in the previous formulations of self, especially in the Upaniṣads. Moreover, it is apparent that of the three Puruṣas the Puruṣottama is the only one which is concrete, the other two being abstract, i.e., an aspect referring to either the individual in the case of the kṣara or Brahma in the case of the akṣara. From the above nature of the three Puruṣas, then, we can definitely state that the Puruṣa never "abides in itself" as in sāṅkhyalaya, simply because it is not the self to be contrasted with the Prakṛti as nature or matter; but rather both Puruṣa and Prakṛti as we have seen[1] are equally of the Puruṣottama. The Prakṛti "his nature" and Puruṣa the core of his being. Akṣara Puruṣa then is still to be associated with Prakṛti, the higher Prakṛti, and, this is why the individual does not achieve laya in the traiguṇyātīta stage. In other words, of the three Puruṣas, the Puruṣottama is the only one having both a Prakṛti referent and a Puruṣa referent; and so is not a "Puruṣa" in the same sense as the other. The Puruṣottama, then, is to be compared to Brahma and the individual rather than to the other Puruṣas. That perhaps is why 'I', 'me' or supreme lord (Parameśvara) is usually used rather than Puruṣottama. We might expect, therefore, that the Puruṣottama sums up the other two Puruṣas not so much by offering something new in the way of Puruṣa, but more by combining both Puruṣas simultaneously with the Prakṛti into a concrete being.

If this much is understood as to the nature of the Puruṣottama in the *Gītā* let us investigate the context in which 'Puruṣottama' occurs, to find in more detail this concept. From a study of the text it is evident that the Puruṣottama is spoken of in three different modes of language. The first is in positive categories such as "His essential nature is called self-knowledge (adhyātma)" (VIII.3); the second is in negative categories such as "the beginningless supreme eternal Brahma. . . can be called neither being nor non-being" (XIII.12); the third is in contradictory terms, e.g., the following "without and within all beings, immovable and also movable; by reason of his subtlety imperceptible, at hand and far away is that" (XIII. 15). We shall want to see just in what way the Puruṣottama is viewed differently in these three languages of expression and also what light may be thrown on the other two Puruṣas in these three modes of discussion.

First there are many passages which link the Puruṣottama to the mutable world[2]. The most important one directly links the Puruṣottama and the Kṣara Purusha, in saying that "An eternal position of my own self, transformed in the world of life into a living in spirit, draweth round itself the senses of which

1. See p. 172.
2. XV. 7-15; X.8, 29-42; IX. 4-10, XIII. 13-17, 22, 27.

the mind is the sixth, veiled in matter" (XV.7). This one verse, as well as the innumerable ones stating the Puruṣottama to be "self (Ātman) seated in the hearts of all beings, the beginnings, the middle and also the end of all beings (X.20)", seems to explain much of the lengthy enumeration Kṛṣṇa makes in the tenth chapter (The details of the Puruṣottama) admitting that "there is no end to details of me" (X.19,40). From such enumeration two questions naturally arise; first if all the enumerations are of the highest qualities (except one) "I am the gambling of the cheat" (X.36), how does all the evil and corruption in the world stand to the Puruṣottama, since admittedly Kṛṣṇa says "whatsoever is glorious, good, beautiful and mighty, understand thou that to go forth from a fragment (aṁśa) of my splendors"? (IX.41). Secondly the one word aṁśa brings a question as to just in what sense is it a "portion" or "fragment". If we can answer these two questions, one aspect of the Puruṣottama, the one using positive categories, will have been elucidated. The first question is partly elucidated by noting the text of XV.79 quoted above which says 'jīvaloke svabhūtaḥ' literally then the Puruśottama has become (bhūtaḥ) a jīva, "a living spirit". This goes a long way toward establishing the idea that this mutable world is an aspect of the Puruṣottama; yet we must note that in "becoming" a jīva, which includes being expressed in aparāprakṛti or lower nature, the Puruṣottama on this level of discourse simply is what we have termed kṣara Puruṣa. This is to say the idea of "becoming" in some way involves a diminution of its capabilities as Puruṣottama and being bound to the guṇa activity of lower nature. This is, perhaps, the meaning of the *Chāndogya* where we are likened to a blind folded man from Gāndhāra who has been carried far away and need directions home.[1]

Thus the source of origin has been lost sight of or at least dimmed in the process of becoming. If this is the case, then, we can see that evil or corruption—the demoniacal—born of the 16th chapter are simply those jīvas following the lower guṇas—tamas and rajas. These latter two can, of course, be used towards constructive purposes but in this case already sattvaguṇa would

1. *C.U.* 6.14.

have entered. The demoniacal are rather those who try to use rajas and tamas without acattva, who reside almost wholly in manas with a resultant desire and aversion ruling the consciousness of self. This then is the answer to the first question; the Puruṣottama has become, been transformed into, the jīva with all its inherent limitations. Our second question can be seen to immediately arise when we ask just what this transformation or becoming constitutes. The elucidation of 'aṁśa' will go a long way toward solving this question. First, however, we might point out the serious nature of the question, Śaṅkara takes the nirguṇa Brahman as the Puruṣottama and makes the mutable world merely an adhyāsa upon the qualityless unmanifest Brahman, primarily because in answer to the above question he can find no basis of transformation or becoming according to his professed vivartavāda view of causation. Rather than considering the process of transformation and its possibility, however, we can immediately see our question as more generic, questioning as it does the nature of what undergoes the transformation in becoming the Jīva. This is simply to say we must decide whether 'aṁśa' means part or fragment in the sense that an army commander would send a detachment or part of his forces to one sector of battle holding the other back; or whether 'aṁśa' might mean part in the sense of a cell organ or limb of the body. In the last case taken apart from the body, the part loses its significance as "part of a body" since the body is an organic whole in which there are no "parts" except in an abstract analysis of it which destroys its "bodiness" in the analysis. Since the Puruṣottama clearly is put forth not as merely an extensive unity of various parts such as our army above would be, but as a being of which Kṛṣṇa is the avatāra. Then it is clear that the peculiar sense of aṁśa as "aspect" or "function" is more exactly what is put forth as the relation of the mutable world of finite souls to the Puruṣottama. The relation of function to whole, is analogus to cell or organ to body. We must not carry this analogy too far, however. The consciousness of self which marks the level of the individual is not as a cell in the body which is God, which seems to be roughly Rāmānuja's view[1]. The above analogy applies only to the

1. See Bhāṣya on V. 18; VI. 8.

mutable world as a whole and strictly as an analogy. We see this brought out in the text in Kṛṣṇa's teachings that, "they who refuged in me, strive for liberation from birth and death, they know the Eternal (Brahma), the whole self knowledge (adhyātmam)" (VII.29), and followed immediately in the next chapter after Arjuna's request for explanation of these, that "the indestructible, the supreme, is the Eternal (Brahman); His essential nature is self knowledge" (adhyātma). Therefore since the individual has the potentiality for the whole adhyātma, he cannot be merely a cell; but in some peculiar way much like a seed contains the potentiality of the entire tree not just a part, the individual must reflect the whole of the Puruṣottama. This sort of relation of aṁśa, then is the Puruṣottama's description in positive categories.

In order to avoid confusing this description of the Puruṣottama for a pantheism the *Gītā,* we must recognize, also uses negative categories saying "I know the beings that are past, that are present, that are to come, O Arjuna, but no one knoweth ME" (VII.26). This then is the attempt to show the Puruṣottama to be in his nature wholly unmanifest (cf. VII.24). Never, however, is the Puruṣottama openly and fully treated in a negative vein, what few passages there are treating the Puruṣottama in negative categories[1] are in context of two sorts; first to avoid a complete identification with the mutable activity. There is a negation as in the second chapter to show the self indestructible, and so to overcome Arjuna's gloom from such identification. This is also shown in the ninth chapter when the Puruṣottama is shown to be the support of all beings yet not rooted in beings (IX.4,5). Secondly there is also negation to avoid identification with a wholly unmanifest Puruṣa. It is this last context that the negative categories point out the widest use of contradictory categories. In the verse quoted above Kṛṣṇa says "the beginningless supreme Eternal Brahma. . .can be called neither being nor non-being" (XIII.12). This is a most significant negation because it says that the Puruṣottama cannot be *sat,* the manifest. This much is quite straight, merely what other negative passages purport. In addition, however, the Puruṣottama is said not to be non-being (*asat*) or unmanifest

1. II 20-25, 29; VIII. 16-21; IX. 4, 5; X. 3; XIII. 31-33; XVIII.20.

either. If both of these categories are negated we immediately wonder what is left. If we can understand that the negation does not intend to be an absolute negation but only a significant negation, i.e., merely saying that the Puruṣottama is not wholly being nor wholly non-being (he cannot be defined by either one) then we can see only the Puruṣottama enveloping all is left. We may conclude then that negative categories are used in the *Gītā* to avoid complete identification with either kṣara or akṣara Puruṣa. This weaker use of negation is quite significant and goes a long way towards avoiding the identification that Yājñavalkya in the *Bṛhadāraṇyaka* and Śaṅkara later make between the nirguṇa Brahman and the Parabrahman. Śaṅkara in his Bhāṣya on the above passage (XIII.12), as is common in passages difficult for him to interpret under his system, avoids the issue completely. The *Gītā*, then, not only makes the neti-neti negation here but also negation of the neti-neti itself, which the immediate monist fails to do.

Immediately following the above passage there are passages describing the Puruṣottama in such contradictory categories as "He is movable and immovable, shining with all sense faculties without any senses" (XIII.14,15). The negation of any quality, then, has the ambiguity of denying that particular predicate of the subject as absolute negation; or denying merely that the subject is to be defined or wholly exhausted by that quality. Where this is the case with negation, clearly the use of contradiction at once avoids this and points out that the subject is a peculiar subject not amenable to the subject-predicate or substance quality mode of expression which is inherent in some languages. Of all the passages seeming to talk of Puruṣottama in contradictory manner,[1] perhaps the following one sums them up in their import :

> "But what is the knowledge of all these details (of his divine glories, positive qualities) to thee O Arjuna? Having pervaded this whole universe with one aṁśa of myself, I remain" (V.42).

Not only is the concept of pervading and supporting (as kṣara and akṣara) all the universe and yet not being altered or traas-

1. VIII. 9; IX. 4, 5; X. 42; XIII. 12-18.

formed, beyond the ordinary categories of language, but it seems that it is just about beyond the ability of intellect to grasp except through the rather inadequate analogies used in discussing "aṁśa". This difficulty was also met in the Upaniṣad attempts to put forth a transcendental Brahman; and here in the *Gītā* although we are not faced with the open opposition between a manifest and unmanifest Brahman, nevertheless we must confess an inability to fully grasp the concept of Puruṣottama except to recognise that the aṁśa that is the mutable and immutable worlds represents the full embodiment of the Puruṣottama into these worlds in each particle of the mutable, and also wholly the immutable; yet the Puruṣottama while being both the mutable and immutable cannot be defined as either or both together. The contradictory quality of this expression along with the confessed lack of ability to define the Puruṣottama more clearly, casts this expression of the Puruṣottama as at least only an intellectual analogy for a referent which lies outside intellect. Śaṅkara has recognised this in his commentary on the unknowability of Brahman and only anubhava is possible.

The *Gītā*, then, presents the Puruṣottama in three different realms of discourse, in positive categories, negative and contradictory categories. Only in the latter, however, does the *Gītā* rest its concept of Puruṣottama, the positive being negated by the negative terms and the latter only culminates in contradictory terms being cast in the form of a significant negation. The first two are, by and large, more intellectually graspable and perhaps explain why they are generally more widely taken as the model for expressing Brahman than the last, the contradictory categories. In religious terms this is simply the observation that God is more widely understood as pantheistic or theistic than panentheistic, which leaves the intellect baffled and unsatisfied. The *Gītā* does not balk at this intellectual incompleteness, however, and clearly puts forth, as observed above, the remark that the individual, so long as he is bound to use reason, cannot pierce the Puruṣottama's "Yogamāyā" which hides him from this world.

Perhaps it is partially to fill this obvious intellectual gap that the concept of Vibhūti and avatāra are put forth in the *Gītā*. These two link the Puruṣottama even to the mutable world in both an impersonal and personal way. First we note from the tenth chapter that 'Vibhūti' is translated by Śaṅkara (X.7) as "Vistara", literally extension or expansion. By Rāmānuja it is translated "aiśvaryaṃ", i.e., indicating his dominion or lordship over the mutable world (X.7). Radhakrishnan[1] explains it as right feeling, real, faith, glory. Only the last term really fits the meaning, which is roughly the best or most glorious which that race, quality, item or power produces. It is the lack of appreciation of this term as shown by 'Śaṅkara and Rāmānuja's bhāṣya which prevents them from overcoming the metaphysical incompleteness of Puruṣottama. In the text there is clear indication of its meanings such as in the following verses: "Of Vedas I am Sāmaveda; I am Vāsava of the devas and of senses I am mind (manaḥ); I am of living beings the intelligence (cetanā) (X.22)", "of Vṛṣṇis Vasudeva am I; of Pāṇḍavas Dhanañjaya; of sages I am Vyāsa; of poets Uśanas the poet" (X.37).

In the case of the human, then, the Vibhūti is the man who has risen above common humanity (bound to the guṇas) and reaches towards divine humanity (triguṇātīta or centered in the akṣara). All this can be summed up as "that entity or person which most completely expresses the svadharma and svabhāva of his race or kind". Sri Aurobindo perhaps has characterized this best[2] in saying the vibhūti is "a pre-eminence in the inner and other achievement, a greater power of divine quality, an effective energy is always the sign" and in reference to the human vibhūti "Every great man who rises above our average level, rises by that very fact over common humanity; he is a living assurance of our divine light and a breath of the divine power". The above intellectual gap in understanding the Puruṣottama as the core of mutable existence and at the same time wholly immutable, is partially overcome at least from the standpoint of the mutable world by showing the vibhūti to be, personal or impersonal, more than a creation or fragment of the divine made human; but in someway, to be described only by "aṁśa", it is the very workings of the Puruṣottama itself not as a "*deus ex machina*" but as the core and essence of our being itself.

1. See also Radhakrishnan, *Bhagavad Gītā*, p. 253.
2. Essays on the Gītā (American Edition), p. 143.

The vibhūti concept closes the gap left in our thinking about Puruṣottama from one side, by supplying a concrete example of the link of the mutable and the Puruṣottama through the growth of the mutable being into his full svabhāva. While this is the case, there is no doubt that the Gītā's real contribution is in the concept of avatāra. It is this more than anything else which will show the Puruṣottama to be more than the metaphysical absolute reached by a logico-psychological dialectics of contradiction or the like. The first thing that strikes the reader of the *Gītā* on the avatāra makes just this point, i.e., Kṛṣṇa throughout the *Gītā* speaks of the Puruṣottama in the first person. There is the definite statement in one passage that the Puruṣottama has taken by his own creative powers (Ātmamāyā IV. 6; Yogamāyā VII.25). The extent to which the Puruṣottama is spoken of in the *Gītā* in the first person is shown by the fact that Kṛṣṇa claims it is "I who am" the source of forthgoing of the whole universe and likewise the place of its dissolving (VII.6). "I pervade the whole universe" and "am its support (IX.4,10,8 XV.17). Kṛṣṇa goes even further claiming that all this universe is only a small part of his nature[1]. These claims all lead to the eleventh chapter in which Arjuna is given the "psychic sight" "Divya-cakṣu" to see Kṛṣṇa's "Viśvarūpa", it seems that this vision of the form of the Puruṣottama could be divided into three groups. First, the forms as Īśvara (XI.10-12), secondly the form as the Supreme (XI.13-21) and lastly the terrible aspect as the source of dissolution (XI.22-30). The very fact, then, that Arjuna sees Kṛṣṇa in his divine form, tempers the statement elsewhere that "no one knows me" (māṁ veda na kaś cana) making its meaning simply 'no one knows me with ordinary human knowledge (vidyā) but only with divine knowledge.' This last knowledge' as the vision in the 11th chapter, comes as grace crowning Arjuna's worthiness not simply as something acquired. Here as in the Upaniṣads there is general agreement among the ācāryas and modern philosophers on the special nature of the "knowledge"[2]. Therefore, when

1. Cf. "All things are rooted in me, not, in them". (IX.4) cf. also X. 42.

2. See Bhāṣyas on VII. 6, 25; also Dasgupta, *Hist. of Indian Philos.* II. 499, 523 f.

Kṛṣṇa is mistaken as merely human and not taken as supreme (XX.11,12) this very mistake illumines not only the nature of the avatāra but also the nature of the human in its relation to the avatāra. Perhaps a key to all the passages on the avatāra is given in 5 succinct passages of the fourth chapter which because of their vital importance to the *Gītā's* doctrine of Puruṣottama are worth quoting to call them to mind :

> "Many have been my past birth and many have been thine, O Arjuna! I know them all, but thou knowest not thine" (IV.5).
>
> "Though unborn, the imperishable self, and also the lord of all beings, brooding (adhiṣṭhāya) over nature which is mine own, yet I am born through my own power (ātmamāyayā)". (IV.6).
>
> "Whenever there is decay of righteousness—and exaltation of unrighteousness, then I create (send forth, sṛjāmi) myself" (IV.7).
>
> "For protection of the good and destruction of evil doers, for the sake of firmly establishing righteousness I am born from age to age" (V.8).
>
> "He who thus knoweth my divine birth and action, in its essence, having abandoned the body, cometh not to birth again, but cometh unto Me. . ." (III.9).

Thus, when it is said elsewhere that knowledge of self (adhyātma-vidyā) brings this beatitude (VII.29), here it is said "if one knows my divine birth and action". It is clear, then, that if man can grow into the vibhūti and the Puruṣottama can become man in the avatāra then the intellectual gap in the Puruṣottama is closed in religious terms where it could not be in metaphysical terms. The above passages tell us three things which explain the avatāra (birth); first, both the individual and the Puruṣottama undergo many births, only the Puruṣottama has full understanding of them; secondly, the Puruṣottama is born for a specific purpose which is not simply the purpose of humans (svabhāva) but more specific and immediate, and thirdly through the term 'adhiṣṭhāya (established in or on, III. 6) we can see that the birth of the avatāra is voluntary and not involuntary, driven by prakṛti through ignorance, as human beings are so born. Thus it is ātmamāyā, not the power of avidyā, that brought the avatāra to birth. We might characterise this by saying that the prakṛti is infused with puruṣa rather than the reverse as in ordinary birth, and hence the meaning of adhiṣṭhāya as more "a standing on" than "involved in". Aurobindo has summarised this characteristic of the avatāra perhaps in the clearest fashion when he says "it is the manifestation from above of that which we have to develop from below; it is the descent of God into that divine birth of the human being into which we mortal creatures must climb, it is the attracting divine example given by God to man in the very type and form and perfected model of human existence"[1]. The most important observation arising from our understanding of the avatāra then, is that the difference between the human-being and the Puruṣottama is not a difference in kind, a vast chasm which a theism would in its dualism set up. Rather activistically conceived it is a difference in the "direction" of action, one from below the other from above.

Even though we may now understand the nature of the avatāra in relation to the human, still there are some problems. Basically there are four questions which we should want answered by this theory of avatāra. First we must inquire whether Kṛṣṇa really is to be considered human or divine, i.e., just to what degree can Kṛṣṇa be an example to man if he is not to be considered human. In our discussion of the birth of the avatāra above we found that there was a subtle difference. In the case of the avatāra we remember puruṣa infused prakṛti in a fully voluntary manner which is the reverse for the ordinary human birth. Thus the avatāra and the human are both individuals, and are identical in all respects except consciousness of which the latter is centered in the Puruṣottama and the former in the guṇa action of lower nature. Perhaps this is the import of the passage quoted above[2]. "Many have been my past births and many have been thine, O Arjuna ! I know them all, but thou knowest not thine. . ." In answer to our question, then, we can see that Kṛṣṇa is as truly human as Arjuna, that is his purpose as avatāra to become human. The real difference between

1. *Essays on Gītā*, p. 140.
2. IV. 5; see p. 185.

them lay in their consciousness of self which are poles apart, one involved in becoming the other resting in being fully directing his actions in the becoming.

Another question, relating to the above, seems to arise, i.e., "in what way is Krishna as the avatāra related to the guṇas ?" Such a question arises because the human is involved in the guṇas and even bound to them; the triguṇātīta even though freed, continues to use the guṇas instrumentally. It would seem in comparing these two human states with the avatāra that the *Gītā* would support the doctrine of prārabdha karma since the traiguṇyātīta is said to be freed upon death (VIII.5-10). This is also shown by the emphasis that the self abides in itself; and the guṇas then play among themselves. What we want to ask, then, is whether in the avatāra the "guṇas play among themselves", merely being directed through the will of the self; or whether the guṇa action is at all modified in view of the difference in birth. Thus since in the avatāra the Prakṛti is infused with the Puruṣa, in birth then one would expect that the guṇas are not moved by prārabdha or by ignorance, but the purposeful direction of the guṇas. In the avatāra's case then it should be that the guṇas are more directly controlled by Puruṣa than in the case of the human which can only supply final and formal causation to the guṇa activity. In answer to the second question, then, it would seem that the guṇas are not left to themselves to colour the Puruṣa as in the human birth; but in the avatāra Prakṛti itself is coloured, by, and more directly controlled under the Puruṣa. Kṛṣṇa, the Avatāra, then, is the divinised human at once divine yet also the human made perfect. Rāmānuja is the only one of the Ācāryas who fully appreciate this difference in Prakṛti orientation.

Another question arises from the above passage saying "many have been my past births". If the avatāra is not involved in guṇa activity what is the reason for the "many births?" This, of course, is answered in the two verses following this (IV.7,8), i.e., "For the sake of firmly establishing righteousness" but here the real question is that if the Puruṣottama is seated in the hearts of all beings, why is such a direct descent into birth necessary ? This question is related to our fourth question; and we might ask both of them as, "what is it about the avatāra" that the vibhūti cannot so achieve by his enlightened guidance ? Clearly if the Puruṣottama chooses to achieve its purposes through the avatāra rather than by some "supernormal" miracle of awakening in the hearts of all, then he must be achieving something as a divine-human which he would not achieve as merely divine; yet if this is the case why could not the vibhūti, the *evolved* of the race, achieve the same since these latter must be responsive to the supreme seated in the heart even if the ordinary man has lost the truth, to use a Upaniṣad phrase[1]. This is a most difficult question, and does not seem immediately answerable by the *Gītā*, and perhaps may be a defect in the whole avatāra theory. Aurobindo who carefully distinguishes between the Vibhūti and the avatāra[2] gives the example of Caitanya whom he considers an ordinary jīva (perhaps a vibhūti). Caitanya in ordinary consciousness was a devotee of God but in certain ecstatic states "became in these abnormal moments the lord himself". Thus the vibhūti in an ecstatic state may actually reach the consciousness of the avatāra. If so, even more should the vibhūti serve the redemptive purpose of the avatāra. The only answer which could be given to this difficult problem, and actually that which the *Gītā* does indirectly give, is that it is not so much the Jñāna imparted to the race by the avatāra which constitutes the redemptive purpose, but more concrete symbol of the God-head; to evolve through bhakti the response from the heart of the individual. The *Gītā* does emphasise bhakti in relation to Kṛṣṇa; and this at least seems a partial answer to our double question of the incarnations of the Puruṣottama and why the vibhūti would not serve this redemptive purpose.

There are differences of views among the various ācāryas over the avatāra theory in the *Gītā* which arise through the use of personal terms ('I', 'me', etc.) by Kṛṣṇa. Rāmānuja (XV. 17-19) like Radhakrishnan[3] seems to view the Puruṣottama in

1. See R.B, XIII. 2, 16 esp. VII. 4-7, cf. Ś.B. on some passages and esp. VII. 4-7.
2. *C.U.* 6, 8, *passim*.
3. *Essays on the Gītā*, p.143.
4. Radhakrishnan, *Indian Philosophy*, I. 533-6, *Bhagavad Gītā*, p. 204, (VI.30).

the image of Kṛṣṇa by their using the term "personal". To view the Puruṣottama as personal is to miss the real import of the avatāra and the Puruṣottama, and put the reader in danger of thinking in terms of the personal-impersonal, and God's personality and human personality as dualities. Although true, the Puruṣottama in the form of the avatāra can be called personal, nevertheless to consider the Puruṣottama "personal" is to lose sight of the very decent which the avatāra stands for. To consider the Puruṣottama personal, then, is anthropomorphic, and to avoid this we can at best say it is a "transpersonal personality". Śaṅkara avoids difficulty with the avatāra concept through his double truth standard theory[1] which otherwise would be difficult to reconcile with his leaning towards the impersonal. The *Gītā* does intend to put forward the Puruṣottama as having the qualities of personality-impersonality and yet transcending it; that this is true, we have found in two different contexts, one a metaphysical consideration ending in a dialectical concept largely intellectually incomplete, and now in consideration of the vibhūti and the avatāra. Perhaps it is accepting either one of these contexts as the dominant thread (Mahāvākya) and neglecting the other which causes the difficulties which many commentators find in the *Gītā*. In our discussion we have found that it is the vibhūti-avatāra passages which have largely closed the intellectual gap in grasping the transpersonal nature of the Puruṣottama, largely in terms of bhakti. The Puruṣottama, we also found, largely summed up the positions of the other two Puruṣas, kṣara and akṣara; and the Puruṣottama might in the end be said to be the *Gītā's* teachings on self.

C. *Summary : The Description of Self :*

Before going on to consider the Sādhana portions of the *Gītā*, which we must consider in order to more fully ascertain to what degree the above description is in fact a single concept of self, let us briefly sum up what we have concluded so far.

In this chapter we have considered the concept of self from two aspects, Prakṛti and Puruṣa. First, let us take Prakṛti; we

1. See Ś.B. on *Muṇḍaka Upaniṣad* 1. 1.4, also Ś.B. on VIII. 11, II.49.

Sāṅkhya Classification	Elements	Vedānta Classification	Gītā Classification
Neither Prakṛti nor Vikṛti	Puruṣa	(1) Superior form parabrahman	Parāprakṛti
Fundamental Prakṛti (1)	Prakṛti	(2) The inferior form parabrahman (eightfold)	Aparāprakṛti 8 subdivisions
(7) Prakṛti-Vikṛti	(Mahan (1) (Ahaṅkāra (2) (Tanmātras (3)		
(16) Vikāra	(Manas (1) (Jñānendriyas (5) (Karmendriyas (5) (Mahabhūtas (5)	The 16 elements are not looked upon by Vedānta as fundamental elements as they are vikāras or evolutes.	Vikāra

have two Prakṛtis, one, the lower Prakṛti, was conceived largely along the lines of Sāṅkhya and the Upaniṣads as eight-fold. The *Gītā*'s view of Aparāprakṛti compared to others has been given in a handy chart by Tilak[1].

We note that Tilak has made the same identification of higher or Parāprakṛti with Puruṣa that was criticized in our discussion. The *Gītā* accepted the Sāṅkhya pluralism of finite selves, we recall, on the level of lower Prakṛti. These finite selves were subject to domination by the guṇas or three fundamental modes of Prakṛti.

There was another Prakṛti, the Parāprakṛti which was : the support or impersonal sanction to the lower Prakṛti. In our discussion the comparison was made of the Parāprakṛti to the Vedic idea of Ṛta. This higher nature was connected with self on the level of Īśvara or akṣara Puruṣa.

The *Gītā* classified the Puruṣa under three headings the kṣara, the akṣara and the Puruṣottama. Each was spoken of separately, although the first two we summed up under the third. The kṣara Puruṣa was that concept of soul associated with the lower Prakṛti and in a multiple-mutable state. The akṣara was the underlying and also aloof unmutable self associated in the unitary Īśvara with the higher nature. The Puruṣottama was said to be both of these at the same time yet transcending such distinctions. This formulation was presented largely in terms' of contradictory categories while the mutable-immutable was spoken of in positive and negative categories, respectively. This contradiction was the terminus of the metaphysical discussion of the Puruṣottama. The intellectual gap left in the readers mind between these contradictory formulations of the Puruṣottama was bridged in the *Gītā* in the concepts of the vibhūti and the avatāra. The following table sums up the main points in the description of self in the *Gītā* :—

1. *Gītā Rahasya* I, p. 249. *VS*. p. 190.

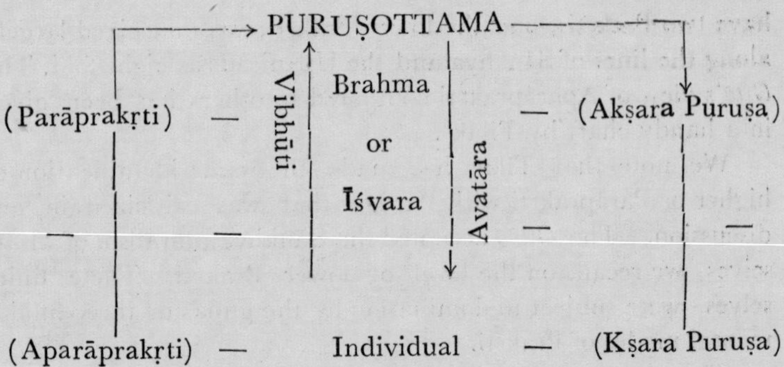
PURUṢOTTAMA
(Parāprakṛti)
Vibhūti
Brahma
or
Īśvara
Avatāra
(Akṣara Puruṣa)
(Aparāprakṛti)
Individual
(Kṣara Puruṣa)

CHAPTER III

THE ADHYĀTMAVIDYĀ SĀDHANA

A. *Introduction* :

So far in our study of the concept of self we have found three such concepts—the individual, Īśvara and the Puruṣottama, all which in some sense might be called self. The *Gītā*, we can see, accepts a pluralism when talking of the individual and yet maintains one Īśvara and Puruṣottama. Moreover, we spent some time considering to what degree the latter summed up the former two. Metaphysically, the concept of Puruṣottama is meant to do just that, provide the ground for the completion of the conflicting natures of the mutable and immutable. In more religious language we found that the vibhūti and the avatāra gave a more satisfactory picture of the Puruṣottama than the metaphysical one which was left in openly contradictory terms, unsatisfactory to the intellect.

Nevertheless, we have yet three concepts of self unless in some way we can show that the *Gītā* is saying that the individual by growth of some kind becomes the Īśvara and the Puruṣottama, thereby making the Puruṣottama somewhat of a telos of all becoming. The answer to this is found in the various paths to action Arjuna is given. These paths are intended not only for Arjuna's specific problem, the battle at hand; but also apply to the doctrine of self already described. This broader application is shown by the lengthy discussion of the path of meditation and abstraction given in the 5th and 6th chapters, a discussion not immediately applicable to Arjuna's problems, and seemingly only given to round out the discussion of the sādhana especially in respect of the akṣara Puruṣa. Before critically evaluating the concept of self in the *Gītā*, then, let us briefly consider the various mārgas given in the *Gītā* for the individual towards orienting this growth to either the Īśvara or Puruṣottama.

B. The Path of Karma :

The individual and all creation, we remember, are cast into the guṇa activity as part of their nature. The path of karma is the one most directly concerned with the guṇa activity, and corresponding to our two individuals, one bound to the guṇas and the other traiguṇyātīta. There are, then, two views of karma in the *Gītā*. One might call them the lower path of karma and the higher path.

The lower path is the familiar one from the Upaniṣads that of "Vedic works" which the *Gītā* casts in rather denunciating terms (II.41-46). The followers of this path are the "deluded who are attached to the guṇas" (III. 25-27,29) and also the "demoniacal born" (XVI.4; VII.24). We might say this is the man who has turned his attention away from any higher purposiveness to sense attractions, what in Christian theology is termed the unrepented man[1]. Arjuna's despondency seems to be over such a posture to action although the *Gītā* does not stress this. Clearly the motives of Arjuna for rejecting the action ultimately are found to rest in an egoism (I.28-37) based on consideration of pleasure (1.33,36), enjoyment (I.32-33), desires (I.31) etc. This observation as to Arjuna's despondency is justified by the passages in the second chapter where Arjuna is incited to action by rewards and threats (II.32-37). That is, we might infer that Kṛṣṇa is here testing Arjuna just as Yama tested Naciketas in the *Kaṭhopaniṣad* first by rewards and the like. It is precisely the failure of this test to attract Arjuna that shows his despondence to be a bankruptcy of his existing posture to karma. The *Gītā* says, that the road to the higher path of karma is through bankruptcy of the existing egocentric orientation; and this is an inevitable occurrence (XVIII.59).

Once this simple posture of desire to action is broken, there are two postures one might adopt. The first is abstinence from action, sannyāsa, which the *Gītā* takes up under Jñāna Mārga. The second is the *Gītā's* own teachings on karma, niṣkāma karma, which we remember was partially anticipated in the *Īśopaniṣad*. We might recall the observation that the *Gītā's*

1. Frank, E., *Philosophical Understanding and Religious Truth*, Oxford, 1945, 158 f.

metaphysics clearly claims that all creation (both men and the devas) are bound to action since they are in Prakṛti. Therefore, as we shall see even further later, the *Gītā* rejects the first possibility. There can be no complete sannyāsa. According to this second doctrine, one performs action relinquishing (tyāga) the fruits of the action. If this were all we would have the Kantian dictum of "duty for duty's sake". Indeed, there are passages which seem to advocate this[1]. This is one of the senses in which the word 'yoga' appears, as "skill in action" (II.60). Basically, we can conclude, that the *Gītā* puts forth karmayoga as "duty for duty's sake" as action done without desire (niṣkāma), without attachment (vairāgya) and can be summed up as "Niṣkāma Karma". This conclusion is what Tilak[2] and Gandhi seem to think is the *Gītā*'s "message".

That the *Gītā* does not stop at pure karma as its message, however, is plainly shown in the *Gītā* itself by such passages as "Far lower than the yoga of discrimination (buddhi yoga) is action" (II.49). Karma, then, seems only the base, only the posture to action of non-attachment. The path pursued by itself would seem to lack all purposiveness; and it perhaps is this that leads the *Gītā* to the above observation of Buddhi.

C. *The Path of Jñāna* :

The first alternative mentioned above after bankruptcy of the lower path of karma, was Sannyāsa. This is the formulation of the Jñāna Mārga to be found especially in the 5th and 6th chapters (esp. V. 21-29, VI.).

There are different formulations of Jñāna, however, depending upon the degree of other mārgas present in the Jñāna. The one formulation which is the purest Jñāna seems to be that path of Sannyāsa close to the one formulated in the Yājñavalkya-Maitreyī portion of the *Bṛhadāraṇyaka Upaniṣad*[3]. These passages are largely formulated in comparison to the lower Karma in the senses. In this case the word 'yoga' is again used. In one context it is defined as "disconnection from union with pain" (VI.23). In this sense 'yoga' seems more to be sāṅkhya in the

1. II.47, 48; III. 19, 22; XVIII. 59. etc.
2. *Gītā Rahasya*, I. XXV.
3. Cf. IV.22, 23, 33-42; V. 8, 9, 12-14, 16, 25-28; VI. 3-23.

modern sense; and this is the defining position of Sāṅkhya in the *Sāṅkhya Kārikā* (I and II). Usually in the *Gītā*, however, wisdom is the culmination of yoga in a third sense which we shall take up shortly, and is the definition of Jñāna below (III. 38). Jñāna is defined in the *Gītā* in the five following ways, some of them representing the more integral path which the *Gītā* is continuously blending into its discussion of any one path :

1. Jñāna is renunciation (V.8-9, 14-16, 25-28, 34,35; IV. 22,23, 33-42; VI. 3-29).
2. Jñāna is inner equilibrium, mind poise (IV.24-27; V. 18-20; VI. 8-9).
3. Jñāna is knowing self and self (VI. 5-7) subduing thought and fixing on self (VI. 18-23).
4. Jñāna is finding delight in self (VI.19-21).
5. Jñāna as the flame which burns up karma (VI.36,37).

Of these five the first two can be seen to be more generic concepts of which the others are specifications. The first is defined in negative terms as "when a man feeleth no attachment either for the objects of sense or for actions, renouncing the formative will (Saṅkalpanam), then he is said to be enthroned in yoga" (VI.3). This is the path leading to the akṣara or Īśvara, the retreat from karma and the kṣara. The second seems to be largely what Yoga has come to mean in the darśana, mind poise; "Little by little let him gain tranquility by means of reason controlled by steadiness; having made mind abide in self, let him not think of anything. As often as the wavering and unsteady mind runneth away, so often reining it in, let him bring it under control of self" (VI.6). We note a significant difference from the darśana, however; the above passage does not mean merely "cittavṛtti-nirodha"[1] as for Patañjali's yoga; but subduing the mind and placing it under control of the self.

These two statements on Jñāna are significantly different. The first seems to have been made in terms of the senses and the lower path of karma, while the latter view is cast more directly in terms of Jñāna alone. Which view the *Gītā* in its synthetic attempts favours is quite clear when we recall that it is stated that all creatures cast into Prakṛti are bound to activity. Thus

1. As in *Yoga Sūtras*, I.2.

sannyāsa is impossible, and the first view openly contradicts this statement. It is at such points that scholars such as Otto[1] and Garbe[2] criticize the *Gītā*. Our hypothesis, according to our introductory discussion, is that the *Gītā* is bound to describe all the paths according to its plot. If our hypothesis is correct, then, after describing sannyāsa there should be clear indication that it quickly shows its own preference. Proof can be seen in such verses as "Among all Yogīs too, he who, full of faith, with inner self abiding in me, adoreth me, he is considered by Me to be the most completely harmonised" (VI.47, cf. V. 6,7,10). We shall see this much clearer when discussing the integral path of the *Gītā* in section E. At the moment it suffices to recognise that the *Gītā* presents two views of Jñāna, one the monistic view of sannyāsa which we found in such Upaniṣads as *Bṛhadāraṇyaka*, *Muṇḍaka* and *Kaṭha*, the other its own theory of mind poise. The former contradicts the *Gītā*'s metaphysics of Prakṛti, discussed in the last chapter, whereas the latter is used more widely as the basis for the *Gītā*'s own conclusions in the integral path.

D. The Pāth of Bhakti:

So far the paths of karma and Jñāna have been largely those found in the Upaniṣads. It is in bhakti that the synthesising element is found; and this element, although found to a degree in Upaniṣads, especially the more Brāhmaṇic material, is vastly expanded and refined in the *Gītā*. We might infer from this that the attempts towards a philosophical synthesis made in the later Upaniṣads, were considered by the authors of the *Gītā* to have failed their purpose in confining this synthetic attempt exclusively to a metaphysics which was necessarily cast in contradictory terms. Whether the *Gītā*'s attempt in using bhakti is any more successful we shall attempt to find out in the conclusions; here we have only to critically develop the concept of Bhakti, and see in what way it leads to an integral path, and to what degree the integral path succeeds in making a single concept of self out of the three, we have uncovered in the last chapter.

1, 2. See introductory Chapter, p. 126 *ad passim*.

In various contexts presenting Bhakti in the *Gītā* we might conclude two different but related concepts:

1. Bhakti as sacrifice (IX.20,21; III.10-13,30,31; IV.25-33; XVII.11-14).
2. Bhakti as devotion (XI.54,55; IV.24; VII.1; VI.31; IX.13-35).

These two forms may seem at first to be the same since usually sacrifice requires a sacrificer, the sacrificed, and one to whom sacrifice is directed; and devotion requires also such a three-fold division, involving the same participants; and so a bhakta who was a sacrificer would also be a devotee; actually, however, the stress is different. In the case of mīmāṁsā (pūrva-mīmāṁsā) for instance the sacrifice has assumed such an importance that it largely occludes the one to whom the sacrifice is directed[1], whereas devotion is always a goal directed action, i.e., one is always a devotee of some God or the Puruṣottama. The *Gītā*, however, makes clear that both are necessary for the Bhakti path; and this combination of the two illustrates the fundamentally soteriological orientation of the whole bhakti element in the *Gītā* (VII.16,17,18). We might expect then that Bhakti would have equivalents for each level of the individual of the last chapter, all the way from manas to Vijñāna. This expectation is borne out in the 12th chapter in the 4 levels of Bhakti (XII.8-12).

(1) Fixing the mind on the Puruṣottama (Buddhi) (XII.8).

(2) If (1) above is impossible, then through practice (XII.9).

(3) If (2) is impossible, perform actions for his sake (XII.10).

(4) Refuge in me and renunciation of fruits if (3) is impossible. (XII.11).

In other words devotion through buddhi (determinate reason) is the highest and most complete form of Bhakti; following this in abhyāsa or practice which gradually cultivates the manas away from desire and aversion and leads to the devotion of (1). This constant practice is the simple idea of devotion to the lord as the goal of all activities. The third path is open to those of the

1. Radhakrishnan, *Indian Philosophy*, II. 424 ff., 428 ff.

lower path of karma, these bound to actions for whom constant practice is impossible. This is the simple conception of bhakti as service to the lord and can be seen to be also a posture to karma. The last posture, that of renouncing actions and taking refuge in the lord, seems out of place below service, and indeed the next passage seems to openly refute the previous order. We might, therefore, place (4) first. We can see, in addition to the soteriological orientation of bhakti, another point, that devotion to the lord is placed above sacrifice as is shown by the lst 2 steps being efforts conceived devotionally with the lord as their goal, whereas the third and possibly the fourth, depending upon its position, is largely a sacrifice of actions or fruits of actions to the Puruṣottama.

This devotion and sacrifice is characteristic, then, of Bhakti as conceived in the *Gītā*. We have discovered, however, in the soteriological orientation of bhakti evidences of the interweaving of karma and jñāna as is evident from the (3) and (1) of the above levels of bhakti. Bhakti, then, more clearly than karma or jñāna, therefore, involves other factors than worship alone; and it is through this observation that the *Gītā*'s attempts to integrate all the paths most often is brought into the dialogue. When the *Gītā* does try to present bhakti as pure worship, it seems to cast it in somewhat derogatory terms (VII.21-23, 28-30).

E. Attempts in the Gītā towards an Integral Path:

Two points of the above discussion clearly necessitate some sort of more complete consideration of the sādhana. First, the path of karma as well as jñāna seemed conspicuously incomplete as a sādhana. We found, for instance, that karma conceived as niṣkāma karma left a dictum of duty for duty's sake which reduced the motives for action to almost an automation level; likewise jñāna as sannyāsa was clearly impossible according to the *Gītā*'s metaphysics and the view of jñāna as mind poise was likewise incomplete as a discipline. Second, the path of bhakti showed clear signs of a hierarchy of interpretation which crossed the boundaries of bhakti itself, and took up karma and jñāna into its ken. These blendings seem necessary from the very nature of the *Gītā* as a concrete expression of an individual problem. Thus we can say that the *Gītā*'s more complete pragmatism brings the discussion of self and self development out of the realm of cosmological and abstract psychological presentation of the Upaniṣads and embodies it dramatically in the problem of the concrete individual. An investigation of the broader contexts in which the above margas were given immediately shows how the *Gītā* uses the above paths as bases for various blendings.

The table below sums up the contexts of the three basic paths and shows the broader context in which they have been interwoven:—

Path :	*Hints at an integral Path* :
Karma:	
II.39-48	II.48;—all three, complete statements
III.4-9	III; (Generally)—karma and jñāna
	III.9-16, 30; karma and bhakti
XVII.23-28	XVIII. 2-11; karma and jñāna
	56-60; karma and bhakti.
Jñāna:	
II.12-38,49-53	II.54-72; complete description of triguṇātīta in terms of all three.
IV.20-23,38,40-42	IV.5-10; jñāna and bhakti
	IV.11; complete path in terms of bhakti.
	IV.13-19; jñāna and karma
	IV.24-32; bhakti and karma
	IV.39, Goal of jñāna
V.6-29	V.2; jñāna and karma
VI.4-26	VI.3; karma leads to jñāna
	VI.27-31; Puruṣottama goal of Jñāna
	XII.1-20; Jñāna and bhakti
XVIII.50-53	XIII. 10; XVIII. 54-55; jñāna and bhakti

Bhakti :

VII.21-23, 28-30, 16-18	
VIII.5-7	VIII. 8, 11-16; bhakti and jñāna
IX.13, 20-27, 29-34	IX.14-15; bhakti and jñāna
Chap. XI (whole)	IX.28 complete statement of path
XVIII.61-62, 65-66	

Rather interesting conclusions arise from the above table. First we note three major movements. In the third chapter karma is presented generally with jñāna interwoven and also some element of bhakti. In the fourth, fifth and sixth chapters there is a transition to jñāna where it is also generally interwoven with karma and small elements of bhakti. From seventh chapter to twelfth chapter the major portion of the bhakti element is the basis of discussion, again interwoven with the other two elements. Moreover from the above table and our discussion of bhakti we can see that the *Gītā*'s approach to the sādhana as an integral path, like its metaphysics and concept of vibhūti and avatāra is two-pronged; on the one hand from a blending of karman and jñāna in the early chapters, bhakti is interwoven; thereby the karma jñāna combination brought in through the Gītā's yoga and through the notion of mind poise is given purpose and direction towards the supreme. On the other hand, the middle chapters are devoted to bhakti primarily interwoven with jñāna in bringing the goal of the Puruṣottama into the ken of the individual. From this we might conclude a hierarchy of possible paths starting in lower karma and through the higher karma blending into bhakti through the intermediary of jñāna (as mind poise). If this is the case, we might say that the *Gītā*'s integral path is basically a bhakti highly modified by karma and jñāna elements. Also it is evident that the *Gītā* is claiming that all three paths discussed above lead into this integral path as their natural conclusion.

That this is the conclusion of the *Gītā*'s sādhana, we might now briefly undertake to prove, holding in mind our discussions in the last chapter and so far in the present discussion. The *Gītā* in the 5th and 6th chapters seems to be saying that pure yoga (in the sense of karma) like pure Sāṅkhya (in the sense of jñāna) is impossible in man because he partakes of both puruṣa and Prakṛti—eternal aspects of the Puruṣottama. This seems to be saying, then, that it not only is impossible but even undesirable to remove all desire and act like an automat in karma; rather when the desires are destroyed in the senses and manas, then higher purposes of which the desires were only restricted distortions appear. These higher purposes carry the seat of action up into the buddhi and so into jñāna. The *Gītā* says this in so many words in the passage quoted above "Far lower than buddhi yoga is action... Take thou refuge in pure reason (buddhi) pitiable are they who work for fruit" (II.49). Thus in one stroke Kṛṣṇa says one should not work for fruit (desires) and also should follow buddhi yoga. We must not take fruits (phalam) literally as the results of action, only as rewards, as accomplishments of the desires seated in the mind. Judgment seated in the reason, indeed, works for purposes; but these are not the limited desires of ego and so to be considered phalam. Kṛṣṇa says as the Puruṣottama that there is nothing that he needs yet to accomplish, yet he engages in action; for otherwise the world would fall to ruin. This is seen also to support the integration of karma and jñāna; for truly the Puruṣottama has purposes in acting but not desires. We may conclude from this that the lower karma is the base from which many paths branch out. Once the limited base for actions in the guṇas is passed beyond one does not act as an automat; rather one passes into jñāna as the seat of action. Moreover, from the opposite point of jñāna, pure sannyāsa is impossible in the world of Prakṛti and so the jñānī, is "forced helpless to action" (III. 5; XVIII.40). Therefore, the *Gītā* recommends "yoga" (as mind poise, inner equilibrium) whereby the action done through the senses does not disturb the equipoise of buddhi. Therefore, instead of trying to shut all activity from buddhi which the sannyāsī tries, the *Gītā* recognizes along with Sāṅkhya that the buddhi itself partakes of Prakṛti whose nature is action. By letting the "senses play among the senses" (V.9) action is not a distraction to the buddhi in equilibrium (not "Cittavṛttinirodha" but in dynamic equipoise). This is the attempt of the *Gītā*, then, in the first six chapters to show that as soon as lower karma is transcended then one of necessity must partake of both karma and jñāna. The key to understand this is given in the concept of yoga as mind poise in the sixth chapter.

The *Gītā* also adds another element to this combined path that of purposiveness or action directed towards Puruṣottama as a goal of development. This is quite definitely stated in such passages as the following which is typical of many (XVIII.55; VI.27-31; VII.1): "He who established in Unity worshippeth me, abi ding in all beings, that yogi liveth in Me, whatever his mode of living" (VI.31). In the first six chapters this is introduced only in a minor way; but from 7 to 12 chapters we notice that a full-fledged bhakti is introduced. The *Gītā*, however, seems quick to subordinate a karma-bhakti combination to a bhakti of wisdom (XII.8-12). Thus, although it is possible to do actions merely as a service to the lord, renouncing the fruits for oneself, it is not held as important as a full devotion of knowledge by the wise. Clearly this revolves around the difference between sacrifice and devotion mentioned above. Bhakti without jñāna then does not serve a soteriological function but only a liturgical one; and it is this which the *Gītā* seems to want to avoid. This bhakti seems, then, to be a devotion in which the devotee and the lord achieve an ultimate union in some sense, much like the lover and beloved. This is, precisely, the figure of Kṛṣṇa as the lover and beloved in the Bhakti-cult. This bhakti requires jñāna, an enlightened understanding of lover and beloved and so is vastly different from the worshipped and the worshipper, which might be the bhakti when performed by one in lower karma.

We can see, then, the two-fold nature of the integral path; on the one hand the sādhana of combined karma and jñāna, and on the other the goal of the supreme brought to the individual consciousness, through bhakti-jñāna. The *Gītā* states the complete path in a few passages such as the following three (II.48; IV.11; IX.27;28) :—

> "Perform action, O Dhanañjaya ! dwelling in union with the divine, renouncing attachments and balanced evenly in success and failure; equilibrium is called Yoga" (XI. 48).
>
> "Whatsoever thou doest, whatsoever thou eatest, whatsoever thou offerest, whatsoever thou givest; whatsoever

> thou doest of austerity ... do thou that as an offering unto me" (IX.27).
>
> "Thus shalt thou be liberated from the bonds of action, yielding good and evil fruits, thyself harmonized by the yoga of renunciation (Sannyāsa), thou shalt come into Me when set free" (IX.28).

If we understand the integral path both as another choice for Arjuna to make among the already given karma, jñāna and bhakti, and also understand it as the core of philosophical synthesis which the *Gītā* offers, then the basic reason for the *Gītā* putting forth such a sādhana is clear. If the metaphysics of Puruṣa and Prakṛti are accepted, then, since there is some dynamic interaction between various levels of Puruṣa and Prakṛti, and moreover since growth is not a growth out of Prakṛti into pure Puruṣa, then the individual is required to make a dynamic effort in all aspects of his being, both Puruṣa and Prakṛti, and both jñāna and karma. Since Puruṣa and Prakṛti are eternally distinct aspects of the Puruṣottama, therefore, the *Gītā* is saying that this effort can be best made by performing both karma and jñāna, as bhakti, as sacrifice—devotion to the supreme self. If this is the integral path and the sādhana put forth in the *Gītā*, let us see in what way the concept of self in the *Gītā* is so influenced by it.

F. The Mārgas and the Concept of Self:

We are now in a somewhat better position to assess the relations between the three concepts of self—the individual, Īśvara and the Puruṣottama. It is clear from the discussion in the last chapter that the Puruṣottama was the reality behind the individual and the Īśvara—"all beings are rooted in me not I in them" (IX. 4)—and moreover the avatāra showed the Puruṣottama to be more than an impersonal absolute, and could only be called at best a trans-personal personality. In the last chapter we also found in the metaphysical discussion and in the idea of the vibhūti, that the individuals were not eternal atoms of personality, but themselves reaching towards the Īśvara, towards the divine and out of the human. This is the point at which the discussion of the Sādhana entered. In what way is there this reaching out? From the integral path as presented above it is clear that the individual has union with the Puruṣottama as the goal of his efforts. This point is also recognized in two different contexts:—

(1) Contexts where Puruṣottama is spoken of as Supreme self (II.18-26,30,72; III. 14; IV.15, VIII. 8, 10,21-22; XIII. 2, 34).

(2) Contexts where Kṛṣṇa speaks in first person (II.61; IV. 9-11; VI.15,30-31; VI. 14,17,19,23; VIII. 14-16; IX 7,25,28,34; X.10; XII. 8-10; XIII. 18; XIV. 2, 19; XVIII. 62,65,66,68).

In the first context speaking of the supreme self, liberation is said to be a reaching, going, or entering the supreme. Likewise in the first person passages similar terms are used. They are correlated in the table below:—

Puruṣottama as Param:		*Puruṣottama as I or Me*,
Āpnoti	(IV.19) obtains	XIV.19
Adhigacchati	(VI.15) attains	Adhigacchati (VI.15) X.10
Yāti	(XIII.8) goes	Yānti (VII.25; IX.7,25) XVIII.65, 68
Upaiti	(VIII.10) goes	Upetya (I.15;16 IX. 28,34)
	approaches, becomes fit for	Prapadyate (VII.14, 19; XIII.18)
	becomes (of like nature)	Āgataḥ (Sādharmyam) (III.10; IV.9).
	come	Vraja (XVIII. 66).
	dwell	Nivasiṣyasi (XII.8)
	easily obtain	Sulabhaḥ (VIII. 14)
	this supreme	Matparaḥ (II.61)
	goal is in me	Mayi Vartate (VI.31)

Thus there is no question that there is some union with the Puruṣottama as the goal of man's endeavours according to the *Gītā*; but it is quite careful never to use terms identifying the Puruṣottama with the liberated man, it is always a "dwelling in," "is in", "obtains" or "goes". This conclusion is to be contrasted with the passages speaking of the eternal (Brahma) as man's goal which are more numerous than the supreme (param) as the goal. These passages are listed below:—

Adhigacchati	attains (V.6)
gantavyam	to be attained (IV.24)
Sarvabhūtātma-bhūtātmā	whose self is self of all beings (V. 7)
Tadātmanaḥ	merged in that (V.17)
Tanniṣṭhaḥ	established in that
Brahmaṇi sthiṭaḥ	established in Brahma (V.20)
Brahmabhūtaḥ	become brahma (V.24; VI. 27; 18.54)
Brahma saṁsparśam	contact with brahma (VI.28)
Brahmabhūyāya	fit to become brahma (XIV. 25, XVIII.53)
Brahma sampadyate	becomes brahma (XIII.31)
Āpnoti, Avāpnoti	obtains. (XVIII. 50,56)

By the frequency of the terms implying becoming or an intimate oneness, we can fairly well conclude that the individual becomes the Brahma or Īśvara, the eternal. The contexts speaking of the supreme, the Puruṣottama, however, never use such intimate terms. This can mean one or both of two things either the *Gītā* maintains a pantheism and not a monism, i.e., there is some difference between the Puruṣottama and the individual at the end of his becoming; or else the *Gītā* merely holds that due to the akṣara nature of the Brahma there is unity or homogeneity, whereas the Puruṣottama cannot be spoken of in such terms simply because its dynamity and transcendental nature does not admit of unity or oneness in this simple mathematical, homogeneous sense. Which one of these alternatives we are to choose, while vitally important to our concept of self, is rather difficult to decide. We can note, however, that Kṛṣṇa as the Puruṣottama claims to be the creator, preserver and source of dissolution of all beings and they enter (Yānti) him at the close of a Brahmic day. If all beings eventually enter Brahma to be reborn again at the beginning of a Brahmic day, then the sage or Mahātmā must "enter" him in an entirely different way. Moreover, in a very interesting passage he says : "udārāḥ sarva evaite, jñānī vātmaiva me mataḥ; āsthitaḥ sa hi yuktātmā māmevānuttamāṃ gatim"— "Noble are all these, but I hold the wise as verily Myself; he, self united, is fixed in me, the highest path" (VII.18). This passage is interesting in two ways, first he uses the verb "is" and the derivative "yukta" or fixed, joined; and second he says the one "fixed in me" as "the highest path". Thus implying that whatever the Union with the Puruṣottama it is not a static union but a dynamic one such that when fixed in me there is still a "path". If this latter passage is considered along with the difference in "entering" of the mahātmā and the dissolved beings. then we could perhaps at best say that the *Gītā* intended an ultimate monism and not a dualism between individual-cum-brahma and the Puruṣottama. Yet we must admit that overall the *Gītā* really remains vague on matters of eschatology and any definite conclusions can only be speculation.

We can conclude our study of the *Gītā*'s concept of self by recognising that the three concepts of self in the *Gītā* are actually one loosely knit concept which is subsumed under the Puruṣottama as that towards which all beings merge. Exactly what this mergence entails must remain unanswered but the ultimate identity of the Brahma and the "Realised" individual is unequivocal. We shall have occasion in the concluding portion of the present work to even more critically examine such words as "Unity", "Oneness", etc. when considering these terms in the broader context of the whole early Vedānta literature.

CHAPTER IV

CONCLUSIONS TO THE STUDY OF THE GĪTĀ

A. *Summary of the Concept of Self*:

We found three senses of self in the *Gītā*—individuals, Īśvara or Brahma and the Puruṣottama. These three were loosely summed up under the Purṣottama. This summing up does not reduce the former into the latter, for the *Gītā* seems to want to maintain that there will be always individuals and Brahma (XI. 12); but in a teleological manner the Puruṣottama is the goal of the becoming of the other two.

In keeping with this teleological orientation there were a wide range of levels among the individuals which were summed up under the two heads either demonic (asura) or divine (deva). In the one case we had the individual doing work in terms of lower karma and worship of the type found in the Vedic ritual (II.42-46). According to the dramatic orientation of the *Gītā* this is Arjuna before coming to the battle-field. The *Gītā* starts, then, with the assumption that eventually such a limited view of self and environment will come to bankruptcy by the uniting character of its own categories, as Arjuna's despondency shows. Yet another sense of individuality is set before us as the perfected individual, the vibhūti, the traiguṇyātīta. Through an effort of combined karma and Jñāna and with a bhakti orientation, the individual is brought to recognize the self as brahma, whereupon the guṇas lose their hold upon him; and he becomes the sage, the mahātmā.

Both senses of individuality are built around a concept of Prakṛti largely in the Sāṅkhyan manner of action cast in terms of the three guṇas. Associated with this prakṛti is Kṣara or mutable Puruṣa, which is roughly the soul or jīva bound to the body and making the rounds of death and birth. Instead of following the Sāṅkhya and making Prakṛti merely extend only to this, the *Gītā* extends the notion of Prakṛti and gives a higher meaning to it. This higher Prakṛti is the supporting life element. In the case of the individual, when he becomes perfected he raises kṣara Puruṣa, bound as it is to the guṇas, out of lower Prakṛti and so becomes akṣara Puruṣa or immutable (still embodied, however, in lower Prakṛti). This, then, is the nature of the vibhūti, the muni or jñānī. The *Gītā* seems to say eschatologically that the realized individual upon death becomes Brahma in dropping lower Prakṛti, the physical body, and taking up the higher Prakṛti which is the impersonal support, life force, for all phenomenality and roughly that Rāmānuja calls the body of God (RB VII. 8-12). Because Brahma is conceived as both Puruṣa and Prakṛti one does not arrive at an unmanifest Brahma nor to a pure being. Rather Brahma is conceived as the immutable, the unchanging substratum on which all change is dependent and derivative, the one universal self from which all the mutable individuals derive their sense of individuality. Although it would seem that such an unchanging-changing dichotomy would require no further concept to complete it, we can see that the *Gītā* needs a third, a Puruṣottama, insofar as it maintains that, although immutable and both manifest and unmanifest, Brahma is in the end impermanent. "The worlds up to Brahma are impermanent; they come and they go" claims the text. The one touch of cosmology in the *Gītā* is this concept of Brahmic day and night, periods of going forth and withdrawal. The Puruṣottama is the third concept supplying a foundation for this mutable-immutable couple and the brahmic day and night. The *Gītā* does not cast the Puruṣottama, however, merely as a transcendent impersonal ground for the mutable and immutable worlds, but goes further and adds a personal element, the Puruṣottama as a transpersonal personality which is active in both worlds as the avatāra in this world and Brahma in the other. This is the case in addition to being both impersonally their ground (prakṛti), and as inner guide "seated in the hearts of all" (Puruṣa). This results in a similar perspective to the worlds as the Turīya concept in the Upaniṣads, i.e., from the standpoint of the mutable world there are two worlds, this world and the unchanging ground, the immutable world; and from standpoint of the Brahma there is only the immutable and the ephemeral impermanent mutable world. From the standpoint of the Puruṣottama like that of the turīya there is supposedly only *one world.* The self of this world is ultimately the supreme self. To what degree this supreme self is the end of the development of the other concepts, the *Gītā* did not seeme ither consistent in putting forth or even ultimately concerned except to teach Arjuna that in terms of his immediate awareness of self there was not the identity in the Puruṣottama that there was in the immutable Brahma. Whether this less intimate union was due to the nature of the Puruṣottama itself or a less monistic feeling in the teachings there was little ground to decide.

B. Critical Reflections :

One naturally first wishes to know whether the situation in which Arjuna finds himself and forms the basis of the *Gītā*'s inquiry into self is a conceivable situation; that is, "does the *Gītā's*, inquiry into self really start from what we normally think self to be or from some hypothetical basis which would make the self a conditional construct"? In the latter category we have only to recall Hobbes' or Locke's philosophy to be furnished an example. Our ordinary common sense view of self is that of a personality; what we might call an "Atom" of awareness around which an alien environment revolves, containing among the objects apparently other like atoms of personality. This conception clearly is the basis of individuality with which the *Gītā* starts, as can be seen from the ethical considerations Arjuna uses in rejecting his duty. He has conflicting ethical commitments, on the one hand to family support and on the other hand to fight these same kinsmen. Such crises situations point out the inadequacy if not the incompleteness of such a concept of self. The *Gītā* as a drama has made the most of this situation, and upon the ruins of this common sense concept is built the above metaphysical structure regarding self. We note in support of the *Gītā*'s basis of inquiry that such crises situations viewed as crises in one's sense of self are not peculiar to the *Gītā*, and the reader of Kirkegaard[1] is undoubtedly familar with such crises situations as times of fundamental reorganisation in the concept of self; and Arjuna indeed is passing in Kirkegaard's language from the ethical stage to the religious stage. Even more familiar is Descartes' familiar crisis which gave birth to his system of thought.

1. *Stages on Life's way.*

The *Gītā*, then, starts on familiar lines in its inquiry of self. We note another significant factor in Arjuna's crisis, namely, that he becomes despondent and rejects everything which before was the core of his sense of self-duty, family, etc. In this observation we have an indication perhaps why immediate monism, although not found in as many contexts as other thought in the Prasthānatraya, held such a strong sway over later thinking, i.e., the neti-neti process is the natural outcome of the bankruptcy of the atomistic concept of self. Thus the individual feels an atom of personality from his identification with family and environment in general; but when this fails he becomes aware of another sense of self which is also common experience, namely, that permanent unchanging feeling of self which tells him that is the same self that experienced childhood, youth, marriage, etc. This is the introspection common to many philosophies ultimately leading to an unchanging universal being as the only reality. The philosophy of Paramenides might be a very simple example compared to the philosophy of change of Heraclitus or better the comparison between Advaita Vedānta and the Central concept of change in Buddhism. At first such conflicts between change and the unchanging are often conceived by projection into the environment cosmologically as the manifest and unmanifest. It seems another step to analyse the manifest to see that more fundamentally it is a conflict between the changing and the unchanging in sentiment beings. The *Gītā* has made this step over the Upaniṣads; and the changing and unchanging is the basis of the concept of self it builds from Arjuna's despondency.

The philosophical inquiry into self, then, starts where common sense, bankrupt, leaves off. One has the choice of building a metaphysical system explaining self, much as Aristotle does in his *De Anima* or he has the choice of pragmatically building from experience. It is this latter choice which establishes the *Gītā* as a religious text perhaps more than a philosophical one. The teachings on self purport to be the experience of one who claims to be the supreme, the Avatāra, the divine incarnation. The reader on the other hand must take these teachings as revealed writings and follow them, only consequently finding a basis for them in his own experience.

Perhaps to supply this basis till experience can be had of the teachings is the reason for the bhakti element which so distinguishes the *Gītā* from the other of the Prasthānatraya. Since our purpose is a philosophical one, this posture to the *Gītā* will not suffice; indeed our job was mainly to develop the metaphysics of self in the *Gītā*. In this difference of interest perhaps can be seen the ultimate failure of all philosophical attempts to investigate a religious text; for the *Gītā* by a subtle combination, characteristic of the dialogue form, teaches a concept of self embodying a complicated metaphysics; and at the same time embeds it in the concrete problems of the interlocuoter. This dialogue form, however, suffers from the defect, as we found in our analysis, of aiming specifically at Arjuna's problems. This is to say, although a quite complex metaphysics is developed, only that part relevant to Arjuna's and man's immediate problems is at all made clear. Thus we found the development of the individual into the muni and eventually into brahman quite clearly amplified along with a quite definite sādhana of yoga (mind poise); but the rest of the metaphysics was not amplified, and was even made vague in a language which refused consistency and definite concepts; thereby the reader was left indefinite on exactly in what way there was a development of all becoming into the supreme. This eschatological vagueness is not limited to the *Gītā*, however, and we found a similar inadequacy in the transcendental concept of Brahman in the Upaniṣads. We shall try to explore the purpose for this vagueness further in the General conclusions. Suffice it here to recognize that it is the heavy weight placed upon experience by the early Vedānta which seems to demand an experience of eschatological matters not a metaphysical grasp. If we understand the basis and limitations of the *Gītā*'s inquiry into self, let us proceed to evaluate its concept of self according to the logical criteria set up in the introduction. When we consider the three aspects of the concept of self-individuals, Brahman and the Supreme, there is a clear increase in completeness in the concept. Thus the bankruptcy of extreme individuality leads to a more complete sense of self because of its position as the unchanging support of the former state. Moreover, as Monism shows, it is capable of being put forth as the only reality. This is to say that while change might require an unchanging support, the reverse is not the case. The unchanging can only support in a seeming gratuitous manner change, not requiring itself change. The giveness of the changing world however, seems to impress the *Gītā* enough that it cannot make it just phenomenal as Vedānta and Sāṅkhya so made it and so a third concept is required when the change is taken as more than an adhyāsa upon the unchanging as the monist so takes it. This third concept completes these two conflicting ones and gives both a telos. The completeness of the third concept is such as to answer most any question asked of it of an ethical, metaphysical or soteriological nature. It is only in eschatological questions that any sense of incompleteness is felt. This is not an incompleteness in that eschatological problems have no place in the concept, but only that there is vagueness surrounding its answer which seems largely intentionally conceived and also partly perhaps that our language breaks down to the point contradictory predicates must be used to convey anything at all.

While the Puruṣottama like the transcendental Brahman of the Upaniṣads seems complete enough to answer any question that might be asked of a concept of self, it is apparent that it is complete only because it includes all of imaginable reality ultimately within its scope. Unfortunately once we reject the most common sense idea of self, we have virtually no other standard than our introspection and experience by which to judge whether the concept, in order to be complete, has overstepped the limits which we would ultimately wish to assign to the sense of self.

We can at best only consider its coherence psychologically and logically to make certain that it is not, in its attempt to be complete, merely a hotch-potch of contradictory elements. This factor of coherence, we remember, was the difficulty we found in the Upaniṣadic concept of self. Logically the two elements of changing or mutable self and the immutable or unchanging self do not literally contradict one another such as the manifest and unmanifest did in the Upaniṣads. This is to say it is not like predicating both yellow and blue to the same subject. Unless we can show the self in some other manner to be a loose knit organization, we must admit that both change and permanency cannot be logically predicated of self in the same sense without being openly contradictory. Here, however, we seem to be able to make the distinction Hegel seems to have made[1] between an abstract system and a factual system which is being analysed. In the latter where there are statements of facts and statements of possibility based upon fact, we have a dialectical analysis and more exactly the law of contradiction is applicable. Thus if we said "the bird is yellow" "the bird is blue", although the statement has factual components namely bird and colour, nevertheless the concept of colour prevents both being predicated of the same subject, whereas change and permanence do not immediately strike one in that same way when predicated of self; and indeed as we noted above, change may well require an unchanging substratum. Therefore, in our case this dialectical synthesis is exactly what the concept in its attempt for completeness is purported to do. We can conclude, then, that logically conceived, the concept of self is loosely coherent in a dialectical fashion when the indicated synthesis is achieved. The *Gītā*'s concept of self, like the Upaniṣads, however, purports to be a pragmatic treatment. Therefore, we might go further and ask : Is it psychologically coherent, i.e., can this synthesis really be made experientially. It is clear that such experiences of an unchanging and changing self cannot stand to one another as thesis and antithesis since both really are experiences which when one is having, seem to have equal claim to the same 'I' and the same "World". Nevertheless we do not have both experiences at the same time; and they do seem to oppose one another in their import. Such "tensions" in experience are not uncommon, however, and may be what Pascal was implying when he said "man is a mean between infinity and nothingness".[2] To overcome such "tensions", however, it seems impossible in terms of subject-object consciousness, common to the mind and intellect. We

1. Hegel, *Phenomologie of Mind*, 454, also "Wer Denkt Abstract" in *Vermische Schriften*, II. 402.

2. Parcal, *Pensee*, 72.

must conclude that unless one can achieve some "insight" or "Immediate experience", the concept of self in the *Gītā* remains a distinctive couple of the changing self and unchanging self, even though logically such a synthesis seems conceivable. In the final conclusions when considering the relations between the concept of self in our texts and later Indian philosophy we shall see that it is the failure of coherence, perhaps which leads to the bifurcation into the darśanas in an attempt to find intellectual satisfaction.

The *Gītā*'s concept of self is not by any means unique. In western philosophy in Leibnitz' monadism we have hints at such a transcendental synthesis into a monism, insofar as the monads may ultimately be conceived analogously "as perspectives would be of the whole city"[1]. This idea was taken up and vastly overhauled in recent times by Whitehead whose theory of God very strongly resembles the *Gītā*'s.[2] Whitehead also maintains an immediate pluralism and consequent or ultimate monism. The German idealism especially in F. Schlegel[3] with his finite, infinite and return of the finite to the infinite carries a similar thought to that of the *Gītā*. We can only note, however, that like the German idealism which ended by being thrown over for more realistic systems of Fewerbach, Marx and Schliermachar, so the *Gītā*'s synthesis seems to have been thrown over by Buddhism. Most of these European systems like the *Gītā* appeal to intuition, and use a very vague descriptive language when passing beyond the opposition between these elements of experience to make their synthetic attempts.

C. *Monism, Theism and the Concept of Self*:

There have been many commentaries of the *Gītā* both by Western and Indian philosophers. Before closing let us discuss them briefly and examine the *Gītā* again in the light of the most common of their criticisms. Most of these philosophers either do not take up the latter chapters where the bulk of the

1. See Leibnitz, *Monadology*, transl. Oxford (1925) pp. 47-50, 75, 243, cf. also pp. 84-5.

2. Whitehead, *Process and Reality*, Part 1, Ch. III, cf. Northrop and Cross Whitehead, *Analogy*, p. 599, also pp. 49, 523, 572-873.

3. *Philosophische Verlasung*, edited by Windishmann, discussed by Windelband, *History of Philosophy*, London (1923), p. 617.

metaphysical description is given (what we have termed the description of self) or at least seem to find little controversy there. Most of the difference seems to be over the earlier monistic passages (V. 6-29, VI. 4-26) and the later theistic passages. Some take one or the other of these elements as the "teachings of the *Gītā*'s or the "original" teachings of the *Gītā*. Much of this difficulty has been bypassed in our study by basing the discussions of the Mārgas or the Sādhana upon the metaphysics in spite of the greater interest in the Mārgas shown in the *Gītā* itself. This mechanism bypassed the difficulty found in the theistic language used by Kṛṣṇa when speaking as the Puruṣottama as compared to the third person metaphysical language.

Let us, then, investigate these theories of others to see in what way the theism and monism have been reconciled. First to consider the main Western commentators on the *Gītā*, the following list gives an example of the variety of opinions on the subject:—

1. *Otto* (*Original Gītā*) : Gītā originally part of an epic poem later worked over by doctrinists and theists. Thinks Bhakti original element and not in Vedic tradition. Sāṅkhya, Yoga and Vedānta elements later.
2. *Garbe* (*Indian Antiquity*) 47 (1918), (Sup.) : Originally the *Gītā* taught Sāṅkhya-Yoga which Kṛṣṇa-Vāsudeva cult associated till 300 B.C. when Brahmanized.
3. *Hopkins* (JRAS (1905) p. 384-9) : Kṛṣṇa version of an old Viṣṇu poem and in turn first a non-sectarian work, perhaps an Upaniṣad.
4. *Farquhar* (Outlines of the general literature of India, (1920) Section 95 : Upaniṣad worked up into *Gītā*).
5. *Holtzmann*: (Garbe, *loc. cit*) : Original *Gītā*, a pantheistic poem a philosophico-poetical episode of the *Mahābhārata*.

1. Esp. chapters VII-XII.

6. *Hill*, W.D.P. (Intr. to Trans. of *Gītā*, Allen and Unwin, p. 21). "Some brilliant member of Vāsudeva cult worked up old and new material into *Gītā* quoting *Kaṭha Śvetāśvatara*.

The extreme diversity of opinion here leads one to expect much speculation to be involved. The two theories most developed which must be considered are those of Garbe and Otto; and indeed treatment of their theories will apply largely ipso-facto to the others. First Garbe thinks that own beliefs of Sāṅkhya, Yoga and the Vāsudeva cults regarding Kṛṣṇa are the original *Gītā*. He goes through the *Gītā* and separates out passages he believes to be later Vedāntic interpolations. Belvalkar in his *Lectures on Vedānta Philosophy*[1] ably criticises Garbe's selection and shows it to be gratituous leaving much which has equal claim to being Brahmanic. We need not repeat this criticism here, because on a more fundamental level we can recognize a basic error. Garbe assumes the 'Sāṅkhya' and 'Yoga' of the *Gītā* are systematic terms. In our discussions we have shown rather that they were Upaniṣadic. Thus the word 'Yoga' occurs in the *Gītā* in the following meanings :

1. 'Yoga' as Karma—Ch. II.
2. 'Yoga' as Merger with the Supreme.
3. 'Yoga' as mind poise.
4. 'Yoga' as disconnection from union with pain (VI.23). The only meaning at all close to the darśanic meaning is serial No. 3 which is also found in *Kaṭhopaniṣad* and moreover is equilibrium not "Vṛtti Nirodhana" as in Patañjali. Moreover, 'Sāṅkhya' means something closer to scientific or natural knowledge and indeed not anything like the darśanic use as can be seen in examining the passages putting forth what was later to be the Sāṅkhyan cosmology (see Chap. XIII especially); we find 'Sāṅkhya' never used. Therefore, we can say that whatever the mode of composition of the *Gītā*, it was not a Sāṅkhya-Yoga treatise. By this criticism and Belvalker's, Garbe's theory can be seen to have no ground. Otto's theory is much more difficult to deal with because the theistic element in the *Gītā* is, with little doubt, characteristic of Bhāgavata cult as most agree.[2]

1. PP. 89-101.
2. See works 1-6 listed above; also footnote 1.

His idea of later systematic interpretation, however, falls under the same criticism as of Garbe above. Actually the same criticism Belvalkar uses against Garbe, that of gratituousness of selection, also might be made against Otto. Thus, as we can see from the chart of the Mārgas on P. 200 and comparing it to Otto's *Original Gītā* (I,II.I. 13,20,22,24-37, XI.4,8-12,14,17, 19-36, 41,51, XVIII. 58-61, 66, 72, 73) we see much of the earlier portion of Bhakti in the Gītā's eliminated; but more definite than that is the use of "Buddhi yoga" in Ch.X.10, and also X. 11, which hints at grace bringing Jñāna and Mukti. Both of these passages should be eliminated as they require much of the intervening passages in Ch. V and VI to be intelligible. The same applies to Ch. XVIII. 62 which is even more close to Otto's theory than 61 which he retains as one can see :

> "The lord dwelleth in the hearts of all beings, O Arjuna! by his illusion-power, causing all beings to revolve, as though mounted on a māyā-machine" (XVIII.61).
>
> "Flee unto him for shelter with all thy being O Bhārata; by his grace thou shalt obtain supreme peace and the everlasting dwelling place" (XVIII.62).

We can see that Otto's theory is inadequate as presented, whatever the merit of the idea of the original *Gītā*. As remarked in the introduction[1], little can be said of the possibility and form of the *Gītā* in the two earlier workings of the *Mahābhārata*, the *Bhārata* and *the Jaya*. We can say with some conviction now that the *Gītā* is more a synthesis and elaboration of the Upaniṣads than a darśanic intercessor. Before passing on to the Indian philosophers a few words on Hill's idea of the *Gītā* being a "patch work" must be said. Hill gives[2] three reasons for the *Gītā* not being a unitary work :

1. Its metrical form.
2. It is trying to reconcile too many different points of view.
3. Differing meanings given to the same words.

1. See p. 127.
2. Hill, W.D.P., *Bhagvad Gītā*, p. 19 f.

The first point is only made based upon the assumption that the *Gītā* was completed after the metrical form no longer was used. The second makes the above assumption of systematic orientation and overlooks the composer's duty to the plot to give Arjuna a choice. The third is much more formidable criticism, the word 'yoga' above being such an example of different meanings assigned to the same word. Hill, however, is not definite in pointing out such cases; and at best one can only observe that such a change of meaning might be just the poetic license which the Sanskrit poets took to make their works rich in allegory and shades of meaning. The *Gītā* is not an exact piece of philosophical discourse. Therefore, merely different meanings assigned to the same work do not reduce its value as a reconciliation of beliefs unless some of these meanings could be proved contradictory or much later usage in *time*, which Hill does not attempt to do. In general then we say that western philosophers have tended by and large to miss the *Gītā's* dramatic position, and at the same time fail to appreciate the Upaniṣadic leanings of the teachings, both of which gave rise to their feelings of heterodoxy.

The Indian philosophers on the whole are oriented in the opposite direction, attempting to reconcile the theistic and monistic elements into one teaching of the *Gītā*. Because an exhaustive treatment of all commentators on the *Gītā* would be impossible we shall limit our consideration to six : Śaṅkara, Madhva, Rāmānuja, Dnyaneshwar, Tilak and Aurobindo. These six will just about exhaust the theories of the other commentators. Śaṅkara's *Śārīraka Bhāṣya* might be treated best by considering Śaṅkara's central doctrine of the double truth theory. For once we appreciate this theory, Śaṅkara's whole commentary seems to follow, largely along this line. This theory basically said that there were two standards of truth Vyāvahārika and Pāramārthika, the first is applicable to the Brahman with the adhyāsa of the multiple phenomenal world and the other when this adhyāsa is sublated to the Nirguṇa Brahman. This essentially is saying that, so long as we are in māyā, the reports of the senses are true; but to the Jñānī, to one who has pierced Māyā, the unitariness of Brahman as the sole reality is true indeed. Thus in the *Gītā Bhāṣya*, as in the

Upaniṣad Bhāṣyas, there is the "higher and the lower science" for Śaṅkara. The theistic passages advocating worship, sacrifice and devotion to the Puruṣottama along with the passages devoted to Karma are for the "weak minds", and the monistic Passages are for those already fit to take up the path of Jñāna, those whose vāsanās have been worked out. An example of his use of the double truth standard is the elaboration of the 10th and 11th chapter without taking up the serious difficulties it offers his thought. Thus the dual standard of truth allows him simply to develop these passages inimical to his own conclusions as only of the lower truth. It is true the *Gītā* has a preference in the integral path, but this is not solely Jñāna which Śaṅkara seems to support. The passage of the *Gītā* IV. 11 might illustrate another way in which he uses the *Gītā* as a support for his own doctrine. "However men approach me even do I welcome them, for the paths men take from every side are mine" is typical of another approach to the *Gītā*'s difficult passages. Śaṅkara at this point says that all paths are mine means that, "knowledge is the highest, the only one granting liberation, others find only their selfish desires". That this is a highly gratituous addition to the passage and the context is obvious; and this represents largely the posture of all three Ācāryas to the *Gītā*, not one of exegesis solely but using the text to support their own doctrines. We can see, then, that Śaṅkara takes the monistic passages as the Gītā's teaching, claiming that the others are for those not prepared for Jñāna (II.49; VIII. 11). This is partially true in that the *Gītā* does teach all paths and even sets up a heirarchy of paths, but jñāna is not the preference of the *Gītā* as we have seen in our present discussion of the concept of self.

Rāmānuja's Śrī Bhāṣya on the whole seems to be more sensitive to the peculiarity of the monistic character of the teachings of the *Gītā*; but there are many places which seem to show that Rāmānuja's own theory, close though it may in some respect fit the *Gītā*'s conclusion, nevertheless is radically different from the metaphysics of the *Gītā*. One most important example is in his commentary on VII.47. Rāmānuja takes these passages to mean that lower Prakṛti is of jīva and higher Prakṛti is of God. This may seem to be our conclusion on the same points; but in VII. 8-12 he betrays his own theory which does not fit the passage or context. He says (VII.12) the bodies of individual Ātmans serve the purpose of their sustenance whereas God's body is only for Līlā; and moreover these Jīvas are viewed apparently as the body of God, (if this body soul concept here applies). Rāmānuja then agrees that the Ātmans each pervade the others that are not self (VI.8); and in 4 stages the Ātman reaches realisation of a state of common form-knowledge (VI.20) which is as close to monism as Rāmānuja reaches. Nevertheless the Ātman apparently is multiple and dissimilar (VI.8), because unlike the Ātman of God which has never been involved in Prakṛti, the Ātmans are imbedded in Prakṛti and only in knowledge in the state released from Prakṛti can the Ātman feel any equality (but not identity) with God. Such elaborate metaphysics can be seen to have its purpose in Rāmānuja's thoughts to justify Vaiṣṇava theism which is accomplished by forever making the Ātman different from God but equal. The *Gītā*, while not supporting the immediate monism of Śaṅkara, seems not to take the view of either Prakṛti or Ātman (presumably Akṣarakṣara Puruṣa) which Rāmānuja so does. Rāmānuja even quite often openly uses the text in similar system supporting attempts where definitely contrary. For example, in IX.9 where the *Gītā* establishes God as not bound to actions he supports in the world, Rāmānuja uses this to show that God stands aside from the cruelty of inequality; yet the Gītā is insistent elsewhere (IV.13) that varṇa and karma are god-given and so openly contradicts this view of Rāmānuja. We can see that in the end Rāmānuja, while taking a broad view of Bhakti, supports the theistic passages not fully appreciating the monistic ones or the metaphysics of Prakṛti which does not wholly correspond to Rāmānuja's view.

Madhva goes even further in support of the theistic passages and indeed under a dualistic metaphysics little else could be done. One verse shall suffice to show Madhva's commentary as an exposition of the *Gītā* (II.45) "Vedas deal with the Guṇas, be thou above these Guṇas, beyond the pair of opposites, ever steadfast in purity, careless of possessions full of self (Ātman)". Madhva distinguished as does Rāmānuja between

Ātman as God supreme, and Ātman the mind. He says; "Ātman is the God supreme, and to be possessed by him is to be devoted to him in the full facts that he is ever our master and lord. This is the flame of devotion which recognizes that God is ever our master and that we are his slaves, his absolute property. Such a life is Yoga". While the particular verse taken by itself would not prove or disprove Madhva's comment on it, the context is highly inimical to it; and indeed like Rāmānuja, Madhva seems to support his system on a manipulation of 'Ātman'.

Dnyaneshwar seems of all the commentators the most fruitful in his full appreciation of the place of the Yoga in the *Gītā*. We have already observed (see p.182) that the *Gītā* is vague on ultimate problems of metaphysics, and seems to say in the end that the nature of the Puruṣottama cannot be grasped by a metaphysical concept only by some immediate experience. The *Gītā*'s doctrine of "mind poise" is just the method the *Gītā* sets out as the way to acquire this "experience" and indeed forms also the core of Jñāna, Bhakti and Karma. Therefore, Dnyaneshwar in his sensitivity to "mind poise" also seems to be understanding the *Gītā's* doctrine in proper perspective. The one draw-back in the doctrines of Dnyaneshwar seems to be that in the metaphysical passages he seems to support the more extreme monism, which not only in the end fails to do justice to the theism but if our observations on the nature of Vijñāna in the Upaniṣadic discussion are correct, and the effort one makes colors the Vijñāna; then eschatologically Dnyaneshwar would end up with the same Nirguṇa Brahman as Śaṅkara which seems to be the case :[1]

"What is seen in the dream is found real only while the dream lasts, but on awaking there is nothing. So is this illusion (Māyā) which puzzles you. A blow given to a shadow does not cause a wound on the body".

Tilak seems to be one of the first Indian commentators to appreciate the most obvious point of the *Gītā*, its insistence upon Karma. In the introduction to *Gītā Rahasya* he says "The conclusion I have come to is that the *Gītā* advocates the

1. Dnyaneshwar, *Gītā Explained*, tr. by M. Subedar, p. 61.

performance of action in this world even after the actor has achieved the highest union with the supreme deity by Jñāna or bhakti". Outside of the observation in the body of our discussion that the individual did not achieve the highest union with the supreme according to the *Gītā* till after death and "coming unto me", outside of that one difference, this conclusion is largely the conclusion we have come to. Yet Tilak arrives at an interesting metaphysical conclusion that the Parabrahman of the *Gītā* is qualityless or 'nirguṇa' using the passages III. 27-9 to support his thesis. From the standpoint of the entire context of the *Gītā*, which we have tried to present above, this does not seem to be borne out, and indeed Tilak seems largely interested in putting forth the doctrine of Naiṣkarmya karma rather than dealing more broadly with the real soteriological import of the *Gītā* for which he falls back on Śaṅkara; yet this nirguṇa Brahman is hardly compatible with his Naiṣkarmya karma as the means. Tilak, however, has made a fundamental contribution in pointing out the broad context in which the *Gītā's* doctrine of mind poise is not-action done with an inner equilibrium, thus avoiding the Guṇas.

The one commentator on the *Gītā* who has given the fullest scope to the *Gītā's* many-sided teachings is undoubtedly Śrī Aurobindo. His *Essays on the Gītā* is in the strict sense, an independent work. This allows a greater degree of freedom of presentation than the more restricting Bhāṣya style. In Aurobindo we find practically all the elements so far expressed by the other commentators, the theism of Rāmānuja and Madhva with the former's līlā theory, the karma of Tilak and the Yoga of Dnyaneshwar. While not making a point of the dramatic requirement to present the paths to choose between, Aurobindo does try to present the integral path in its full scope. He recognises not only Tilak's Naiṣkarmya Karma but takes these elements into a soteriologically oriented bhakti-jñāna movement. It is this appreciation for both the more theistically oriented Sādhana and the more monistically oriented metaphysics which places Aurobindo's work in such a different light from the others. He seems to appreciate the language of contradiction the *Gītā* uses to present the Puruṣottama and actually pushes beyond it to present in his essays an elaborate metaphysics. This indeed would be the major criticism against Aurobindo. The much more elaborate metaphysics prevents the reader from knowing exactly how far he is presenting the teachings of the *Gītā* and how far he is putting forth his own philosophy; whatever it be, the *Gītā* clearly, as we have noted above, leaves a certain vagueness in the ultimate aspects of its metaphysics. By pushing into elaboration of this apparently neglected side of the *Gītā* Aurobindo is able to make such a synthetic attempt. The relative success of it, then, over the others and even to a degree over the teachings of the *Gītā* itself is this excursion and completion of the idea of monism, found in the latter chapters. Yet at the same time he does not depreciate the Yoga of mind poise, the Sādhana. Aurobindo's conclusion and largely the conclusions of the present work are well summed up in the following quotation from *Essays on the Gītā*[1] which points up the theism of the Sādhana and ultimately some "union" or "oneness" with the supreme as goal: "The mystery of our being implies necessarily a similar supreme mystery of the being of the Puruṣottama . . . It is not an exclusive impersonality of the absolute that is the highest secret. This highest secret is the miracle of a supreme person and apparent vast impersonal that are one, an immutable transcendent self of all things and a spirit that manifests itself here at the very foundation of the cosmos as an infinite and multiple personality acting everywhere".

1. American Edition, p. 490; Indian Edition, p. 531.

PART III

GENERAL CONCLUSIONS

CHAPTER I

THE CONCEPT OF SELF IN EARLY VEDĀNTA

A. The Individual:

Both the Upaniṣads and the *Gītā* started from the same common sense acceptance of self. In the Upaniṣads, we recall, this common sense acceptance was illustrated in the more Brāmaṇic portions where sacrifice, worship and "Vedic works" were enjoined. This was the self conceived as Puruṣa with its various analyses of organs and their deities. This concept in the Upaniṣads was in some places (especially the Brāhmaṇic portions) conceived in such positive terms that there is little doubt that it was put forth as a concept of self. It did serve the purpose of offering a psycho-physical analysis of self from which the more developed concepts started. In the *Gītā* this egocentric concept was roundly condemned in the form of the demonic man (Asura) and it was upon the ruins of this concept of self that the *Gītā* built its own concept. In both the *Upaniṣads* and the *Gītā* we find Brahman worshipped as God much as in the Madhva Master-Slave relation as mentioned above.[1] Thus, Brahman is that which is not self but has some mysterious dominion over selves. In this attitude we find the Brāhmaṇa extolling of sacrifices and rituals and the condemned worship of the unintelligent for fruits, in the *Gītā* (II.43). This, then, is the egocentric basis for self in the Prasthānatraya carrying with it a simple non-teleological theism.

From this material there was in both the texts a broader sense of the individual presented. In the Upaniṣads there were two separate schools of thought branching off: The monism of Yājñavalkya where the developed individual is the one who has overcome desires etc. and has become sannyāsin. The other was the less monistic school which took the Kośa analysis of Puruṣa not as veils of ignorance over the only real Brahman but levels of development[2]. Thus in the Upaniṣads the more

1. See p. 221 ff.
2. See *Taittirīya Upaniṣad*, 2.

developed individual was the one who recognized the Ātman as self and felt this Ātman to be in bondage to the three States and death. The nature of this bondage was fully developed only in the *Gītā* using the guṇa theory which was set out but not developed in the Upanisads. Therefore, while the Upaniṣadic-developed individual was the Jñānī, the one who knew Ātman, for the *Gītā* the developed individual was the traiguṇyātīta.

There were more developed senses of individuality, conceived as one of the steps towards a goal which was termed differently Ātman-Brahman or Puruṣa and conceived roughly alike as the absolute, the foundation for all reality. Most of the ensuing differences in the conception of these higher senses of self seemed to revolve around different conceptions of reality. In all cases, however, this Brahman as we have termed it was viewed not theistically as the earlier Vedic material so conceived it, but as the fountainhead of the self and after death the individual went to, was absorbed in or dwelled in this Brahman.

B. Brahma: The Manifest and Unmanifest Brahman:

We have observed that once the egocentric sense of self became bankrupt some concept of Universal self enters. While the individual is still in the body this necessitated the idea of a universal self that "resided in the hearts of all"[1], what in the Upaniṣads was termed Ātman and in a slightly broader sense the manifest Brahman. Here, in the Upaniṣads, the Brahman was taken as creator, preserver and source of dissolution of all creation. Roughly this is the pantheism found not only in some of the earlier mantras of the *Rgveda* but also brought out in many of the Upaniṣads especially the *Chāndogya*. The pañcakośa analysis came to its full stature here when, for instance, in the *Taittirīya*[2] the culmination of the growth through the various Kośas was bliss in the ether of the heart. Thus the manifest Brahman as a concept of self does not negate individuality, but merely says that after "knowing" (in the sense of Vijñāna) this Brahman there is no more birth uniting one to being an individual. This pantheistic universal self, we

1. See *Gītā*, XV. 15.
2. II. 7; IV. 6.

remember, seemed to suffer the difficulty of all pantheism of not being able to explain in what manner the Brahman could be both individual and multiple yet universal and unitary in its own being. The various "heart" concepts were the Upaniṣad's contribution. Largely because of this feeling of incompleteness the manifest Brahman was not widely supported and tended to be a step towards the transcendental Brahman.

Another school of thought also sprang from the earlier Brahmanic material in the Upaniṣads. This was first put forth by Yājñavalkya in the *Bṛhadāraṇyaka Up.* Disavowing interest in cosmological problems, it sought to understand self by a total negation of all mutable activity. This view advocated removal of the coverings over the Brahman, which in itself was aloof and actionless. Brahman was the true nature of self and what one reached when "knowing" Ātman. We mentioned the direct negation of egocentricism above (see p. 223) as the natural reaction to the bankruptcy of the common sense view of self, and so the unmanifest Brahman was absolute self "one without a second". Therefore only by dropping all activity, all sense of association with the waking world could one attain the unmanifest Brahman, a state analogous to deep sleep.

Even though the Monists seemed to have rejected the cosmological interests of the early brahmanic portions and the manifest Brahman school, nevertheless in conceiving self as a rejection of the egocentric self, they cast it in terms of unmanifest; and this opposition between the manifest and unmanifest appeared to be an open one which was difficult to bridge without cosmology. The *Gītā*, on the other hand, seems to have made a step beyond the Upaniṣads in casting Brahman as both manifest and unmanifest, and also disavowing cosmology as a basis for understanding the Universal self. The *Gītā* worked with the phenomenon of change and the unchanging, familiar to all beings with a sense of self. Since the idea of change more clearly required an unchanging substratum than either the manifest or the unmanifest required each other, then we can see that the schism between an absolutely aloof and unitary Brahman and a universal active brahman was by-passed. Therefore, the place of the individual was much expanded over the Upaniṣads where he seemed at best only to occupy the position of a means to liberation. In the *Gītā*, then, the individuals in the mutable world have as their ultimate sense of self not simply a manifest or unmanifest Brahman but an immutable Puruṣa which is both the aloof Brahman which the monists invoked by their process of neti-neti, as well as the manifest Brahman underlying individuality. This contrast between the world of individuals and the immutable world of Brahman served to focus the conflict between the two orders back on the individual where by and large in the Upaniṣads the conflict had been between the manifest and unmanifest brahman. In the *Gītā* this interest in the world of individuals is focused dramatically on the concept of the Avatāra. The puruṣottama, or supreme, is vitally interested in and a part of the mutable world. We can see, then, that Brahman of the *Gītā* is lying across both of the Upaniṣadic concepts, more nearly approximates the experience of an unchanging self which is in some way involved in yet unchanged by the experiences of our changing immediate consciousness.

In keeping with this broader sense of universal self, the *Gītā* puts forth a much broader programme of possible paths of development since one was not enjoined to remove all distinctions (Jñāna) nor solely the more active taking on of universal qualities (karma, bhakti). In so doing one did not eliminate either the changing or the unchanging in his nature. From what was said in the first part regarding the nature of Vijñāna, it is apparent that if the nature of the effort made, conditions the entire nature of the insight, then this broader conception of Brahman is much more likely to prevent the one-sided rejection of either pole of the experience of changing and the unchanging.

C. *The Turīya-Brahman and the Puruṣottama*:

Both the Turīya-Brahman and the Puruṣottama are obviously synthetic attempts in the Prasthānatraya. It attempts to hold together people of different schools and to patch up the schism between the apparent diversities in the Śruti. Although what these two concepts summed up differs considerably, as we found in the last section, it seems that there was much similarity between these transcendental concepts of self. The Upaniṣadic

Turīya-Brahman tied together three diverse concepts of self in the Upaniṣads, the Puruṣa or individual, the Ātman-Brahman or universal self and the unmanifest Brahman. The transcendental concept of self was found all through the Upaniṣads, although the *Māṇḍūkya* and *Īśa* we found were two Upaniṣads consciously making the attempt to synthesize the divergent elements. The three-fold analysis of the *Māṇḍūkya* perhaps most clearly illustrates the nature of the synthesis. Swami Chinmayananda[1], a modern popular exponent of Śaṅkara's teachings gives the following tabular summary:

Mantras & Om:	Padas of self: Microcosm:	Macrocosm	State	Consciousness.	Enjoyment.	Place of
A	Vaiśvānara 19 parts	Virāṭ 7parts	waking	outer	gross	right eye
U	Taijasa 19 parts	Hiraṇya garbha 7 limbs	dream	inner	subtle	mind (manas)
M	Prājña	Sarveśvara	deep	homogeneous	bliss	heart lotus

Turīya Brahman Amantra

From this table, the synthesis is apparent and of a cosmo-psychological character revolving around the three states of consciousness in man, the waking state as the individual or the Puruṣa, the dream as the dipolar Ātman and the link between the Puruṣa and the unmanifest Brahman of the sleep state. This synthesis around "om" gave us even less to work with than the *Gītā's* Puruṣottama. The conclusion we arrived at in the first part was that the Turīya Brahman was the underlying reality penetrating all three states, making each an aspect or aṁśa of the turīya. The Turīya-Brahman then is a synthesis of the three just as in the case of the individual his self is a synthesis of body, mind and soul. The disadvantage of the concept was that it was "unknowable" in the language of the text, i.e., only through insight would the nature of this transcendental Brahman be understood; and this insight was not obtainable solely through effort. Not having any intellectual

1. *Māṇḍūkya Kārikā, p.* 28.

guide, one was inclined to view this Brahman as impersonal, simply the absolute, which like Om was wholly different than its components, i.e., A, U or M; yet very definitely the Kośa analysis represented an ontological structure in some way representative of the path to the "knowledge" of Turīya-Brahman.

In the case of the Puruṣottama, on the other hand, the synthesis was much simpler—a mutable world of individuals and immutable world of Brahman. These two as we have already seen formed more of a couple than the disjunction of the above three. The Puruṣottama like the Turīya is viewed as making "one world" out of the two divergent ones and indeed Om is an analogy, used by the *Gītā* also[1]. Thus it is plainly evident that both the Upaniṣads and the *Gītā* were working with similar conceptions and similar purposes and similar experiences. The *Gītā's* synthesis is simple, because of its being taken out of the cosmological context it was cast in the Upaniṣads; but more than that, there is an intellectual criterion by which to understand its synthesis and that is the Avatāra. The Puruṣottama descended into human form to restore dharma. In the *Gītā's* synthesis, then, there is no possibility of taking the Puruṣottama as impersonal as was the case in the Upaniṣads. In this sense the Puruṣottama is more of a synthesis than that of the Upaniṣads; for all Upaniṣadic attempts at synthesis of the divergent trends of thought agreed in their leaving out Bhakti and personality as an element. This is to say, the individual was part of the synthesis only in his essential nature. The *Gītā's* synthesis includes this personal element precisely because the *Gītā's* conception of matter was broader; and indeed one could not contrast the "phenomenal" with the "noumenal" because matter was divinised; and rather there were only grades of the "phenomenal". We might say, then, that the *Gītā's* synthesis expands the sense of personality through its conception of Bhakti and the Avatāra. The Puruṣottama, then, is at least a personality but more than that he is a transpersonal personality.

While the *Gītā's* synthesis was much simpler and clearer

1. VIII. 8, IX. 17; XVII. 23, 24.

through the intellectual basis offered by the Avatāra nevertheless it is precisely this which offers a handicap. The impersonal tone of the Upaniṣad synthesis left no doubt that the synthesis ultimately led to a monism, to a union between Brahman and Ātman. In the *Gītā*, however, the theistic language offered a formidable barrier for deriving any conclusion as to final deliverance. We did speculate that from its metaphysics an ultimate monism was intended; but the theistic language Kṛṣṇa uses makes it difficult to arrive at any definite conclusion.

D. Results of the Study of Self:

If this is the nature of the concept of self in our two texts, then we can come to some definite conclusions regarding the nature of the texts themselves. In the case of the Upaniṣads we can say that the teachings regarding self indicate roughly four major schools of thought:

1. The Theistic school—of the earlier Brahmanic material. Foundation of some schools of Vedānta and more realistic schools. The self is viewed as egocentric individual.

2. The Pantheistic school—The universal self ultimately the manifest Ātman-Brahman. Sāṅkhya, the more theistic Vedānta schools largely come from this.

3. The Monistic school—The absolute self as the unmanifest Brahman—Advaita.

4. The school of ultimate Monism—The transcendental Brahman as the inclusive self, the self aloof, unmanifest and the self active and manifest.

Although these four schools are often found expressed in one Upaniṣad, some sort of rough classification of the Upaniṣads according to these schools could be made:

(1) Theistic — *Aitareya*, *Kena*

(2) Pantheistic — *Chāndogya*, *Taittirīya*, *Praśna*

(3) Monistic — *Bṛhadāraṇyaka*, *Muṇḍaka*

(4) Ultimate Monism — *Īśa*, *Māṇḍūkya*, *Kaṭha*

Thus, although highly gratuitous, the above classification tries to represent the predominant interest in the Upaniṣads. The existence of the four schools indicated that even at the time of the closing of the Vedas there were many schools of thought all using the same Weltanschaungs and roughly the same concepts.

The *Gītā*, coming at the closing of the Upaniṣadic period attempted as some of the later Upaniṣads also did, to fuse these schools of thought into one system. Just as the Upaniṣads brought metaphysical psychology to the Vedic thought, so the *Gītā* adds an element virtually foreign, in its form, to the *Upaniṣads*, that of the Avatāra by the Bhakti of the Bhāgavatas. Its synthesis was unequivocally more cogent than the Upaniṣadic attempts, yet the Bhakti element served to keep it as a devotional text and the philosophical schools seem to have by-passed it largely for the *Brahmasūtras* as the Vedic foundation for the darśanas. Thus the *Gītā*'s main failure lay in the ultimate splitting of the Sāṅkhya-Yoga-and Vedāntic trends in the Upaniṣads which the *Gītā*'s metaphysics tried to reconcile and this splitting up was perhaps aided by the *Gītā*'s more clear statement of each of these elements. The truth of this failure was seen in the lesser interest in the metaphysics of the *Gītā* in comparison to its Sādhana by philosophers even upto contemporary times. Some of the difficulty which led to the *Gītā*'s failure in metaphysics and the greater interest in the Sādhana portion could perhaps be laid to difficulties in the language discussing its metaphysics. Let us proceed to summarise the linguistic problems connected with the concept of self.

CHAPTER II

THE CONCEPT OF SELF AND THE LANGUAGE OF ITS EXPRESSION

A. *Negative Concepts and the Natuie of Brahman* :

We have already felt the inadequacy in our texts of language as a tool to express the concepts which claim an intuitive origin. Perhaps this is characteristic of much of metaphysics and theology. Some metaphysicians and theologians admit this and are aware of the inadequacy of language to express the thought they wish to convey (see Aurobindo, *Life Divine* p. 28). More often, however, the ramifications of their expressed thoughts are never realised. In both the East and the West examples are not wanting. The different schools built up around the different interpretations of Brahman and the means of realizing it, is of direct concern to our present work. It is here that the inadequacy of language is most apparent, even such an astoundingly rich language, philophically as Sanskrit.

When one contemplates 'Brahman' and its use, one of the first things which strikes him is the preponderance of negative terms used to describe Brahman or the means of attaining that realisation. Words such as 'vairāgya', 'niṣkāma', 'tyāga', 'sannyāsa', 'nirguṇa' 'neti-neti' and a host of others are examples which require elucidation. Let us examine, then, such concepts as desirelessness, qualitylessness and neti-neti. First, however, we must make clear some of the problems with both negative and positive concepts so that we will know what to look for when examining the above three concepts.

With copulative terms, we are all aware of the problems associated with such words as 'is'. When we say, "The moon is a satellite" we mean that the connotation of the word 'moon' is contained in that of 'satellite'. This, then, may be either a definite statement or a class inclusion statement; but when we say "the moon is a luminous body" we surely cannot assert that the connotation of 'moon' is exhausted or contained in that of 'luminous body'. Rather here we have a descriptive statement. One thing we must watch for in our examination, then, is the descriptive and definite use of 'is'. While the difficulty between these senses does not appear in the above examples, nevertheless when we come to the analysis of the concepts relating to Brahman, we will find that because the subject is either difficult or impossible to define or describe, then, the two meanings of 'is' may become blurred.

An even more difficult problem arises with negative statements, however. If we say "Rāma is absent" we make the obvious remark that after looking about we find Rāma missing. That is a statement denying Rāma's presence; but there are also positive statements involved in the subject 'Rāma'. The first is, that, if Rāma were here we could distinguish him from others; and second that Rāma is an entity which has a locus that does not admit of being in more than one place; that is to say, he could not be both present and absent at the same time. While these two positive statements, asserted by the negative statement 'Rāma is absent', seem in this context obvious and perhaps trite, we can and will see in the analysis of the metaphysical concepts above how the lack of understanding of these positive assertions and of the nature of 'is' may have caused difficulty which could have otherwise been avoided. This difficulty occurs because in the metaphysical concepts the nature of the concept is not so simple that such an obvious statement as the above will analyse the meaning of the concept in full.

We may now proceed to consider the concepts of desirelessness, qualitylessness and neti-neti. In considering 'desirelessness' we should keep in mind that this word is but a model for a host of similar words in Sanskrit and the consideration of 'desirelessness' will apply to both 'niṣkāma' and 'vairāgya' in the above list.

We found in the Yājñavalkya portion of the *Bṛhadāraṇyaka Upaniṣad* a fundamental concept that desire binds the Brahman to the Saṁsāra; and so in order to be freed from such bondage one must achieve the state of being desireless. The usual argument for such a view is that desire implies that we seek something which is lacking, such as when one says "I desire wealth". "Were I to have wealth I would hardly desire it". Such a desire then, implies a lack, a vacancy, which must be filled by the object of desire. The difficulty with 'desirelessness' appears when we apply this idea of avoiding desire, to our actions. Were we to avoid any action at all upon realizing the binding nature of desire, then we would be neither asserting nor denying any object as an object of desire; rather we would be avoiding any possibility of being labelled desireless or desireful. Since this is the case, let us agree that by 'desire' we mean the mental image of our possession of the object. In this way we shall avoid this difficulty. When we say that "Mohan is desireless", then, we say that he should have no mental image of longing for an object. Now calling to mind the two positive statements made in the negative statement "Rāma is absent" we see some statements here also which are part and parcel of the original negative statement that Mohan is desireless. We see that it is saying one of two things; Mohan is disinterested in all matters; and his mental images are not connected with possession of an object, a state of consciousness; or that Mohan has no sense of lack such as when an image comes to mind it is not associated with an object which he does not possess. The first sense one might label a vacuous sense of desirelessness and the latter desireless from completeness. Both of these are statements about the nature of Mohan just as Rāma's absence was a statement about our knowledge of Rāma's identity and nature. Keeping in mind these two natures of 'desirelessness', only one of which can be implied in any given context, let us examine the second statement implied in "Mohan is desireless". We are also saying that Mohan is an entity of such kind that he cannot have a mental image with any longing associated with it and yet he is desireless or lacking in the quality or object of longing. All these statements are, directly or indirectly, statements about the nature of the subject, circumscribing his limits, to either not having a mental image or having a sense of complete possession associated with it. Either one of these may be acceptable if we look upon Mohan as a locus of activity, an ego which excludes everything which is not ego or if he were considered an absolute which was "one without a second" and needed nothing else and seeing, therefore, complete unity in all his consciousness. These two alternatives are not necessarily exhaustive as we can see when applying such considerations to 'Brahman'. Indeed 'desireless' applied to the Sādhana would require a sense of completeness not vacuousness to avoid conceiving Brahman as an ego. This, however, has vastly different implications than Yājñavalkya's use, which is more the vacuous disassociation from all images of their objects.

If we keep in mind the positive assertions of negative terms such as 'desirelessness', then we will be in a position to consider 'qualityless' and 'neti-neti' and so more directly 'Brahman'.

It is stated in the *Bhagavad-Gītā*[1] and some of the early Upaniṣads[2] that Brahman (Parabrahman) is beyond all thought, beyond our conception. If we overlook the difficulties with such a statement for the moment and consider that it is merely saying that there can be no definition of 'Brahman', because whatever term or terms used, Brahman's essential nature would not be exhausted. If this is what it is saying, then, it is all the more perplexing to find such adjectives applied to Brahman such as saguṇa or nirguṇa. Let us however, not talk of aspects of Brahman here, but the Parabrahman, Brahman in its essence or a better term of the Gītā the 'Puruṣottama'. To say, then, that the Brahman or Puruṣottama is qualityless really only brings up more problems than the statement attempts to solve. In this light let us first examine the word 'qualityless' before further consideration of the nature of Brahman. First, we see that 'qualityless' predicated of any subject implied one of two things. First that in no way, in no aspect, can the subject be possessed of qualities. This is what one might term "absolute negation". Second, it might mean that the subject cannot be defined by any quality words because the units of the subjects lie beyond qualities. In this case it would be making an assertion in addition to the negation, namely, that the subject can possess qualities but is not limited to a quality and so some part of the definite or description must be made in non-quality words.

1. II. 25, 29; VII. 25; VIII 20.
2. *Kaṭha Up.* V. 23, VI. 12; *Muṇḍaka Up.* III. 2-3.

This type of negation might be called "significant negation". In addition to the above alternatives another statement is implied in the case of absolute negation, namely that the subject can be defined, i.e., the units of the subject are known such that we can distinguish all predicates which may be applied to the subject from those which do not apply. The sign of not being able to define the subject, i.e., not fully knowing the nature of the subject is only being able to predicate a significant negation of 'qualityless'. Then, we either assert an absolute negation of the subject, the limits of which must be known, which implies that the subject can have no quality predicate or we assert a significant negation that the subject could not be defined or exhausted by quality predicates.

We may now proceed to apply this analysis to the subject Brahman. When someone such as Tilak[1] says that "The Parameśvara is qualityless" he seems to be aware of the above distinction, and so limits Brahman by an absolute negation. This is also asserting, as we have found, that Brahman is well known enough to be able to say what predicates apply to it and which do not. As a result of this Tilak reaches the same conclusion that Śaṅkara does, that the Parabrahman is the nirguṇa Brahman and, therefore, the saguṇa Brahman is māyā. This Brahman of exclusion is also reached by Advaitins by the more general process of neti-neti to which the same analysis applied that was made in the case of 'qualityless'. In Śaṅkara and Advaitins the absolute negation seems intended in both cases; that is, no quality word can be predicated of the subject Brahman; or in the neti-neti process no predicate can be made of Brahman which is positive. In other words Brahman is transcendent of the world to which positive language applies or perhaps we should say from a consideration of Śaṅkara's doctrine of māyā, necessary for such an exclusive Brahman, that positive language and all to which it applies is empty of any real meaning in relation to Brahman. Because of the haziness of the doctrine of Māyā, Śaṅkara seems in talking of a conditional Brahman to be using 'qualityless' in the second or significant sense, i.e., that quality words cannot

1. *Gītā Rahasya* 1, p. 288.

exhaust the meaning of 'Brahman'. This sense would be contrary to the first and is highly doubtful whether Śaṅkara fully intended it. Most probably the difficulty lies more generally in the use of such negative concepts when talking of something intended to be absolute.

Śaṅkara is forced by the different use of negative and positive terms in the texts to take one of the two, usually the negative terms and claiming the other, the manifest, term to be a superimposition (adhyāsa) on the quality-less,[1] or in case where two teachings are given, asserting two different audiences, the ignorant and the knowers[2] instead of appreciating the value of possible dialectical meaning. This stretches the original text as many writers have observed.[3]

We can conclude, then, that unless one can say Brahman is wholly known—which would be counter to most of the Prasthānatraya texts, then we cannot apply negative concepts to Brahman in an absolute negation, only in a significant negation which admits also the positive terms as applying but not defining the subject. Before going on to consider the significance of this conclusion in terms of contradictory predication let us first take up positive and devotional terms.

B. Positive and Devotional terms

If we continue to hold in mind the foregoing discussion, especially on the nature of 'is' and the two types of negation, then, we can with advantage investigate such concepts as Yajña, Iṣṭa, Bhakti and any of the positive qualities such as are found in the Gītā X. 21-42 or the famous "brahmaiva idaṁ viśvam". First let us consider 'worship' as representative of the above devotional words and as we shall see in the end the same problem applies to all devotional words.

The word 'worship' is actually a subtly nagative word. It might be said to be a "dualistic" term somewhat like 'desire' which implies a subject desiring and an object desired. In this case we have the worshipped and the worshipper. In its usual connotation it implies God or the worshipped and the worshipper as being separated by often an inexpendable gulf.

1. See Ś.B. XVIII. 13.
2. See esp. Bhāṣya on *Īśa and Māṇḍūkya* Up. I.1.4.
3. Tilak, *loc. cit.*, p. 15, 20; cf also Rāmānuja Bhāṣya, XIII. 2.

In short it seems to carry a dualistic theism built into its meaning. This theism implies that the worshipper is not God and in addition the worshipper knows both God's nature and his own such as the above negation or separation could be made. Buddha made the observation[1] in this connection, illustrating this separation, when he said "one coming to the shore of a broad river would not pray to cross over, rather he would go to the forest and cut logs to float over". So in our case worship could not imply a dualism but that we thought that the Ātman and Brahman were separate. If we did not hold to this separateness, then we would not have this longing or desire to fulfil this realization of true nature. This same sort of difficulty, the assertion that the object worshipped and the worshipper are separate is implied by both 'sacrifice' and 'devotion' although to a lesser degree in these cases, since it is possible to use them in a "pantheistic" way whereby we sacrifice ignorance, let us say, to attain our true state of wisdom; but in this case also there is the assertion of the reality and importance to us of that which is sacrificed by the very act of considering it a "sacrifice".

We can see in this light the lack of devotional terms in the Upaniṣadic concept of self actually aids its professed monism, whereas the *Gītā* using these terms encounters difficulty in keeping an outright theism from resulting. In terms of the above analysis of 'worship' the *Gītā's* position becomes even clearer. The *Gītā* is frankly recognizing an immediate separation between the individual and the Puruṣottama; but asserts that "through worship" not of a ritualistic type but a purificatory, a soteriological type, one reaches the Puruṣottama teleologically. In this case bhakti is highly modified with an ultimately monistic metaphysics rather than the simple dualism which devotional words normally carry. This is why we have criticised above both Śaṅkara and Madhva as falling short of fully understanding the intentions of the *Gītā*.

Positive terms can also be understood in terms of the above distinction between the definite and descriptive sense of 'is'. In the case of the sentence 'brahmedam evaṁ viśvam", we could be saying one of three things:

1. *Majjhima Nikāya*, I. 134-5.

(1) Brahman is included in the class of things denoted by 'world'.

(2) Brahman is coextensive with the world, i.e., is identical to the world.

(3) The word 'world' is one predicate among many which could be predicated of 'Brahman'. In the case of 'Brahman' no one seriously would consider the first. The problem lies in the (2) and (3) cases. One common criticism of positive language speaking of Brahman is that it limits Brahman to qualitied predicates. This common criticism of monists can be seen to be due to the confusion of the above two senses of 'is' the definite or identity sense and the descriptive sense. Kṛṣṇa in speaking of the Vibhūtis in the 10th Chapter of the *Gītā* is clearly using the third sense above as is seen in his remark in X.40-42, where he shows the Vibhūtis are only illustrative of his infinite nature. Thus it would seem that the Pantheist and the monist in their debate over the way of talking about Brahman are not really understanding one another and are using positive terms in different senses. Let us consider contradictory terms predicated of Brahman and how the problem is solved.

C. Contradictory Terms:

Since we are now aware of the difficulty with negative concepts and the difficulty in applying them to Brahman, and also we have a notion of the problems with positive and devotional terms, let us attempt to find a better interpretation of some of the texts on Brahman and Puruṣottama. In the light of the above remarks on absolute and significant negation, perhaps we can avoid the difficulties of talking about Brahman in purely negative or positive terms. The first thing to observe is that were we to talk of Brahman in terms of words such as 'qualityless' in their absolute negation sense, not realising the other sense of significant negation, we would then be forced as Śaṅkara to reject quality subjects as being illusory since they could not be Brahman. One sees in such assumptions a more basic assumption which will show us the way in our consideration of Brahman, namely that there can be nothing outside

Brahman, i.e., there can be nothing that is non-Brahman. This we may take as a standard for our present attempts. From this we can see that we must avoid negative terms by themselves as well as positive terms predicated in a definitive sense, since both will, in the above way, develop an exclusive Brahman. Moreover, if we are not to limit Brahman and thereby set up something which is non-Brahman we must somehow avoid the problems of asserting knowledge of the subject called for in absolute negation or definite assertion. We must then make a significant negation and/or a descriptive assertion without using either, because of the possibility of others confusing this sense of negation, unless well explained, for either absolute negation or definition. These objections may seem insurmountable since we would not necessarily say that Brahman could not be realised such as to know what could be predicated of it, since rather we should say that everything should be predicated of it; since our whole reason for using negative terms would be to point out that Brahman in some way encompasses all and yet is not exhausted by way of these predicates qualitied or non-qualitied. This, of course, was found as one of the interpretations of negation terms above, i.e., significant negation. Still this cannot be used for the above reasons of possible confusion. The way out of such difficulties is either "mauna", the solution of Buḍdha, or to use contradictory predicates. In regard to the last solution we have already observed that the sign of not being able to define the subject is the ability of predicating contradictory terms of the same subject. Now this means that either we have made a mistake and the subject is not a real subject or that the structure of language is inadequate to talk of such subjects. We would accept the latter and use contradictory predicates when talking of Brahman. Contradictory predicates act as a pointer to the fact that the subject of the statement is a peculiar subject in that it will not fit into language and in addition contradictory predicates also point out significant negation. We would be saying of Brahman, when saying "Brahman is qualitied and non-qualitied" that it has qualities but is not limited or exhausted by qualities. The predicate turns out, then, not ultimately to be a contradiction because the absolute negation that Brahman cannot be talked about in quality words is prevented by the positive term. This also seems to be the import of such use of contradictory terms when talking of Brahman in both Smṛti and Śruti. It is true that we find in these works use of negative terms such as by Yājñavalkya in the *Bṛhadāraṇyaka Upaniṣad* when using "neti-neti" (B.U.IV.2.4). He seems to misunderstand the above distinctions and arrives at a nirguṇa Brahman, an exclusive Brahman which in order to be realised must be approached by desirelessness, etc., in the absolute negation sense of vacuousness. The nature of the language, however, is such that the reader cannot be certain of which sense he is using the negative terms and so various interpretations can be made or have been made from these passages. Śaṅkara also, judging from his commentaries on the Upaniṣads and the *Bhagavad Gītā*, does not realise this matter of negative and contradictory predicates, in not avoiding the subtle limiting and yet also excluding of Brahman which using a single negative predicate does.

There is, then, some precedence for talking of Brahman as we have in contradictory terms. Not only does Kṛṣṇa in the *Gītā* use contradictory predicates when talking of the supreme[1] but also the early Upaniṣads used this device in order to talk of supreme Brahman[2]. In modern Indian philosophy Aurobindo, *par excellence*, has recognised this need to talk of Brahman only in the most "plastic and suggestive way"[3] to avoid such narrow and limiting concepts as found above. This Brahman is not merely nirguṇa as compared to saguṇa or akṣara as compared to kṣara; but is the Puruṣottama of the *Gītā* which transcends such opposing categories.[4] With this view of the Parabrahman, one is not forced to make such negative terms as 'tyāga', 'sannyāsa' and 'vairāgya' in their extreme negative sense, the essence of the sādhana. Rather again such a term as 'desireless' would be taken in its oblique sense as desirelessness from a sense of completeness, not in the sense that all objects of desire are illusory and should be avoided, for Brahman is just such a desire ! The way out

1. See for example, XV. 7-9, XIII. 13-16, see our discussion, p. 180.
2. *Kaṭha Up.*, V. 4. 10, 11, 13-15, *Māṇḍūkya Up.* VII. 12.
3. *Life Divine*, 437, 143.
4. See *Gītā*, VII. 17, 18.

according to contradictory language would be a growth to encompass all the qualitied and non-qualitied elements in order to embrace Brahman.

We have seen that in our general consideration of the language used in talking of the Supreme, two major fallacies were the source of much difference of opinion. First there was what one might call the "Labeling fallacy" considering Brahman, because the word is a simple unit of letters, to be a unit like pencil or Rāma or Mohan. As a result of this, one was led into the trap of making absolute negations or identity statements treating 'Brahman' as an ordinary subject. The second error was the confusion of significant and absolute negation as well as identity and descriptive statements. To avoid these errors contradictory predicates were found to be the only solution; yet this language at best only gave description which could never hope to exhaust the subject or to bring it into clearer focus. Perhaps it was this recognition that led both texts to claim 'Brahman was unknowable' implying experience was the only way.

D. *Some Specific Language Problems*:

In the body of our discussion we encountered some difficulties with such words as 'oneness' and 'unity' as well as such statements as 'Ahaṁ Brahma Asmi' which require some consideration at this point.

The problems revolving around such words as 'oneness', 'unity', 'union', etc. are roughly the same. We see this when we ask ourselves the question "Is Brahman unitary like the number one, as an assembly of people is unitary, or as the body is unitary ?" Let us first try to see a few salient senses of unity :

(1)	The unity of the number 1	: Arithmetic Unity
(2)	The unity of a machine to its parts	: Structural Unity
(3)	The unity of a family or clan	: Functioning Unity
(4)	The unity of an assembly	: Purposive Unity

(5) The unity of a symphony or art : Aesthetic Unity

(6) The unity of parts of the body to whole : Organic Unity.

These six meanings indeed apply to vastly different areas of discourse. For instance, the unity of various stratas and minerals in a rock is much different from the unity of parts of a body to the whole, not because merely of any accidental, structural or functional difference, but because the nature of the subject itself is vastly different, expressing itself as it does on a different level of being. Taking arithmetic unity as the basic concept of unity, we can perhaps see that 'unity' in the other cases implied parts or aspects which have different degrees of autonomy such as parts of a machine to the whole, compared to individuals of clan or an assembly. The latter two senses are more senses of unity in extensio such that in most contexts considering the Supreme, especially in the *Gītā*, could not be the meaning. Whichever sense we can conclude both from the *Māṇḍūkya Upaniṣad* and the *Gītā* it must fulfil the following conditions :

(1) Must be a unity in which the whole is prior to the part;

(2) Must be a unity which from the standpoint of the part or aspect seems complete in itself and even may appear contradictory to other parts ;

(3) Must be a unity which can admit of diversity or apparent diversity.

These three may seem like impossible criteria to satisfy and immediately eliminate unities (1) to (4) as obviously not fulfilling the requirements. (6) meets the third requirement as well as the second but fails (1) because the whole cannot be recognized from the part or seen through the part. (5) of all seems closest to fulfilling these requirements. A painting indeed fulfills (3) in its context as well as (2) since any part of the scene if abstracted would not wholly destroy the scene and indeed may appear just as complete in itself as the whole. Moreover, it satisfies (1) since we are aware first of the whole than of any particular "area of interest" in the picture. Further we note an interesting fact about the painting which may be close to being an analogy to the supreme unity, and that fact is that any painting always points outside itself to the scenery "Just over the mountain" or "just beyond the road", etc; yet even though pointing outside itself, is aesthetically complete as a picture. This aesthetic unity may well be the best analogy for the *Gītā* but in the Upaniṣads there may be different senses intended depending upon which of the four schools conceived of Brahman. Monists perhaps best fit (1), pantheists (6), and the Om analogy of *Māṇḍūkya* seems best to fit (5) the aesthetic unity.

One other problem of language must be considered and that is such statements as "Ahaṁ Brahma Asmi". When we say that, do we mean that I right now as John Jones am Brahman ? The Persian religious figure Mansur was hung for such an utterance—"An-al-Haaq". We obviously cannot mean then that 'I' as a personality am Brahman. It would seem that the statement could be made only in some special circumstances :

(1) that there were, even though slight, some differences between "I" and 'Brahman'.

(2) That all "I"s cannot unequivocably make the statement.

We see in regard to the first circumstance if one were to say "I am a human" it would convey no information. Therefore the statement "I" am Brahman if it is to convey anything must involve the circumstances of (1) or the statement will be an emotive statement only expressing an emotion and not conveying information. Indeed not everyone agrees that "I am Brahman" is true, ergo the case above of a religious community executing a pious individual for such a statement. We seem to have, then, only two alternatives. The first, accepting the statement as a mere emotive one and not of an ordinary informative nature. This is about all strict monism could say. The other possibility is to admit the above analysis of 'unitary' involves a dynamic element of becoming such that no matter how small the difference. There is some sense in which I could say also "I am not now identical with Brahman". Were we then to take the statement as saying "in essence", "I am Brahman" or in any true nature I am Brahman, such qualifications make this admission of difference even though ultimately through some Sādhana or merely ontologically there may be ultimate identity.

We have already discussed to some extent the problem of Jñāna and Vijñāna[1] and we have only to recall the dual aspect of Vijñāna for our present purposes. These aspects were grace and effort. We concluded that Vijñāna was more akin to experience than Manas or knowledge, which could be attained solely through effort and the results of the effort showing logical clarity and rational order. In the case of Vijñāna the Grace crowned our efforts and although like experience, the results were not olways according to expectation or efforts, nevertheless it was not wholly independent of effort, much as of the same event two people could have two different experiences according to their backgrounds. If this is the case we see, that the vijñāna of Brahman may differ according to the metaphysical preparation; and this latter is just the difference we have tried to show in the section on linguistic problems. Thus, we could conclude the monist could have truly a vijñāna of a nirguṇa Brahman and the theist of a saguṇa Brahman and yet not be wholly wrong, only because each of them had experience of only that aspect they have prepared themselves to experience. This use is counter perhaps to the common use of vijñāna as complete experience of all reality but if we are to accept all claims even of equal merit to differing vijñāna we have only to reject either vijñāna at all or come to the above conclusion.

1. See page 48ff ; also 158-162.

CHAPTER III

THE CONCEPT OF SELF IN EARLY VEDĀNTA AND ITS RELATION TO LATER SYSTEMATIC BIFURCATION

We have already seen that there were basically four schools of thought on the concept of self in early Vedānta and even some differences in the fourth between the *Gītā* and the Upaniṣads. There never was anything like one school of thought in Indian philosophy. Moreover, of the six Brahmanical systems little of what we have discussed here applies in any extent to Nyāya or Vaiśeṣika. These two systems seem to have somewhat of an independent growth as indeed most realism seems to have. There are some, however[1] who find in the mantras of the *Ṛgveda*, signs of Lokāyata and realism.[2] Certainly the egocentric concept of self in our present study exhibits such realism as is to be found in the two systems but at best here it is only realism applied to religious matters resulting in a simple dualistic theism. Therefore in considering the relation of the early Vedāntic concepts of self to the later systems we can safely confine our attention to the three—Sāṅkhya, Yoga and Vedānta. It will suffice merely to recognise that Mīmāṁsā is the logical outcome of Brāhmaṇic ritualism and has at best only a relation with the first egocentric concepts of self.

Beginning with the Vedānta, we note that it claims, alone of the other systems, orthodoxy. Vedānta, however, is today one of four schools and even many more smaller branches, even though the founding text of the Vedānta is the *Brahma Sūtras* one of the Prasthānatraya. The *Brahma Sūtras* alone, however, of the three has the tersest sūtra style such as to lend itself to many interpretations. In terms of our study of the concept of self we can see the basis of this later division even within Vedānta; for the four concepts of self we have found as the basis of the early Vedānta concept of self were not held together by a rationally complete concept; i.e., the transcen-

1. Radhakrishnan, *Indian Philosophy*, I, 273.
2. *Ṛgveda*, VII. 89. 3-1.

dental Brahman or the Puruṣottama relies upon contradictory predicates for its expression; and only conveys the information that it is indefinable, yet encompassing the conflicting concepts of change-unchanging or manifest-unmanifest. Therefore, for the metaphysician demanding logical completeness, the three concepts of self especially the manifest and unmanifest remain in opposition for him. In the Upaniṣads, except in the *Māṇḍūkya* and *Īśa* and to some extent others, these other three concepts were never associated into one; in other words in the Upaniṣads we already have different schools concerning the three different concepts. Therefore, in the synthetic attempts of the *Īśa* and *Māṇḍūkya* and especially later the *Gītā*, although they bound the three concepts together with a fourth or turīya state, nevertheless, this never did represent a unanimity of opinion. One might conclude, then, that the fourth concept of self in early Vedānta had, at best, appeal to the intuition, could only be accepted from meditation, direct insight, etc. Once the Prasthānatraya is read through from a more metaphysical view, then the systems of Vedānta become obvious—Śaṅkara taking the unmanifest Brahman of the Yājñavalkya philosophy and elsewhere, as the Parabrahman. Rāmānuja becomes sensitive more to the Saguṇa Brahman and Madhva more to the theistic elements. This is the bifurcation of the Prasthānatraya concept of self into later Vedānta.

Another element of the concept of self has split off, and become an independent darśana and that is Sāṅkhya. We recall that the Upaniṣad treatment of self as Puruṣa anticipated much of the Sāṅkhyan metaphysics, most definitely the guṇas and the twenty-five-fold evolution. The Sāṅkhya element was, however, very strong, and became the cornerstone of the *Gītā's* metaphysics. It is clear, however, that the main relations of Sāṅkhya with the Prasthānatraya are with the Upaniṣads, both because of the added theism and the divinization of matter in the *Gītā*. Actually some philosophers have claimed that Sāṅkhya most probably was a Nāstika system probably related to Cārvāka[1] However that may be, we can see that if Sāṅkhyan elements were lifted out of the Upaniṣads there is little left to do to reach the Kapila darśana;

1. Jacobi, in Radhakrishnan, *loc. cit.* II, 251.

since it occurs in the Puruṣa or individual self contexts of the Upaniṣads, usually with cosmological theism. The Puruṣa in its basic sense as we have taken it in the Upaniṣads was pluralistic, and indeed once we eliminate Brahman as the creator of prāṇa and rayi, the puruṣa-prakṛti dualism naturally follows, since prāṇa really is a substratum in the Upaniṣads, a created basic element, it is easy to lose sight of its dependency as a created element. Moreover, Sāṅkhya, as it exists, shows signs of a realistic treatment of something which must have been a much broader conception. We see this best in realising that out of prakṛti a material substratum, the first evolute is mahat, the closest principle to the conception of Brahma to be found in the Sāṅkhya darśana. From a material substratum which clearly Prakṛti is claimed to be, one would expect first the tanmātrās or Pañcamahābhūtas. Moreover, we can't say that the position of the ontologically highest evolute, Mahat, is due to Puruṣa since Sāṅkhya goes to such length to eliminate any activity or any part played by Puruṣa that it seems almost a *deus ex-machina* as indeed the above philosophers claim. Simply it seems an unnecessary addition, without which you would have a materialistic system much closer to Cārvāka. Prakṛti cannot logically be a material substratum for Sāṅkhya; and so we have to conclude either Puruṣa is an addition to the metaphysics and Sāṅkhya is a Nāstika system which the Upaniṣads merely borrowed concepts from for their cosmology, or that dārśanic Sāṅkhya collapsed the Upaniṣadic Sāṅkhya which included another higher teleological element in the evolution—Brahman. If this latter view is accepted, we can see Sāṅkhya in its broader concept in the Upaniṣads lying between the simple egocentric concept of self and the more developed concepts of the teleologically oriented individual. Indeed we found the Kośa analysis merely a deeper insight into the same 25 elements. If we can see Brahman as the goal of the evolution of Sāṅkhya, it changes the entire picture. In this case, Sāṅkhya, in splitting off from the Upaniṣads, was being really more interested in cosmology, and so Sāṅkhya had the choice of either giving the puruṣa the active part of Brahman in creation and Prakṛti the simple material base annam or rayi occupied in the Upaniṣads; either that, or they would have to expand annam to include a conscious mental principle as its nature. Sāṅkhya in the Upaniṣads clearly started with a created dualism in some passages[1] or even a triplicity of elements[2]. Cosmology is more realistic and more difficult of interpretation in terms of a monism which the first choice (Puruṣa, active part) would have offered. Therefore, from the context of the dualism or pluralism of cosmology in the Upaniṣads, if the Sāṅkhya developed from them, then the latter choice it took was the only real option.

Which actually took place--an addition of puruṣa to a materialistic system, or the rejection of Brahman from a somewhat realistic cosmological interest of the Upaniṣads—which took place, it is hard to say exactly, except to note that the Sāṅkhya darśana is unequivocally in its present form as much an Āstika system as present Vedānta can really claim from the Prasthānatraya; moreover cosmology was also an interest of the Vedic Ṛṣis so the Upaniṣadic Sāṅkhya is conceivably a natural outgrowth. Also we have noted in our conclusions that the Upaniṣads really had little place for the individual except as a lowest step in the teleological structure and moreover the synthesis in the Upaniṣads was largely between the unmanifest and manifest Brahman and did not ultimately concern the individual except to change the nature of the goal. If this is recognised then it is obvious that if the concepts of self we have noted were to be taken out of the Upaniṣads which kept them under one heading, "early Vedānta", then the cosmology along with the individual in a teleological orientation would be largely left out of the other two concepts. This is precisely the basic difference between dārśanic Vedānta and early Vedānta with the exception of Rāmānuja who brings in the Bhāgvata theism to his system. This difference is a lack of teleological orientation. We see the truth of this in the darśanas in the treatment of the Pañcamayakośas, although accepted as part of the Śruti, they really had a devolving interest for Śaṅkara rather than their teleological position in the *Taittirīya* and anticipated in the *Chāndogya*. Thus the placing of Sāṅkhya in the bifurcation of the early Vedānta into the darśanas is a fair

1. *P.U.* 1.4-10 *B.U.* 1.4.
2. Cf. esp. *C.U.* VI.

speculation as the origin for Sāṅkhya; and we have seen its effect on both Vedānta and Sāṅkhya in the Prasthānatraya.

From our study yet another point comes to the fore, i.e., that experience (as either anubhava or vijñāna) is the cornerstone of the concepts of self at all levels. What metaphysics is put forth by the Upaniṣads and *Gītā*, then, is put forth towards this end. The very metaphysical incompleteness to the synthetic fourth concept of self in the Upaniṣads and *Gītā* is an example. It seems to have been put forth at best as only a guide to meditation or contemplation as the *Māṇḍūkya* presentation of oṁkāra well illustrates. Yoga has always been just this effort which is assumed by the teachings in the Upaniṣads and explicitly put forth by the *Gītā*. The word 'Yoga' was mentioned in the Upaniṣads[1] and we did see that the basic concepts of its psychology formed the cornerstone of the Upaniṣadic psychology[2]. It was this "mind poise" which the *Gītā* took as the basis of its Sādhana. Although not as explicitly developed in the Upaniṣads as its sister darśana Sāṅkhya, Yoga was the key to developing the experience of Brahman in both our texts.

When we look at the yoga darśana, we immediately note that in the darśanas as in the Prasthānatrya, Yoga is not on a logical par with the other systems and elements. The darśana has not a developed metaphysics of its own and borrows some elements from Sāṅkhya. This latter seems largely a matter of choice, however, since Vedānta also uses Yoga as well as Sāṅkhya and even the Buddhists borrow much from it. Indeed the position of Īśvara in the Yoga system forever differentiates it from Sāṅkhya. It is to be concluded, then, that Yoga is the Sādhana of most of the systems and this is the position it occupied in the Prasthānatraya. Yoga insofar as it eschews metaphysics, really preserves of all the darśanas the atmosphere of the Prasthānatraya and indeed this is all the more clear when the position of Īśvara is properly evaluated as the goal of the sādhana and as the nature of yoga—mind poise. Why yoga, when it really is so different

1. *Kaṭha Up.* II. 12; VI. 11, 18; *T. U.* 24, *Śvetāśvatara Up.* II. 11; VI. 13.
2. See page 53ff.

from the other darśanas, should be considered logical with them, it is hard to determine except the tradition which makes a particular work, the origin and foundation of a system. Whatever be the motive it is reasonable that Patañjali did not set forth his work as an alternative to other darśanas or even as a wholly independent work. What was set forth, however, was geared to developing an experience of Īśvara or at least getting around the barrier of the ordinary mind and perceptions and "draṣṭuḥ svarūpe avasthānam"—dwelling in himself.

CHAPTER IV

PHILOSOPHICAL PSYCHOLOGY OF SELF

If Yoga preserves the essential characteristics of the early Vedāntic teachings regarding self, then let us see just in what way this is so and in what ways yoga is different from other systems. We want here to inquire just what is peculiar about the concept of self which would prevent an elaborate metaphysics from satisfying our inquiry. This peculiar nature has been seen in both of our texts. One way is that one must meditate etc., to acquire an immediate experience of what was set forth from those who claimed such experience. Likewise in the *Gītā* we were told to have a devotional attitude while developing mind poise etc., so as to more directly experience this transcendental Supreme self. There is general agreement in both our texts, that in our immediate awareness of self we are like the blind-folded man who has been led far away from his native place and the blindfold removed[1]. We need directions from one who knows the way in order to reach home.

Yoga darśana as well as yoga of the *Gītā*, alone of the systems, put most of its emphasis on a philosophical psychology. The central concept of this psychology is the idea of mind poise Essentially it is saying that the mind makes images or mental copies of the sense objects and moreover it is like a double-sided mirror in that it not only reflects the objective side but also the subjective. In other words, the self also is reflected into mind and there we make the confused identification of "I saw an object" due to the identification of the self reflected in mind with the self which is much broader in its reaches. This is what the Upaniṣads call "avidyā". It seems to be viewed as a continual process. We might observe that this identification of self with a given mental impression is the basis for the egocentric sense of self which is self largely conceived in terms of environmental and experiential bonds. The idea of mind poise is bringing this mind activity to an equipoise or cessation

1. *C.U.* VI. 14.

and thus the self can be experienced directly and not in terms of any one of its images. The whole concept of avidyā and the consequent effort to know Ātman in the Upaniṣads is centred around this sort of psychology[1]. In the *Gītā* the core of its yoga is just this psychological structure[2].

Important conclusions about the concept of self arise from these considerations. First we note that self, in that it is part of the image in the mind in any experience, colours that experience. Thus we can say that the manner in which we conceive self will largely colour the experience. This is at least what this psychology would seem to say in explaining why two different persons experiencing the same event could have such vastly different experiences. Moreover, it can also be concluded from this view that self is largely a metaphysical experience.

The phenomenon of maturation would illustrate this conclusion. The child's experience and the adult's would not differ so much in the objective reflection of the objects in the mind so much as the experience of self would be different. These conclusions perhaps could be summed up in the view that self as the subject of experience is not directly known or knowable since in making it known it becomes an object of experience. This sort of unknowable subject is not peculiar to yoga or the Prasthānatraya. It is largely the philosophy of Descartes and especially the existentialists such as Pascal. What is peculiar to yoga and early Vedānta is the more detailed psychological understanding of the basis for this peculiar subject-object mode of awareness. Thus while Descartes or most existentialists did not conceive experience or knowledge of self outside this active subject-object mode, the early Vedānta is unanimous in the idea that this is actually avidyā. Vidyā (or Jñāna and Vijñāna of self), on the other hand, can only be had by taking the awareness out of the manas where this discursive mode of consciousness holds sway, and bring it to the buddhi or higher levels of mind. This is done through the discipline of mind-poise.

1. *B.U.* II.4; also Radhakrishnan, *loc. cit.* I.2-6 ff; also Śāṅkara and Mādhva Bhāṣya on the above *Kaṭha* and other verses.
2. See Radhakrishnan *loc. cit.* II, 345-9 for discussion of Yoga psychology.

The Philosophical psychology which grew up around yoga then is making the simple claim that self cannot be understood without discipline, much as objective phenomena cannot be properly understood until we learn co-ordinated and efficient use of the senses. The discoveries of science are just this sort of discipline and training of the sense to co-ordinated endeavour. The discipline of yoga, embryonic in the Upaniṣads and somewhat more developed in the *Gītā*, attempts just this sort of discipline subjectively.

The concept of self, then, in our texts, is not simply a description of various beliefs of an idealistic metaphysics which purport no relation to either our common sense or our aspirations. Rather there are two sides to the presentation, the description of the various levels of self and at the same time the emphasis on a discipline to achieve experience of these claims. Most of us for whom such transcendental concepts of self can only appear abstract, can only consider it philosophically on the basis of intellectual criteria of judgment. The psychological basis of the sādhana recommended, however, has definite links to our ordinary understanding of self; and so in a broader sense the early Vedānta concept of self can have only this psychological importance for most of us, the description of the various concepts of self only gives some idea of possible goals if one has the devotion and faith in the revelatory character of the literature in which it was written. For this reason, then, yoga darśana perhaps carries the main import of the early Vedānta concept of self. The psychology showed the need for discipline—since in both texts metaphysics was not as highly developed as in later darśanas; and so what was given was presented primarily as a guide to experience. In other words the early Vedānta concept of self insofar as it was a discipline, required one to attain the intuition of the nature of self; then early Vedānta is primarily not rationally oriented but is a mysticism. This is the mystical character of both texts which most modern philosophers have recognised.[1]

1. Dasgupta, *Indian Idealism*, 67 ff. Radhakrishnan, *loc. cit.* I. 139 ff. esp. 176-8.
Ranade, *Constructive Survey of Upaniṣadic Philosophy*, p. 6, 15.
Deussen, *Philosophy of Upaniṣads*, 398 ff.

CHAPTER V

THE CONCEPT OF SELF AS A TOOL OF PHILOSOPHICAL STUDY

We can now perhaps see broader values in our study of self. Not only has the study thrown light on the early Vedānta beliefs regarding self, but in addition, the broad purposes and foundations for its metaphysics have come to light simply through the language used regarding self or the conclusions regarding the highest sense of self. Indeed, also some calculated guesses have been possible as regards the history and development of the later darśanas. Upon reflection it is evident that the development of thought, for example as put forth in the introduction, could well be interpreted as a progressive development in the understanding of self. Thus the levels of (1) theology, (2) cosmology, (3) psychology, (4) Mysticism, as we have seen, are also roughly the levels we found in the Upaniṣads and the *Gītā* as levels of self. The early interest in theology and cosmology is often a projection of the conception of self. It really becomes self conscious in the psychological stage as an attempt to understand self. This was especially noted in the *Bṛhadāraṇyaka Upaniṣad* in the sudden changes from cosmotheology to psychology in the second chapter. A more obvious example of the development of thought as a development in understanding of self is the comparison of the mosaic laws with the christian synthesis of them into "Love thy neighbour as thy self". This one commandment summed up all the other ten and moreover showed a greater insight into one's self. The Vedāntic claim might further sum that up by observing that thy neighbour is or ultimately is thyself. It is expected, then, that a study of the concept of self will, if the above is true, show the development or disintegration of a broad field of thought in religion, metaphysics as well as ethics.

The concept of self serves another purpose; and that is, it affords a judgment as to the adequacy of a system of thought to answer the ordinary philosophical questions which confront the intelligent man; for example, we have compared Sāṅkhya and Vedānta by such a study. We see that Vedānta is in a position to answer these questions, a few of which might be the following :—

(1) Is the self a substance ?

(2) Is it continuous and permanent or momentary ?

(3) If the self is transpersonal, how could it face the seeming subjective orientation of man's awareness ?

(4) What about apparent growth in time, birth, death, etc.?

From our study the answers to such questions become clear. The first question, for example, was considered in both of our texts especially in the search for a substratum in the Upaniṣads. The first question is answered by early Vedānta by pointing out that the self is both a substance (Akṣara Puruṣa or Universal Ātman) and a quality (Kṣara Puruṣa) and yet not to be confused as Aristotle seems linguistically to have done as a subject of a sentence which can only be a subject.

Our study has broad implications in the problem of momentariness in Buddhism and possible answers to it. Thus as regards the second question, the metaphysics of both texts, as well as the psychology above, would question the psychological possibility and indeed the metaphysical possibility of memory connecting the momentary particles of phenomena and satisfying all the problems regarding self. In regard to the third question, the psychology above of a self limited in its reflection into manas, illustrates such a limiting of self. This answer also accords with much data of modern psychology and parapsychology on the nature of "unconscious" areas of man's personality. The fourth question is the one question which seems only the two syntheses can answer without fully negating; for if one adopts the unchanging as the sense of self, there can be no growth, time or death. If the changing is adopted, death, time and growth become real problems which can be only purposeless or solved by the Buddhist momentariness. Only in the synthetic concepts can death and growth be reconciled. These are just a few of countless questions which any concept of self should answer; and in our study, by evaluating the concepts according to completeness and coherence, just such a comparison was made on a broad basis.

Perhaps, it is in religion that the study of self is most important. It seems a perennial problem which many enlightened individuals sought to solve. Socrates, for example, sought such understanding with his incessant questioning. His inquiry obtained for him many followers and many enemies. The former profited by his teachings and loved him; but the latter hated him enough to poison him. Why should such a wide discrepancy in reaction be found in such a small community of people. An example even more recent and closer to our experience is that of Mahatma Gandhi. He yet lives in the minds of most of his followers, yet what is it in his teachings that has caused such enmity that someone should shoot him ? The difference in understanding of self and its consequent relation to its environment is the answer our study would give. Such evaluation of different levels in understanding self was what we attempted in the present work.

BIBLIOGRAPHY

Attreya, B.L., *The Philosophy of Yoga-Vāsiṣṭha*, Adyar (1934).

Aristotle, *Metaphysics*, in McKeon Edition, Chicago (1943).

Aurobindo, *Eight Upaniṣads*, text and transl., Pondicherry (1953).

———, *Essays on the Gītā*, New York (1950).

———, *Īśa Upaniṣad*, Pondicherry (1921).

———, *Kena Upaniṣad*, Pondicherry (1952).

———, *Letters*, (First Series), Bombay (1947).

———, *Letters*, (Second Series), Bombay (1949).

———, *Letters*, (Fourth Series), Bombay (1951).

———, *Life Divine*, New York (1949).

———, *Synthesis of Yoga*, Pondicherry (1955).

Bādarāyaṇa, *Brahma-Sūtras*, text, transl. and commentary, by Swami Viresvarananda, Calcutta (1948).

———, *Brahma-Sūtras--Śāṅkara-Bhāṣya*, transl. by Thibaut, *S.B.E.* Vol. XXXIV, Oxford, (1904).

Bhandarkar, *Vaishnavism, Shaivism and Minor Religious Systems*, Strassburg (1913).

Belvalkar, *Lectures on Vedānta Philosophy*, Poona (1929).

Besant and Das, *Bhagavad-Gītā*, text and transl., Adyar (1950).

Bloomfield, *Vedic Concordance*, Boston, (1906).

Chakravarti, *Philosophy of the Upaniṣads*, Calcutta (1935).

Chaudhuri, H., *Philosophy of Integralism*, Calcutta (1954).

Chinmayananda, *Discourses on Māṇḍūkya Upaniṣad and Kārikā*, text and transl., Delhi (1953).

Dasgupta, S.N., *History of Indian Philosophy*, 5 Volumes, Cambridge, (1930-50).

———, S.N., *Indian Idealism*.

———, *Yoga Philosophy*, Calcutta (1930).

Desai, M., *Gītā According to Gandhi*, Allahabad (1951).

Deussen, P., *Philosophy of the Upaniṣads*, Edinburgh (1906).

———, *System of Vedānta*, Leipzig (1883).

Dnyaneswar, *Gītā Explained*, transl. by M. Subedar, Bombay (1945).

Driesch, H., *Man and the Universe*, London (1929).

Farquhar, *Outlines of the Religious Literature of India* (1928).
Frank, E., *Philosophical Understanding and Religious Truth*, Oxford (1945).
Garbe, R., "Introduction to the "Bhagavad Gītā", *Indian Antiquary XLVII* (1918) Supplement.
Gauḍapāda, *Āgama Śāstra*, transl. by Bhattacharya, Calcutta.
Guneon, R., *Man and His Becoming According to Vedānta.*
Hegel, *Phenomenology of Mind*, Oxford (1884).
Hill, W.D.P., *Bhagavad-Gītā*, Oxford (1947).
Hopkins, *Journal of the Royal Asiatic Society*, pp. 384-9. (1905),
Hume, R. E., *Thirteen Principal Upanishads*, transl., Oxford, (1921).
Īśādyaṣṭottaraśatopaniṣadaḥ, text, Banaras (1937).
Īśvarakṛṣṇa, *Sāṅkhya-Kārikā*, texts and transl. by S.S.S. Sastri, Madras (1948).
Jacobs and Stern, *General Anthropology*, New York (1952).
Jaimini, *Mīmāṁsā-Sūtras*, transl. by Thodani, Delhi.
Kant, I., *Kritik der Reine Vernum*, London (1929).
Keith, A.B., *Journal of the Royal Asiatic Society*, pp. 547-50. (1915),
———, *Religion and Philosophy of the Vedas and Upaniṣads*, Boston (1925).
Leibnitz, *Monadology*, Latta transl., Oxford (1925).
Madhva, *Bhāṣya on Bṛhadāraṇyaka Upaniṣad*, transl. Lahore.
———, *Bhāṣya on Eight Major Upaniṣads*, transl. Lahore.
Mahābhārata, 2 Volumes, text, Gorakhapur (no Date).
Mahadevan, T.M.P., *The philosophy of Advaita*, London (1938).
———, *Upaniṣads*, text and transl. Madras (1950).
Moore, G.E., *Ethics*, London (1912).
Mukerjee, A.C., *Nature of Self*, Allahabad (1943).
Muller, F.M., *Upaniṣads*, transl. *SBE* vols. I, XIV, London (1879, 1884).
Narahari, *Ātman in Pre-Upaniṣadic Vedic Philosophy*, Adyar, (1944).
Otto, R., *Original Gītā*, London, (1939).
Pandit, M.P., *Mystical Approach to Vedas and Upaniṣads*, (1952).
Patañjali, *Yoga-Sūtras*, text and transl. by Dvivedi, Adyar (1936).

Plato, *Dialogues*, Jowett, transl. New York (1947).
Radhakrishnan, S., *Bhagavad-Gītā*, (2 Volumes), London (1923, 1927).
———, *Twelve Principal Upaniṣads*, London (1956).
Ramana Maharshi, *Upadeśa-Sāhasrī*, Tiruvanamali (1933).
———, Ramana Maharshi, *Who Am I*, Tiruvanamali (1923).
Rāmānuja, *Brahma-Sūtra-Bhāṣya*, *S.B.E.* Vol., XLVIII, London (1906).
———, *Bhagavad-Gītā Bhāṣya*, text, Gorakhapur (no Date).
Ranade, *Constructive Survey of Upanishadic Philosophy*, Poona (1926).
Rangaramanuja, *Bhāṣya on Īśa and Kaṭha Upaniṣad.*
Ṛgveda-Saṁhitā, text, Max Müller, (1892).
Roer, E. *Twelve Upaniṣads* (3 Volumes), text, transl., and notes from Śaṅkara's Bhāṣya and Ānandagiri's gloss, Adyar (1931).
Runes, D., *Dictionary of Philosophy*, New York (no Date).
Russell, B., *Logical Atomism*, London.
———, *Mysticism and Logic*, London (1955).
Śaṅkara, *Bṛhadāraṇyaka Upaniṣad Bhāṣyas* transl. by Madhavananda, Calcutta (1943).
———, *Chāndogya Upaniṣad Bhāṣya.* transl. by Jha, G., Poona (1943).
———, *Daśopaniṣad* text and Bhāṣya, Gorakhapur (no Date).
———, *Bhagavad Gītā Bhāṣya*, text, Gorakhapur (no Date).
———, *Īśa, Kena, Kaṭha, Taittirīya, Aitareya, Praśna, Muṇḍaka Upaniṣad Bhāṣyas* (5 Volumes), transl. by Jha, G. and Sastri S.S., Madras (1923).
———, *Selected Works*, text and transl., Venkataraman, Madras (no Date).
———, *Vivekacūḍāmaṇi*, text and transl. by Chatterjee, Calcutta (1947).
Sastry, A.M., *Bhagavad-Gītā, Śaṅkara's Bhāṣya.* transl. Madras.
Sastry, K., *Gospel of the Gītā*, Madras.
Sastry, T.V.K., *Lights on the Upaniṣads*, Pondicherry (1947).
———, *Śatapatha Brāhmaṇa*, text, Lahore, (1926).
Schopenhauer, A., *Parerga and Paralipomena.*
Sen, S.C., *Philosophy of the Upaniṣads* (1937).
Sircar, *Hindu Mysticism* (1936).

Stace, W.T., *Time and Eternity*, Princeton (1952).
Tagore, R., *Sādhanā*, London (1954).
Telang, *Bhagavad-Gītā*, *Sanatsujātīya*, and the *Anu Gītā*. transl. in *S.B.E.* vol. VIII, Oxford (1908).
Tilak, B.G. *Orion*, Poona (1893).
———, *Gītā Rahasya*, 2 Volumes, Poona, (1935).
Weber A, History of Sanskrit Literature, (1904).
Whitehead, A.N., *Process and Reality*, in Gross Anthology, Millan (1954)

INDEX

ERRATA

Page	*Read*	*For*
86	espouse	expose
102	Panentheism	Pantheism
211	sentient	sentiment
215	Feuerbach	Fewerbach

[redacted]

[redacted]